Game Developmen and Best Practices

Better games, less hassle

John P. Doran

Matt Casanova

BIRMINGHAM - MUMBAI

Game Development Patterns and Best Practices

First published: April 2017

Production reference: 1180417

Published by Packt Publishing Ltd.
Livery Place
35 Livery Street
Birmingham
B3 2PB, UK.
ISBN 978-1-78712-783-8

www.packtpub.com

Credits

Authors

John P. Doran

Matt Casanova

Reviewers

Francesco Sapio

Josh Wittner

Commissioning Editor

Amarabha Banerjee

Acquisition Editor

Larissa Pinto

Content Development Editor

Arun Nadar

Technical Editor

Sushant S Nadkar

Copy Editor

Safis Editing

Project Coordinator

Ritika Manoj

Proofreader

Safis Editing

Indexer

Francy Puthiry

Graphics

Jason Monteiro

Production Coordinator

Arvindkumar Gupta

About the Authors

John P. Doran is a technical game designer who has been creating games for over 10 years. He has worked on an assortment of games in teams consisting of just himself to over 70 people in student, mod, and professional projects in different roles, from game designer to lead UI programmer. He previously worked at LucasArts on *Star Wars: 1313* as a game designer. He later graduated from DigiPen Institute of Technology in Redmond, WA, with a Bachelor of Science in game design.

John is currently a part of DigiPen's research and development branch in Singapore in addition to DigiPen Game Studios. He is also the lead instructor of the DigiPen-Ubisoft Campus Game Programming Program, instructing graduate-level students in an intensive, advanced-level game programming curriculum. In addition to that, he also tutors and assists students in various subjects and gives lectures on C#, C++, Unreal, Unity, game design, and more.

He is the author of *Unreal Engine Game Development Cookbook*, *Building an FPS Game in Unity*, *Unity Game Development Blueprints*, *Getting Started with UDK*, *UDK Game Development*, and *Mastering UDK Game Development*, and he co-wrote *UDK iOS Game Development Beginner's Guide*, all available from Packt. More information about him can be found at johnpdoran.com.

Matt Casanova has been programming indie games in C++, as well as mobile games and applications in Java and Objective C, for over ten years. For the last seven years he has assumed the role of technical director for his students. He specializes in 2D game engines and tools.

Matt was an instructor for two years at Digipen Institute of Technology's Singapore campus, where he taught *The Advanced Certification in 2D Game Development*. This was a six month graduate-level course that specialized in creating 2D game engines. He then spent five years teaching undergraduate courses such as C++, data structures, and game engine architecture for Digipen's degree in Real Time Interactive Simulation in South Korea. He has helped dozens of student teams make successful game projects and avoid the pitfalls of bad code. He currently works as lead mobile developer at a software company in Las Vegas.

I would like to thank my wife TaeGyeong Lee for listening to me for months on end while I talked about this book. I would also like to the thank Josh Wittner for constantly giving me technical advice and encouraging me to learn programming in the first place.

About the Reviewers

Francesco Sapio obtained his Computer Science and Control Engineering degree from Sapienza University of Rome, Italy, a couple of semesters in advance, scoring *summa cum laude*. He is currently studying a Master of Science in Engineering in Artificial Intelligence and Robotics at the same university.

He is a Unity3D and Unreal expert, a skilled game designer, and an experienced user of the major graphics programs. He developed *Game@School* (Sapienza University of Rome), an educational game for high school students to learn the concepts of physics, and *Sticker Book (series)* (Dataware Games), a cross-platform series of games for kids. In addition, he worked as consultant for the (successfully funded by Kickstarter) game *Prosperity – Italy 1434* (Entertainment Game Apps, Inc), and for the open online collaborative ideation system titled *Innovoice* (Sapienza University of Rome). Moreover, he has been involved in different research projects such as *Belief-Driven-Pathfinding* (Sapienza University of Rome), a new technique of pathfinding in videogames that was presented as a paper at the *DiGRA-FDG Conference 2016*; and *perfekt.ID* (Royal Melbourne Institute of Technology), which included developing a recommendation system for games.

He is an active writer on the topic of game development. Recently, he authored the book *Getting Started with Unity 5.x 2D Game Development* (Packt Publishing), which takes your hand and guide you through the amazing journey of game development; the successful *Unity UI Cookbook* (Packt Publishing), which has been translated into other languages, and which teaches readers how to develop exciting and practical user interfaces for games within Unity; and a short e-guide *What do you need to know about Unity* (Packt Publishing). In addition, he co-authored the book *Unity 5.x 2D Game Development Blueprints* (Packt Publishing). Furthermore, he has also been a reviewer for the following books: *Game Physics Cookbook* (Packt Publishing), *Mastering Unity 5.x* (Packt Publishing), *Unity 5.x by Example* (Packt Publishing), and *Unity Game Development Scripting* (Packt Publishing).

Francesco is also a musician and a composer, especially of soundtracks for short films and video games. For several years, he worked as an actor and dancer, where he was a guest of honor at the Brancaccio theater in Rome. In addition, he is a very active person, having volunteered as a children's entertainer at the Associazione Culturale Torraccia in Rome.

Finally, Francesco loves math, philosophy, logic, and puzzle solving, but most of all, creating video games—thanks to his passion for game designing and programming.

You can find him at www.francescosapio.com.

> I'm deeply thankful to my parents for their infinite patience, enthusiasm, and support throughout my life. Moreover, I'm thankful to the rest of my family, in particular to my grandparents, since they have always encouraged me to do better in my life with the Latin expressions "*Ad maiora*" and "*Per aspera ad astra.*"
>
> Finally, a huge thanks to all the special people around me whom I love, in particular to my girlfriend; I'm grateful for all of your help in everything. I do love you.

At work **Josh Wittner** is currently applying a decade's worth of experience developing real-time simulations in the video game industry to mixing virtual with actual reality through holographic applications. At home, he's the father of a wonderful daughter and the husband to a wonderful wife.

> I'd like to thank my wife and daughter for helping me stay focused.

www.PacktPub.com

For support files and downloads related to your book, please visit www.PacktPub.com.

Did you know that Packt offers eBook versions of every book published, with PDF and ePub files available? You can upgrade to the eBook version at www.PacktPub.com and as a print book customer, you are entitled to a discount on the eBook copy. Get in touch with us at service@packtpub.com for more details.

At www.PacktPub.com, you can also read a collection of free technical articles, sign up for a range of free newsletters and receive exclusive discounts and offers on Packt books and eBooks.

https://www.packtpub.com/mapt

Get the most in-demand software skills with Mapt. Mapt gives you full access to all Packt books and video courses, as well as industry-leading tools to help you plan your personal development and advance your career.

Why subscribe?

- Fully searchable across every book published by Packt
- Copy and paste, print, and bookmark content
- On demand and accessible via a web browser

Customer Feedback

Thanks for purchasing this Packt book. At Packt, quality is at the heart of our editorial process. To help us improve, please leave us an honest review on this book's Amazon page at https://www.amazon.com/dp/1787127834.

If you'd like to join our team of regular reviewers, you can e-mail us at customerreviews@packtpub.com. We award our regular reviewers with free eBooks and videos in exchange for their valuable feedback. Help us be relentless in improving our products!

Table of Contents

Preface

As your programs get larger, it is critical that you understand how to write code in such a way that classes and modules can communicate with each other in an intelligent way. Knowing how to write code that is clean and extensible is critical for the success of medium to large scale projects, especially if there are multiple programmers involved. We don't want to spend time rewriting another programmer's code because it is easier than figuring out how the original code works. Likewise, we don't want other programmers to be confused by our code and rewrite solutions to problems that we already solved.

This book explores the ins and outs of the most common ways to design code so that it can be understood, reused, maintained, and extended if necessary. These common design patterns will make communication between classes simple and clean. Whether you are using a commercial game engine or writing your own from scratch, knowledge of these patterns will make your game project more likely to succeed.

Each chapter of this book explores one of the most used design patterns for games. Together we discuss the problems that we are trying to solve and how a specific pattern can be of use to us. Within each chapter, we also cover the pros and cons of the pattern so you are better equipped to know when to use it. This book is not a "cook book". Using a pattern in your project isn't as simple as copying some code that we provide. Instead of learning recipes for code, we are going to learn the fundamentals of how a game engine should be written. We will do this by looking at lots of code examples. As we said, these example, can't simply be copy and pasted into any project. However, by understanding how these examples fit into the specific project for this book, you can implement them in any project.

What this book covers

Chapter 1, *Introduction to Design Patterns*, introduces the concept of design patterns and how they can benefit our projects. We also dive into learning about the advantages of compartmentalizing our code and set up a sample project that we can use to build upon in the book.

Chapter 2, *One Instance to Rule Them All – Singletons*, discusses the well-known singleton pattern, explaining common arguments for and against having a single instance that's accessible globally within our game.

Chapter 3, *Creating Flexibility with the Component Object Model*, explores how to create a large amount of different game object types while minimizing code duplication.

Chapter 4, *Artificial Intelligence Using the State Pattern*, shows the usage of states to allow a game object to change its behavior and functionality due to different stimuli in your game. We discuss and apply how we can use this concept in both player behavior and artificial intelligence.

Chapter 5, *Decoupling Code via the Factory Method Pattern*, explains how we separate our specific game objects from our game engine. This will allow us to reuse all or at least part of our game engine for future games.

Chapter 6, *Creating Objects with the Prototype Pattern*, covers another way to reduce dependencies within our game engine. We learn how to create objects through their base classes. In addition, we cover how to read object data from a file.

Chapter 7, *Improving Performance with Object Pools*, covers a way to improve memory costs in our games by reusing objects that we've created dynamically by making use of a manager to control what is and isn't being used at the moment.

Chapter 8, *Controlling the UI via the Command Pattern*, discusses how to create reusable actions that can be utilized for UI button clicks or input devices such as keyboard or controller.

Chapter 9, *Decoupling Gameplay via the Observer Pattern*, explains multiple ways that classes can communicate and share data without using global variables.

Chapter 10, *Sharing Objects with the Flyweight Pattern*, discusses how we can design our objects to be as lightweight as possible by separating data that can and can't be shared. We use this knowledge to create a particle system which produces smaller objects developed to simulate things like fire, explosions, and smoke.

Chapter 11, *Understanding Graphics and Animation*, provides a low-level explanation of how graphics and rendering work so that you are better able to implement it in your game.

Chapter 12, *Best Practices*, covers a number of topics that will improve your code and game projects in the future, touching on things like how to improve your code quality, use the const keyword correctly, how iteration is a great way to improve game and code design, and when you should consider adding scripting to your game.

What you need for this book

To write code, all you really need is a text editor, but for serious development you'll need to use an IDE (Integrated Developer Environment). We use Microsoft Visual Studio 2015 and C++ in this book using a Windows computer but, the concepts taught can be used within any programming language as well. For those of you that do not have Visual Studio installed, but are using Windows we do go over how to install the free Visual Studio Community version and set it up with our project in Chapter 1, *Introduction to Design Patterns*.

Who this book is for

This book is for anyone who wants to learn how to write better, cleaner code. While design patterns in general do not require any specific programming language, the examples in this book are written in C++. Readers will get much more out of this book if they are already familiar with C++ and STL containers. The project that is included with this book was written and compiled using Microsoft Visual Studio 2015, so familiarity with that IDE will be very helpful as well.

Conventions

In this book, you will find a number of text styles that distinguish between different kinds of information. Here are some examples of these styles and an explanation of their meaning.

Code words in text, database table names, folder names, filenames, file extensions, pathnames, dummy URLs, user input, and Twitter handles are shown as follows: "I'm going to update the ChasePlayerComponent class that already exists in the EngineTest project."

A block of code is set as follows:

```
class Animal
{
  public:
    virtual void Speak(void) const //virtual in the base class
    {
      //Using the Mach 5 console print
      M5DEBUG_PRINT("...\n");
    }
};
```

When we wish to draw your attention to a particular part of a code block, the relevant lines or items are set in bold:

```
class StaticExamples
{
  public:
    static float classVariable;

    static void StaticFunction()
    {
// Note, can only use static variables and functions within
        // static function
        std::string toDisplay = "\n I can be called anywhere!
        classVariable value: " +
        std::to_string(classVariable);

        printf(toDisplay.c_str());
    }

    void InFunction()
    {
        static int enemyCount = 0;

        // Increase the value of enemyCount
        enemyCount += 10;

        std::string toDisplay = "\n Value of enemyCount: " +
        std::to_string(enemyCount);

        printf(toDisplay.c_str());
    }
};
```

New terms and **important words** are shown in bold. Words that you see on the screen, for example, in menus or dialog boxes, appear in the text like this: "In order to download new modules, we will go to **Files** | **Settings** | **Project Name** | **Project Interpreter**."

Warnings or important notes appear in a box like this.

Tips and tricks appear like this.

Reader feedback

Feedback from our readers is always welcome. Let us know what you think about this book-what you liked or disliked. Reader feedback is important for us as it helps us develop titles that you will really get the most out of.

To send us general feedback, simply e-mail feedback@packtpub.com, and mention the book's title in the subject of your message.

If there is a topic that you have expertise in and you are interested in either writing or contributing to a book, see our author guide at www.packtpub.com/authors.

Customer support

Now that you are the proud owner of a Packt book, we have a number of things to help you to get the most from your purchase.

Downloading the example code

You can download the example code files for this book from your account at http://www.packtpub.com. If you purchased this book elsewhere, you can visit http://www.packtpub.com/support and register to have the files e-mailed directly to you.

You can download the code files by following these steps:

1. Log in or register to our website using your e-mail address and password.
2. Hover the mouse pointer on the **SUPPORT** tab at the top.
3. Click on **Code Downloads & Errata**.
4. Enter the name of the book in the **Search** box.
5. Select the book for which you're looking to download the code files.
6. Choose from the drop-down menu where you purchased this book from.
7. Click on **Code Download**.

Once the file is downloaded, please make sure that you unzip or extract the folder using the latest version of:

- WinRAR / 7-Zip for Windows
- Zipeg / iZip / UnRarX for Mac
- 7-Zip / PeaZip for Linux

The code bundle for the book is also hosted on GitHub at `https://github.com/PacktPubl ishing/Game-Development-Patterns-and-Best-Practices`. We also have other code bundles from our rich catalog of books and videos available at `https://github.com/Packt Publishing/`. Check them out!

Downloading the color images of this book

We also provide you with a PDF file that has color images of the screenshots/diagrams used in this book. The color images will help you better understand the changes in the output. You can download this file from `https://www.packtpub.com/sites/default/files/down loads/GameDevelopmentPatternsandBestPractices_ColorImages.pdf`.

Errata

Although we have taken every care to ensure the accuracy of our content, mistakes do happen. If you find a mistake in one of our books--maybe a mistake in the text or the code-- we would be grateful if you could report this to us. By doing so, you can save other readers from frustration and help us improve subsequent versions of this book. If you find any errata, please report them by visiting `http://www.packtpub.com/submit-errata`, selecting your book, clicking on the **Errata Submission Form** link, and entering the details of your errata. Once your errata are verified, your submission will be accepted and the errata will be uploaded to our website or added to any list of existing errata under the Errata section of that title.

To view the previously submitted errata, go to `https://www.packtpub.com/books/conten t/support` and enter the name of the book in the search field. The required information will appear under the **Errata** section.

Piracy

Piracy of copyrighted material on the Internet is an ongoing problem across all media. At Packt, we take the protection of our copyright and licenses very seriously. If you come across any illegal copies of our works in any form on the Internet, please provide us with the location address or website name immediately so that we can pursue a remedy.

Please contact us at `copyright@packtpub.com` with a link to the suspected pirated material.

We appreciate your help in protecting our authors and our ability to bring you valuable content.

Questions

If you have a problem with any aspect of this book, you can contact us at questions@packtpub.com, and we will do our best to address the problem.

1
Introduction to Design Patterns

You've learned how to program, and you've probably created some simple games at this point, but now you want to start building something larger. Perhaps you have tried building an interesting project but you felt like the code was hacked together. Maybe you worked with a team of programmers and you couldn't see eye-to-eye on how to solve problems. Maybe your code didn't integrate well, or features were constantly being added that didn't fit with your original design. Maybe there wasn't a design to begin with. When building larger game projects, it's important that you break apart your problems, focus on writing quality code, and spend your time solving problems unique to your game, as opposed to common programming problems that already have a solution. The old advice *don't reinvent the wheel* applies to programming as well. One could say that instead of just being someone that writes code, you now need to think like a game developer or software engineer.

Knowing how to program is very similar to knowing a language. It's one thing to use a language to make conversation, but it's quite different if you're trying to create a novel or write poetry. In much the same way as when programmers are writing code in their game projects, you'll need to pick the right parts of the language to use at the best time. To organize your code well, as well as to solve problems that arise time and time again, you'll need to have certain tools. These tools, design patterns, are exactly what this book is about.

Chapter overview

Over the course of this chapter, we will be discussing the idea of design patterns as well as the thought processes to be going through when deciding to use them. We will also be setting up our project and installing everything necessary to work with the Mach5 engine, which was written by one of the authors.

Your objective

This chapter will be split into a number of topics. It will contain a simple step-by-step process from beginning to end. Here is the outline of our tasks:

- What are design patterns?
- Why you should plan for change
- Separating the what and how
- An introduction to interfaces
- The advantages of compartmentalizing code
- The problems with using design patterns in games
- Project setup

What are design patterns

Famously documented in the book *Design Patterns: Elements of Reusable Object-Oriented Software* by *Erich Gamma, John Vlissides, Ralph Johnson,* and *Richard Helm,* also known as the **Gang of Four** (**GoF** for short), design patterns are solutions for common programming problems. More than that, they are solutions that were designed and redesigned as developers tried to get more flexibility and reuse from their code. You don't need to have read the Gang of Four's book in order to understand this book, but after finishing you may wish to read or reread that book to gain additional insights.

As the Gang of Four title suggests, design patterns are reusable, meaning the implemented solution can be reused in the same project, or a completely new one. As programmers, we want to be as efficient as possible. We don't want to spend time writing the same code over and over, and we shouldn't want to spend time solving a problem that already has an answer. An important programming principle to follow is the **DRY** principle, **Don't Repeat Yourself**. By using and reusing design patterns, we can prevent issues or silly mistakes that would cause problems down the road. In addition, design patterns can improve the readability of your code not only by breaking apart sections that you would have put together, but also by using solutions that other developers are (hopefully) familiar with.

When you understand and use design patterns, you can shorten the length of a discussion with another developer. It is much easier to tell another programmer that they should implement a factory than to go into a lengthy discussion involving diagrams and a whiteboard. In the best-case scenario, you both know about design patters well enough that there doesn't need to be a discussion, because the solution would be obvious.

Although design patterns are important, they aren't just a library that we can just plug into our game. Rather, they are a level above libraries. They are methods for solving common problems, but the details of implementing them is always going to be unique to your project. However, once you have a good working knowledge of patterns, implementing them is easy and will feel natural. You can apply them when first designing your project, using them like a blueprint or starting point. You can also use them to rework old code if you notice that it's becoming jumbled (something we refer to as spaghetti code). Either way, it is worth studying patterns so your code quality will improve and your programming *toolbox* will grow larger.

With this *toolbox*, the number of ways to solve a problem is limited only by your imagination. It can sometimes be difficult to think of the *best* solution right off the bat. It can be difficult to know the *best* place or *best* pattern to use in a given situation. Unfortunately, when implemented in the wrong place, design patterns can create many problems, such as needlessly increasing the complexity of your project with little gain. As I mentioned before, software design is similar to writing poetry in that they are both an art. There will be advantages and disadvantages to the choices you make.

That means in order to use patterns effectively, you first need to know what problem you are trying to solve in your project. Then you must know the design patterns well enough to understand which one will help you. Finally, you'll need to know the specific pattern you are using well enough so you can adapt it to your project and your situation. The goal of this book is to provide you with this in-depth knowledge so you can always use the correct tool for the job.

There are many design patterns out there, including the foundational patterns from the Gang of Four book, architectural patterns, and many more. We will only be touching on the ones that we feel are best used for game development. We feel it is better to supply you with deep knowledge of a select few patterns than to give you a primer on every possible pattern out there. If you're interested in learning more about all of the ones out there, feel free to visit

`https://en.wikipedia.org/wiki/Software_design_pattern`.

Why you should plan for change

In my many years doing game development, one thing that has always been constant is that a project never ends up 100% the same as it was imagined in the pre-production phase. Features are added and removed at a moment's notice and things that you think are pivotal to the game experience will get replaced with something completely different. Many people can be involved in game development, such as producers, game directors, designers, quality assurance, or even marketing, so we can never tell who, where, or when those changes will be made to the project.

Since we never can tell what will be changed, it's a good practice to always write your code so it can be easily modified. This will involve planning ahead much more than you might be used to, and typically involves either a drawn flowchart, some form of pseudocode, or possibly both. However, this planning will get you much further much faster than jumping straight to coding.

Sometimes you may be starting a project from scratch; other times you may be joining a game team and using an existing framework. Either way, it is important to start coding with a plan. Writing code is called software engineering for a reason. The structure of code is often likened to building or architecting. However, let's think in smaller terms for now. Let's say you want to build some furniture from IKEA.

When you buy your furniture, you receive it unassembled with an instruction manual. If you were to start building it without following the instructions, it is possible you wouldn't finish it at all. Even if you did eventually finish, you may have assembled things out of order, causing much more work. It's much better to have a blueprint that shows you every step along the way.

Unfortunately, building a game is not exactly like following an instruction manual for furniture. In the case of games and software of any kind, the requirements from the client might constantly change. Our *client* might be the producer that has an updated timeline for us to follow. It might be our designer that just thought of a new feature we *must* have. It might even be our play testers. If they don't think the game is fun, we shouldn't just keep moving along making a bad game. We need to stop, think about our design, and try something new.

Having a plan and knowing a project will change seem to be in opposition to each other. How can we have a plan if we don't know what our end product will be like? The answer is to plan for that change. That means writing code in such a way that making changes to the design is fast and easy. We want to write code so that changing the starting location on the second level doesn't force us to edit code and rebuild all the configurations of the project. Instead, it should be as simple as changing a text file, or better yet, letting a designer control everything from a tool.

Writing code like this takes work and planning. We need to think about the design of the code and make sure it can handle change. Oftentimes this planning will involve other programmers. If you are working on a team, it helps if everyone can understand the goal of each class and how it connects with every other class. It is important to have some standards in place so others can start on or continue with the project without you there.

Understanding UML class diagrams

Software developers have their own form of blueprints as well, but they look different from what you may be used to. In order to create them, developers use a format called **Unified Markup Language**, or **UML** for short. This simple diagramming style was primarily created by Jim Rumbaugh, Grady Booch, and Ivar Jacobson and has become a standard in software development due to the fact that it works with any programming language. We will be using them when we need to display details or concepts to you via diagrams.

Design patterns are usually best explained through the use of class diagrams, as you're able to give a demonstration of the idea while remaining abstracted. Let's consider the following class:

```
class Enemy
{
  public:
    void GetHealth(void) const;
    void SetHealth(int);
  private:
    int currentHealth;
    int maxHealth;
};
```

Converted to UML, it would look something like this:

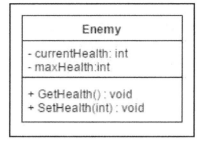

Basic UML diagrams consist of three boxes that represent classes and the data that they contain. The top box is the name of the class. Going down, you'll see the properties or variables the class will have (also referred to as the data members) and then in the bottom box you'll see the functions that it will have. A plus symbol (+) to the left of the property means that it is going to be public, while a minus symbol (-) means it'll be private. For functions, you'll see that whatever is to the right of the colon symbol (:) is the return type of the function. It can also include parentheses, which will show the input parameters for the functions. Some functions don't need them, so we don't need to place them. Also, note in this case I did add `void` as the return type for both functions, but that is optional.

Relationships between classes

Of course, that class was fairly simple. In most programs, we also have multiple classes and they can relate to each other in different ways. Here's a more in-depth example, showing the relationships between classes.

Inheritance

First of all, we have inheritance, which shows the IS-A relationship between classes.

```
class FlyingEnemy: public Enemy
{
  public:
    void Fly(void);
  private:
    int flySpeed;
};
```

When an object inherits from another object, it has all of the methods and fields that are contained in the parent class, while also adding their own content and features. In this instance, we have a special `FlyingEnemy`, which has the ability to fly in addition to all of the functionality of the `Enemy` class.

In UML, this is normally shown by a solid line with a hollow arrow and looks like the following:

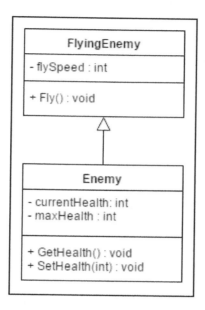

Aggregation

The next idea is aggregation, which is designated by the HAS-A relationship. This is when a single class contains a collection of instances of other classes that are obtained from somewhere else in your program. These are considered to have a weak HAS-A relationship as they can exist outside of the confines of the class.

In this case, I created a new class called `CombatEncounter` which can have an unlimited number of enemies that can be added to it. However when using aggregation, those enemies will exist before the `CombatEncounter` starts; and when it finishes, they will also still exist. Through code it would look something like this:

```
class CombatEncounter
{
  public:
    void AddEnemy(Enemy* pEnemy);
  private:
    std::list<Enemy*> enemies;

};
```

Inside of UML, it would look like this:

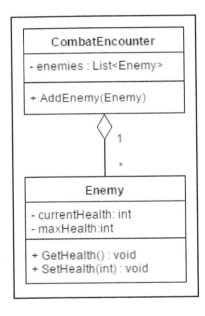

Composition

When using composition, this is a strong HAS-A relationship, and this is when a class contains one or more instances of another class. Unlike aggregation, these instances are not created on their own but, instead, are created in the constructor of the class and then destroyed by its destructor. Put into layman's terms, they can't exist separately from the whole.

In this case, we have created some new properties for the Enemy class, adding in combat skills that it can use, as in the Pokémon series. In this case, for every one enemy, there are four skills that the enemy will be able to have:

```
class AttackSkill
{
  public:
    void UseAttack(void);
  private:
    int damage;
    float cooldown;
};

class Enemy
{
  public:
    void GetHealth(void) const;
    void SetHealth(int);
  private:
    int         currentHealth;
    int         maxHealth;
    AttackSkill skill1;
    AttackSkill skill2;
    AttackSkill skill3;
    AttackSkill skill4;
};
```

The line in the diagram looks similar to aggregation, aside from the fact that the diamond is filled in:

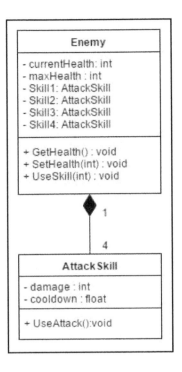

Implements

Finally, we have implements, which we will talk about in the *Introduction to interfaces* section.

The advantage to this form of communication is that the ideas presented will work the same way no matter what programming language you're using and without a specific implementation. That's not to say that a specific implementation isn't valuable, which is why we will also include the implementation for problems in code as well.

There's a lot more information out there about UML and there are various different formats that different people like to use. A nice guide that I found that may be of interest can be found at
https://cppcodetips.wordpress.com/2013/12/23/uml-class-diagram-explained-with-c-samples/.

Separating the why and the how

When creating games, we have many different systems that need to be juggled around in order to provide the entire game experience. We need to have objects that are drawn to the screen, need to have realistic physics, react when they hit each other, animate, have gameplay behavior and, on top of all that, we then need to make sure that it runs well 60 times every second.

Understanding the separation of concerns

Each of these different aspects is a problem of its own, and trying to solve all of these issues at once would be quite a headache. One of the most important concepts to learn as a developer is the idea of compartmentalizing problems, and breaking them apart into simpler and simpler pieces until they're all manageable. In computer science, there is a design principle known as the separation of concerns which deals with this issue. In this aspect, a concern would be something that will change the code of a program. Keeping this in mind, we would separate each of these concerns into their own distinct sections, with as little overlap in functionality as possible. Alternatively, we can make it so that each section solves a separate concern.

Now when we mention concerns, they are a distinct feature or a distinct section. Keeping that in mind, it can either be something as high level as an entire class or as low level as a function. By breaking apart these concerns into self-contained pieces that can work entirely on their own, we gain some distinct advantages. By separating each system and making it so they do not depend on each other, we can alter or extend any part of our project with minimal hassle. This concept creates the basis for almost every single design pattern that we'll be discussing.

By using this separation effectively, we can create code that is flexible, modular, and easy to understand. It'll also allow us to build the project in a much more iterative way because each class and function has its own clearly defined purpose. We won't have to worry nearly as much about adding new features that would break previously written code because the dependencies are on the existing functional classes, and never the other way around. This means we can to easily expand the game with things like **Downloadable Content (DLC)**. This might include new game types, additional players, or new enemies with their own unique artificial intelligence. Finally, we can take things we've already written and decouple them from the engine so we can use them for future projects, saving time and development costs.

An Introduction to interfaces

One of the main features of using design patterns is the idea of always programming to an interface and not to an implementation. In other words, the top of any class hierarchy should have an abstract class or an interface.

Polymorphism refresher

In Hollywood, lots of actors and actresses take on many different roles when filming movies. They can be the hero of a story, a villain, or anything else as they inhabit a role. No matter what role they've gotten, when they are being filmed they are acting even if what they do specifically can be quite different. This kind of behavior acts similarly to the idea of polymorphism.

Polymorphism is one of the three pillars of an object-oriented language (along with encapsulation and inheritance). It comes from the words *poly* meaning many and *morph* meaning change.

Polymorphism is a way to call different specific class functions in an inheritance hierarchy, even though our code only uses a single type. That single type, the base class reference, will be changed many ways depending on the derived type. Continuing with the Hollywood example, we can tell an actor to act out a role and, based on what they've been cast in, they will do something different.

By using the `virtual` keyword on a base class function and overriding that function in a derived class, we can gain the ability to call that derived class function from a base class reference. While it may seem a bit complex at first, this will seem clearer with an example. For instance, if we have the following class:

```
class Animal
{
  public:
    virtual void Speak(void) const //virtual in the base class
    {
      //Using the Mach 5 console print
      M5DEBUG_PRINT("...\n");
    }
};
```

I could create a derived class with its own method, without modifying the base class in any way. In addition, we have the ability to replace or override a method within a derived class without affecting the base class. Let's say I wanted to change this function:

```
class Cat: public Animal
  {
  public:
    void Speak(void) const //overridden in the derived class
    {
  M5DEBUG_PRINT("Meow\n");
  }

void Purr(void) const //unrelated function
  {
    M5DEBUG_PRINT("*purr*\n");
  }
};
class Dog: public Animal
  {
    public:
    void Speak(void) const //overridden in the derived class
    {
      M5DEBUG_PRINT("Woof\n");
    }
};
```

Since a derived class can be used anywhere a base class is needed, we can refer to derived classes using a base class pointer or an array of pointers and call the correct function at runtime. Let's have a look at the following code:

```
void SomeFunction(void)
{
  const int SIZE = 2;
  Cat cat;
  Dog dog;
  Animal* animals[SIZE] = {&cat, &dog};

  for(int i = 0; i < SIZE; ++i)
  {
    animals[i]->Speak();
  }
}
```

The following is the output of the preceding code:

```
Meow
Woof
```

As you can see, even though we have an array of base class pointers, the correct derived class function is called. If the functions weren't marked as virtual, or if the derived classes didn't override the correct functions, polymorphism wouldn't work.

Understanding interfaces

An interface implements no functions, but simply declares the methods that the class will support. Then, all of the derived classes will do the implementation. In this way, the developer will have more freedom to implement the functions to fit each instance, while having things work correctly due to the nature of using an object-oriented language.

Interfaces may contain only static final variables, and they may contain only abstract methods, which means that they cannot be implemented within the class. However, we can have interfaces that inherit from other interfaces. When creating theses classes, we can implement whatever number of interfaces we want to. This allows us to make classes become even more polymorphic but, by doing so, we are agreeing that we will implement each of the functions defined in the interface. Because a class that implements an interface extends from that base class, we would say that it has an IS-A relationship with that type.

Now, interfaces have one disadvantage, and that's the fact that they tend to require a lot of coding to implement each of the different versions as needed, but we will talk about ways to adjust and/or fix this issue over the course of this book.

In C++, there isn't an official concept of interfaces, but you can simulate the behavior of interfaces by creating an abstract class.

Here's a simple example of an interface, and an implementation of it:

```
class Enemy
{
  public:
    virtual ~Enemy(void) {/*Empty virtual destructor*/}
    virtual void DisplayInfo(void) = 0;
    virtual void Attack(void)      = 0;
    virtual void Move(void)        = 0;
};

class FakeEnemy: public Enemy
{
```

```
public:
virtual void DisplayInfo(void)
{
  M5DEBUG_PRINT("I am a FAKE enemy");
}

virtual void Attack(void)
  {
    M5DEBUG_PRINT("I cannot attack");
  }

virtual void Move(void)
{
  M5DEBUG_PRINT("I cannot move");
}
};
```

And here's how it looks in UML:

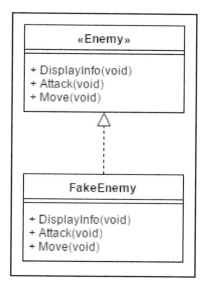

The advantages of compartmentalizing code

One important difference between procedural programming (think C-style) and object-oriented programming is the ability to encapsulate or compartmentalize code. Oftentimes we think of this as just data hiding: making variables private. In a C-style program, the functions and data are separate, but it is hard to reuse any one function because it might depend on other functions or other pieces of data in the program. In object-oriented programming, we are allowed to group the data and function together into reusable pieces. That means we can (hopefully) take a class or module and place it in a new project. This also means that since the data is private, a variable can be easily changed as long as the interface or public methods don't change. These concepts of encapsulation are important, but they aren't showing us all of the power that this provides us.

The goal of writing object-oriented code is to create objects that are responsible for themselves. Using a lot of if/else or switch statements within your code can be a symptom of bad design. For example, if I have three classes that need to read data from a text file, I have the choice of using a switch statement to read the data differently for each class type, or passing the text file to a class method and letting the class read the data itself. This is even more powerful when combined with the power of inheritance and polymorphism.

By making the classes responsible for themselves, the classes can change without breaking other code, and the other code can change without breaking the classes. We can all imagine how fragile the code would be if a game was written entirely in the main function. Anything that is added or removed is likely to break other code. Anytime a new member joined the team, they would need to understand absolutely every line and every variable in the game before they could be trusted to write anything.

By separating code into functions or classes, we are making the code easier to read, test, debug, and maintain. Anyone joining the team would of course need to understand some pieces of the code, but it might not be necessary to understand all of graphics if they are working on game logic or file loading.

Design patterns are solutions to common programming problems flexible enough to handle change. They do this by compartmentalizing sections of code. This isn't by accident. For the purposes of this book, the definition of good design is encapsulated, flexible, reusable code. So it should come as no surprise that these solutions are organized into classes or groups of classes that encapsulate the changing sections of your code.

The structure of the Mach5 engine

Throughout this book, we will be using design patterns to solve common game programming problems. The best way to do this is by example, and so we will be examining how these problems arise and implementing the solutions using the Mach5 engine, a 2D game engine designed in C++ by *Matt Casanova*. By looking at the entire source code for a game, we will be able to see how many of the patterns work together to create powerful and easy-to-use systems.

However, before we can dive into the patterns, we should spend a little time explaining the structure of the engine. You don't need to understand every line of source code, but it is important to understand some of the core engine components and how they are used. This way we can better understand the problems we will be facing and how the solution fits together.

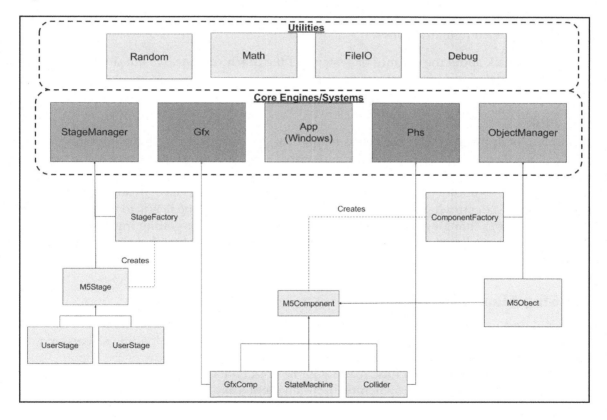

While looking at the diagram, it may seem a little confusing at first, so let's examine each piece of the engine separately.

Mach5 core engines and systems

The meaning of engine is getting a little blurred these days. Often when people talk of engines they think of entire game creation tools such as Unreal or Unity. While these are engines, the term didn't always require a tool. Game engines such as Id Software's Quake Engine or Valve Corporation's Source engine existed independently of tools, although the latter did have tools including the Hammer Editor for creating levels.

The term engine is also used to refer to components within the larger code base. This includes things like a rendering engine, audio engine, or physics engine. Even these can be created completely separate from a larger code base. Orge 3D is an open source 3D graphics engine, while the Havok Physics engine is proprietary software created by the Havok company and used in many games.

So, when we talk about the engines or systems of the Mach5 engine, we are simply referring to groups of related code for performing a specific task.

The app

The M5App or application layer is a class responsible for interfacing with the operating system. Since we are trying to write clean, reusable code, it is important that we don't mix our game code with any operating system function calls. If we did this, our game would be difficult to port to another system. The M5App class is created in WinMain and responsible for creating and destroying every other system. Anytime our game needs to interact with the OS, including changing resolution, switching to full screen, or getting input from a device, we will use the M5App class. In our case, the operating system that we will be using will be Windows.

The StageManager

The M5StageManager class is responsible for controlling the logic of each stage. We consider things such as the main menu, credits screen, options menu, loading screen, and playable levels to be stages. They contain behaviors that control the flow of the game. Examples of stage behavior include reading game object data from files, spawning units after specific time intervals, or switching between menus and levels.

StageManager is certainly not a standardized name. In other engines, this section of code may be called the game logic engine; however, most of our game logic will be separated into components so this name doesn't fit. No matter what it is called, this class will control which objects need to be created for the current stage, as well as when to switch to the next stage or quit the game altogether.

Even though this uses the name *manager* instead of *engine*, it serves as one of the core systems of the game. This class controls the main game loop and manages the collection of user stages. In order to make a game, users must derive at least one class from the base M5Stage class and overload the virtual functions to implement their game logic.

The ObjectManager

The M5ObjectManager is responsible for creating, destroying, updating, and searching for game objects. A game object is anything visible or invisible in the game. This could include the player, bullets, enemies, and triggers--the invisible regions in a game that cause events when collided with. The derived M5Stage classes will use the M5ObjectManager to create the appropriate objects for the stage. They can also search for specific game objects to update game logic. For example, a stage may search for a player object. If one doesn't exist, the manager will switch to the game over stage.

As seen in the previous diagram, our game will use components. This means the M5ObjectManager will be responsible for creating those as well.

The graphics engine

This book isn't about creating a graphics engine but we do need one to draw to the screen. Similar to how the M5App class encapsulates important OS function calls, our M5Gfx class encapsulates our graphics API. We want to make sure there is a clear separation between any API calls and our game logic. This is important so we can port our game to another system. For example, we may want to develop our game for PC, XBox One, and PlayStation 4. This will mean supporting multiple graphics APIs since a single API isn't available for all platforms. If our game logic contains API code, then those files will need to be modified for every platform.

We won't be going deep into the details of how to implement a full graphics engine, but we give an overview of how graphics works. Think of this as a primer to the world of graphics engines.

This class allows us manipulate and draw textures, as well as control the game camera and find the visible extents of the world. `M5Gfx` also manages two arrays of graphics components, one for world space and one for screen space. The most common use of the screen space components is for creating **User Interface (UI)** elements such as buttons.

Tools and utilities

Besides the core engines and systems for a game, every engine should provide some basics tools and support code. The Mach5 engine includes a few categories for tools:

- **Debug Tools**: This includes debug asserts, message windows, and creating a debug console
- **Random**: Helper functions to create random `int` or `float` from min/max values
- **Math**: This includes 2D vectors and 4 x 4 matrices, as well some more general math helper functions
- **FileIO**: Support for reading and writing `.ini` files

The problems with using design patterns in games

Unfortunately, there are also some issues that may come into play from using design patterns exactly as described. It's often said that the fastest executing code is the code that is never called, and using design patterns will typically require you to add more code to your project than what you would have done otherwise. This will have a performance cost as well, as there will likely need to be more calculations done whenever you're using a part of your engine.

For instance, using some principles will cause some classes that you write to become extremely bloated with extra code. Design patterns are another form of complexity to add to your project. If the problem itself is simple, it can be a much better idea to focus on the simpler solutions before going straight into implementing a design pattern just because you have heard of it.

Sometimes it's better to follow the simple rule of **K.I.S.S.** and remember that it is the knowledge of the pattern that holds the most important value, not using the pattern itself.

Setting up the project

Now that we've gotten a good understanding of why we would want to use design patterns, let's get set up the game engine that we will be using over the course of the book: the Mach5 engine. Now in order to get started, we will need to download the engine as well as the software needed to run the project. Perform the following steps:

1. Open up your web browser of choice and visit the following website: `https://beta.visualstudio.com/downloads/`. Once there, move to the **Visual Studio Community** version on the left and then click on the **Free download** option, as shown in the following screenshot:

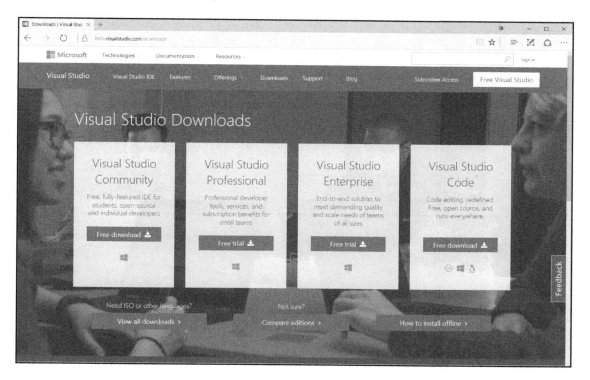

2. If you get a window asking what to do with the file, go ahead and open it or save and then open it by clicking on the **Run** button:

3. From there, wait until the installer pops up, then select **Custom**, and then click on **Next** to start downloading the program:

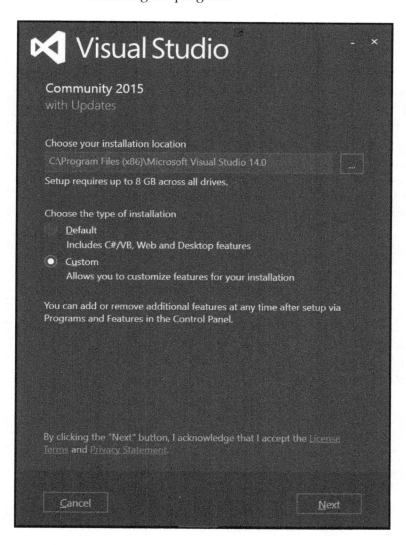

4. Now once you get to the **Features** section, uncheck whatever is selected and then open up the **Programming Languages** tab and check **Visual C++**. You may go ahead and remove the other options, as we will not be using them. Then go ahead and click on the **Next** button, then **Install**, and allow it to make changes to your computer:

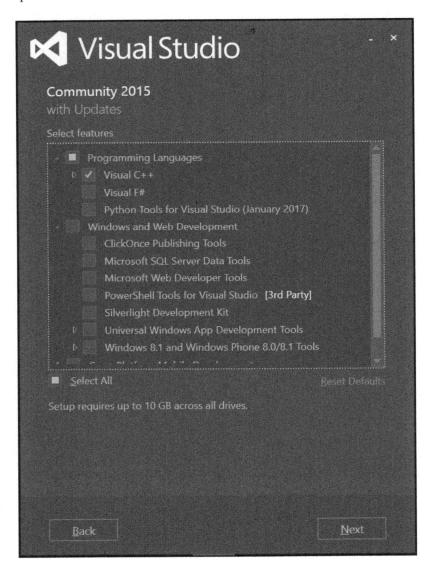

You may need to wait a while at this point, so go ahead and get yourself a coffee, and once it's finished you'll need to restart your computer. After that, go ahead and continue with the project.

5. Once you've finished installing, you next need to actually install the engine itself. With that in mind, go over to `https://github.com/mattCasanova/Mach5` and from there, click on the **Clone or download** section and then click on **Download ZIP**:

6. Once you're finished with the download, go ahead and unzip the file to a folder of your choice; then open up the `Mach5-master\EngineTest` folder, double-click on the `EngineTest.sln` file, and start up Visual Studio.

7. You may get a login screen asking you to log in; go ahead and sign up or press the **Not now, maybe later** option on the bottom of the screen. You can then pick a color theme; then click **Start Visual Studio**.

8. Upon starting, you may get a security warning asking if you'd still like to open this project. This is displayed from any Visual Studio solution that wasn't made on your machine, so it wants to make sure that you know where it came from, but in this case the project is perfectly safe. Go ahead and uncheck the **Ask me for every project in this solution option** and then select **OK**:

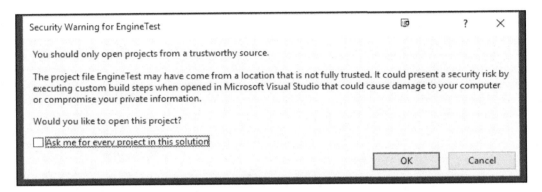

9. Once it's finished loading, you should finally see the Visual Studio interface, which should look like this:

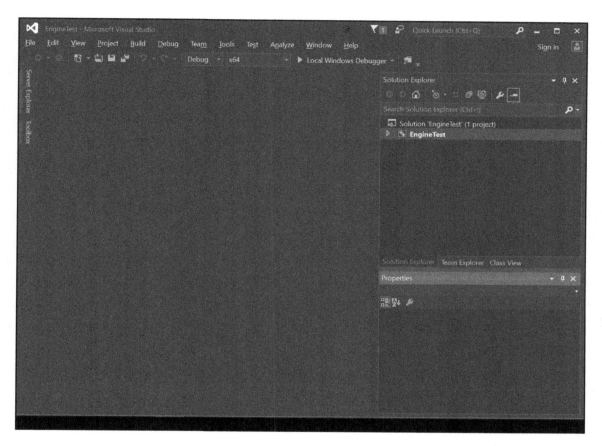

Visual Studio is a very powerful tool and, for developers, it can be quite useful to learn all of the functionality that it has. We'll be discussing the features as we use them, but this book shouldn't be considered the end-all book on Visual Studio.

 If you're interested in learning more about the Visual Studio interface, check out: https://msdn.microsoft.com/en-us/library/jj620919.aspxa.

10. The engine is built to work on 32-bit processors, so change the x64 dropdown to x86 and then click the **Play** button or press *F5*. It will then ask if you wish to rebuild the project. Go ahead and say **Yes**. If all goes well, you should eventually see a debug window and a gameplay window as well. After a few seconds, it should transition to a simple default project:

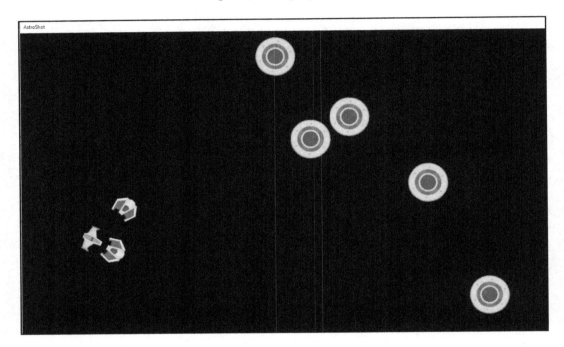

You can play around by using the *W*, *A*, and *D* keys to move the character around and the *Spacebar* to shoot bullets at enemies. Once you're finished playing around, go ahead and hit the *Esc* key to go to the menu, and then click on the **Quit** button to leave the project and go back to the editor!

Summary

And there we have it! In this first chapter, you've learned some fundamentals about design patterns and also got the Mach5 engine running on your computer.

Specifically, we learned that design patterns are solutions for common programming problems. There are a lot of reasons why we should use them, but in order to use patterns effectively, you first need to know what problem you are trying to solve and which ones can help you in that instance, which is what this book intends to teach you.

We learned how game development is always changing and how important it is to have a plan, as well as an architecture that can support those changes. With that in mind, we learned about various aspects of coding that will be used in the creation of our architecture.

We dived into learning about the separation of concerns principle and how important it is for us to separate the what and how; making it so they do not depend on each other allows us to alter or extend any part of our project with minimal hassle. Afterwards, we explored what interfaces were and how they are useful in giving us a foundation we can build on. Later, we dived into the Mach5 engine, saw an example of how compartmentalized code worked, and the advantages of it. We also saw how using design patterns in games can be a great thing, as well as the problems that they have.

Finally, we downloaded the Mach5 engine ourselves and made sure that it worked correctly. Moving on, in the next chapter, we will tackle our first design pattern, the Singleton, and see how it can be useful to us!

One Instance to Rule Them All - Singletons

2

Now that we've learned what a design pattern is, as well as why we'd want to use them, let's first talk about a design pattern that most people learn, the Singleton pattern.

The Singleton pattern is probably the most well-known pattern and it is also the one out there that is most often misused. It definitely has the most controversy surrounding it, so when discussing this pattern it is as important (or even more important) to know when not to apply it.

Chapter overview

In this chapter, we will explain about the pattern and many arguments for and against it. We will describe how and why core systems within the Mach5 engine such as the Graphics Engine and Object Manager are utilized as Singletons. Finally, we will explain a number of different ways to implement this in C++, along with the pros and cons of each choice.

Your objective

This chapter will be split into a number of topics. It will contain a simple step-by-step process from beginning to end. Here is the outline of our tasks:

- An overview of class access specifiers
- Pros and cons of global access
- Understanding the `static` keyword

- What is a Singleton?
- Learning about templates
- Templatizing Singletons
- The advantages and disadvantages of only one instance
- The Singleton in action: the `Application` class
- Design decisions

An overview on class access specifiers

When using an object-oriented programming language, one of the most important features included is the ability to hide data, preventing classes from accessing properties and functions of another class type by default. By using access specifiers such as `public`, `private`, and `protected`, we can dictate specifically how the data and/or functions can be accessed from other classes:

```
class ModifierExamples
{
  public int publicInteger;
  private void PrivateMethod() {}
  protected float protectedNumber;
};
```

A class can have unlimited variables or functions that are `public`, `private`, or `protected` and can even control access to entire sections of the class:

```
class MoreModifierExamples
{
  public:
    // until we reach another tag, all variables and functions
    // will be public
    int publicIntegar;
    int anotherExample;

  private:
    // Now, they'll be private
    void PrivateFunction() {}
    double safeValue;

  protected:
    // And now... protected
    float protectedNumber;
    int AlsoProtected() { return 0; }
};
```

When you place a labelled section with an access modifier's name and a : next to it, until there is another section label, all of the parts of the class that are listed will use that specific one.

When we use the `public` access modifier, we are saying that this variable or function can be used or accessed from anywhere within our program, even outside of the class we've created. Declaring a variable outside of a function or class, or marking a variable as `public` and `static`, is often referred to as being a global variable. We will be talking about global variables in the next section, but for right now, let's go over the other access specifiers as well.

When `private` is used, we are restricting the usage of our variable or function to being allowed only inside of the class, or from `friend` functions. By default, all of the variables and functions in a class are `private`.

 For more information on friend functions, check out
http://en.cppreference.com/w/cpp/language/friend.

The third type, `protected`, is the same as a `private` type except that it can still be accessed by child (or derived) classes. This can be quite useful when using inheritance so you can still access those variables and/or functions.

The static keyword

Another thing that is important to know before diving into the Singleton pattern is what the `static` keyword means, as it's something that we will be using the functionality of when building this pattern. When we use the `static` keyword, there are three main contexts that it'll be used in:

- Inside a function
- Inside a class definition
- In front of a global variable in a program with multiple files

Static keyword inside a function

The first one, being used inside of a function, basically means that once the variable has been initialized, it will stay in the computer's memory until the end of the program, keeping the value that it has through multiple runs of the function. A simple example would be something like this:

```
#include <string>

class StaticExamples
{
public:
  void InFunction()
  {
    static int enemyCount = 0;

    // Increase the value of enemyCount
    enemyCount += 10;

    std::string toDisplay = "\n Value of enemyCount:   " +
            std::to_string(enemyCount);

    printf(toDisplay.c_str());
  }
};
```

Now if we were to call this, it would look something like the following:

```
StaticExamples se;

se.InFunction();
se.InFunction();
```

And when we call it, the following would be displayed:

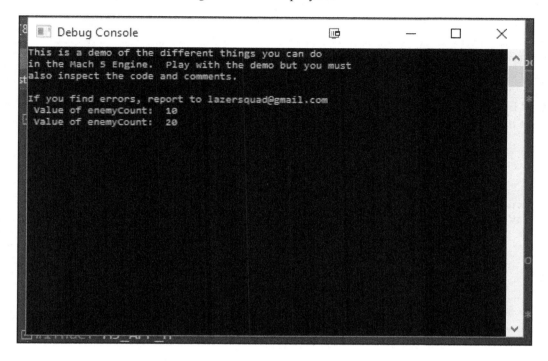

As you can see, the value continues to exist, and we can access and/or modify its contents as we see fit in the function. This could be used for a number of things, such as maybe needing to know what happened the last time that you called this function, or to store any kind of data between any calls. It's also worth noting that static variables are shared by all instances of the class, and due to that, if we had two variables of type StaticExamples, they would both display the same enemyCount. We will utilize the fact that, if an object is created this way, it will always be available later on in this chapter.

Static keyword in class definitions

The second way is by having a variable or function in a class being defined as `static`. Normally, when you create an instance of a class, the compiler has to set aside additional memory for each variable that is contained inside of the class in consecutive blocks of memory. When we declare something as `static`, instead of creating a new variable to hold data, a single variable is shared by all of the instances of the class. In addition, since it's shared by all of the copies, you don't need to have an instance of the class to call it. Take a look at the following bolded code to create our variable:

```cpp
class StaticExamples

{
public:
    static float classVariable;
    static void StaticFunction()
    {
        // Note, can only use static variables and functions within
        // static function
        std::string toDisplay = "\n I can be called anywhere!
        classVariable value: " + std::to_string(classVariable);

        printf(toDisplay.c_str());
    }

    void InFunction()
    {
        static int enemyCount = 0;

        // Increase the value of enemyCount
        enemyCount += 10;

        std::string toDisplay = "\n Value of enemyCount:   " +
                    std::to_string(enemyCount);

        printf(toDisplay.c_str());
    }
};
```

Now, in the preceding code we define a variable and a function, but this isn't all the prep work we need to do. When creating a static variable, you cannot initialize it from within the class, and instead need to do it in a `.cpp` file instead of the `.h` file we could use for the class definition. You'll get errors if you do not initialize it, so it's a good idea to do that. In our case, it'd look like the following:

```
// StaticExamples.cpp
float StaticExamples::classVariable = 2.5f;
```

Note that, when we initialize, we also need to include the type, but we use the `ClassName::variableName` template similar to how you define functions in `.cpp` files. Now that everything's set up, let's see how we can access them inside our normal code:

```
StaticExamples::StaticFunction();
StaticExamples::classVariable = 5;
StaticExamples::StaticFunction();
```

Note that instead of accessing it via creating a variable, we can instead just use the class name followed by the scope operator (`::`) and then select which static variable or function we'd like to use. When we run it, it'll look like this:

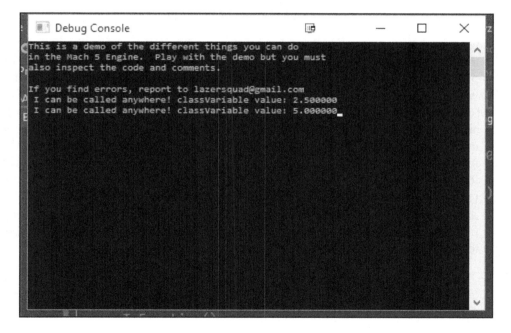

As you can see, it works perfectly!

Static as a file global variable

As you may be aware, C++ is a programming language closely related to the C programming language. C++ was designed to have most of the same functionality that C had and then added more things to it. C was not object-oriented, and so, when it created the `static` keyword, it was used to indicate that source code in other files that are part of your project cannot access the variable, and that only code inside of your file can use it. This was designed to create class-like behavior in C. Since we have classes in C++ we don't typically use it, but I felt I should mention it for completeness.

Pros and cons of global variables

To reiterate, a global variable is a variable that is declared outside of a function or class. Doing this makes our variable accessible in every function, hence us calling it global. When being taught programming in school, we were often told that global variables are a bad thing or at least, that modifying global variables in a function is considered to be poor programming practice.

There are numerous reasons why using global variables is a bad idea:

- Source code is the easiest to understand when the scope of the elements used is limited. Adding in global variables that can be read or modified anywhere in the program makes it much harder to keep track of where things are being done, as well as making it harder to comprehend when bringing on new developers.
- Since a global variable can be modified anywhere, we lose any control over being able to confirm that the data contained in the variable is valid. For instance, you may only want to support up to a certain number, but as a global variable this is impossible to stop. Generally, we advise using `getter/setter` functions instead for this reason.
- Using global variables tightens how coupled our programs are, making it difficult to reuse aspects of our projects as we need to grab from a lot of different places to make things work. Grouping things that are connected to each other tends to improve projects.

- When working with the linker, if your global variable names are common, you'll often have issues when compiling your project. Thankfully, you'll get an error and have to fix the issue in this case. Unfortunately, you may also have an issue where you are trying to use a locally scoped variable in a project but end up selecting the global version due to mistyping the name or relying too heavily on intelligence and selecting the first thing you see, which I see students doing on multiple occasions.
- As the size of projects grow, it becomes much harder to do maintenance and/or make changes to/on global variables, as you may need to modify many parts of your code to have it adjust correctly.

This isn't to say that global access is entirely bad. There are some reasons why one would consider using it in their projects:

- Not knowing what a local variable is
- Not understanding how to create classes
- Wanting to save keystrokes
- Not wanting to pass around variables all the time to functions
- Not knowing where to declare a variable, so making it global means anyone can get it
- To simplify our project for components that need to be accessible anywhere within the project

Aside from the last point, those issues are really bad reasons for wanting to use global variables, as they may save you some time up front, but as your projects get larger and larger it'll be a lot more difficult to read your code. In addition, once you make something global it's going to be a lot more difficult to convert it to not be global down the road. Think that, instead of using global variables, you could instead pass parameters to different functions as needed, making it easier to understand what each function does and what it needs to work with to facilitate its functionality.

That's not to say that there isn't any time when using a global variable is a reasonable or even a good idea. When global variables represent components that truly need to be available throughout your project, the use of global variables simplifies the code of your project, which is similar to what we are aiming to accomplish.

 Norm Matloff also has an article explaining times that he feels like global variables are necessary when writing code. If you want to hear an alternative take, check out
http://heather.cs.ucdavis.edu/~matloff/globals.html.

Basically, always limit your variables to the minimal scope needed for the project and not any more. This especially comes to mind when you only ever need one of something, but plan to use that one object with many different things. That's the general idea of the Singleton design pattern and is the reason why it's important that we understand the general usage before moving onwards.

What is a Singleton?

The Singleton pattern in a nutshell is where you have a class that you can access anywhere within your project, due to the fact that only one object (instance) of that class is created (instantiated). The pattern provides a way for programmers to give access to a class's information globally by creating a single instance of an object in your game.

Whereas there are quite a few issues with using global variables, you can think of a Singleton as an *improved* global variable due to the fact that you cannot create more than one. With this in mind, the Singleton pattern is an attractive choice for classes that only have a unique instance in your game project, such as your graphics pipeline and input libraries, as having more than one of these in your projects doesn't make sense.

This single object uses a static variable and static functions to be able to access the object without having to pass it through all of our code.

In the Mach5 engine, Singletons are used for the application's, input, graphics, and physics engines. They are also used for the resource manager, object manager, and the game state manager. We will be taking a much closer look at one of the more foundational ones in the engine, the `Application` class, later on in this chapter. But before we get to it, let's dive into how we can actually create one of our very own.

There are multiple ways to implement the Singleton pattern or to get Singleton-like behavior. We'll go over some of the commonly seen versions and their pros and cons before moving to our final version, which is how the Mach5 engine uses it.

One very common way of implementing the functionality of the Singleton pattern would look something like the following:

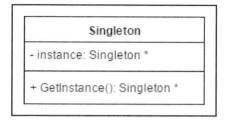

Through code, it will look a little something like this:

```
class Singleton
{
  public:
    static Singleton * GetInstance()
    {
      // If the instance does not exist, create one
      if (!instance)
      {
        instance = new Singleton;
      }

      return instance;
    }

  private:
    static Singleton * instance;
};
```

In this class, we have a function called `GetInstance` and a single property called `instance`. Note that we are using pointers in this instance, and only allocating memory to create our Singleton if we are actually using it. The instance property represents the one and only version of our class, hence it being made `static`. As it is private though, there is no way for others to access its data unless we give them access to it. In order to give this access, we created the `GetInstance` function. This function will first check whether instance exists and if it doesn't yet, it will dynamically allocate the memory to create one, set instance to it, and then return the object.

 This will only work if instance is properly set to 0 or `nullptr` when initialized, which thankfully is the default behavior of static pointers in C++.

Keeping the single in Singleton

As we've mentioned previously, one of the most important parts of the Singleton pattern is the fact that there is only one of those objects. That causes some issues with the original code that we've written, namely that with some simple usage of C++ it is quite easy to have more than one of these classes created by other programmers on your team. First and most obviously, they can just create a `Singleton` variable (a variable of type `Singleton`) like the following:

```
Singleton singleton;
```

In addition, as a higher-level programming language, C++ will try to do some things automatically for you when creating classes to eliminate some of the busy work that would be involved otherwise. One of these things is automatically creating some functionality between classes to enable you to create or copy objects of a custom class that we refer to as a constructor and copy constructor. In our case, you can also create a copy of your current object in the following way:

```
Singleton instanceCopy(*(Singleton::GetInstance()));
```

The compiler will also create a default destructor and an assignment operator, moving the data from one object to the other.

Thankfully, that's a simple enough thing to fix. If we create these functions ourselves (declaring an explicit version), C++ notes that we want to do something special, so it will not create the defaults. So to fix our problem, we will just need to add an assignment operator and some constructors that are private, which you can see in the bold code that we've changed:

```
class Singleton
{
public:
  static Singleton * GetInstance()
  {
    // If the instance does not exist, create one
    if (!instance)
    {
      instance = new Singleton;
    }

    return instance;
  }

private:
  static Singleton * instance;
```

```
// Disable usability of silently generated functions
Singleton();
~Singleton();
Singleton(const Singleton &);
Singleton& operator=(const Singleton&);

};
```

 If you are using C++ 11 or above, it is also possible for us to instead mark the functions we don't want to use as deleted, which would look like this:

```
Singleton() = delete;
~Singleton() = delete;
Singleton(const Singleton &) = delete;
Singleton& operator=(const Singleton&) = delete;
```

For more information on the delete keyword, check out http://www.stro ustrup.com/C++11FAQ.html#default.

Another thing that may possibly be an issue is that instance is a pointer. This is because, as a pointer, our users have the ability to call delete on it and we want to make sure that the object will always be available for our users to access. To minimize this issue, we could change our pointer to be a reference, instead, by changing the function to the following (note the return type and that we use *instance now on the last line):

```
static Singleton& GetInstance()
{
  // If the instance does not exist, create one
  if (!instance)
  {
    instance = new Singleton;
  }

  return *instance;
}
```

Programmers are used to working with references as aliases for objects that exist somewhere else in our project. People would be surprised if they ever saw something like:

```
Singleton& singleton = Singleton::GetInstance();
delete &singleton;
```

While technically doable, programmers won't expect to ever use delete on the address of a reference. The nice thing about using references is that, when you need them in code, you know that they exist because they're managed somewhere else in the code--and you don't need to worry about how they are used.

Deleting our object correctly

People also are used to looking for memory leaks with pointers and not references, so that perhaps leaves us with an issue as, in our current code, we allocate memory but don't actually delete it.

Now, technically, we haven't created a memory leak. Memory leaks appear when you allocate data and lose all of your references to it. Also, modern operating systems take care of deallocating a process's memory when our project is quit.

That's not to say that it's a good thing though. Depending on what information the Singleton class uses, we could have references to things that no longer exist at some point.

To have our object delete itself correctly, we need to destroy the Singleton when our game shuts down. The only issue is we need to make sure that we do it only when we are sure no one will be using the Singleton afterwards.

However, as we want to talk about best practices, it's much better for us to actually solve this issue by removing resource leaks whenever we see them. A solution to this very problem was created by *Scott Meyers* in his book *More Effective C++*, which uses some of the features of the compiler, namely that a static variable located in a function will exist throughout our program's running time. For instance, let's take the following function:

```
void SpawnEnemy()
{
   static int numberOfEnemies = 0;
   ++numberOfEnemies;

   // Spawn the enemy
}
```

The `numberOfEnemies` variable is created and has been initialized before any code in the project has been executed, most likely when the game was being loaded. Then, once `SpawnEnemy` is called for the first time, it will have already been set to `0` (or `nullptr`). Conveniently, as the object is not allocated dynamically, the compiler will also create code so that, when the game exists, it will call the deconstructor for our object automatically.

With that in mind, we can modify our Singleton class to the following:

```
class Singleton
{
  public:
    static Singleton & GetInstance()
    {
      static Singleton instance;
      return instance;
    }

  private:
    // Disable usability of silently generated functions
    Singleton();
    ~Singleton();
    Singleton(const Singleton &);
    Singleton& operator=(const Singleton&);

};
```

Specifically note the changes we've made to the `GetInstance` function and the removal of our class instance variable. This method provides the simplest way to destroy the `Singleton` class automatically and it works fine for most purposes.

Learning about templates

Another technique to add to your toolbox of programming concepts that we will use in the next section is the idea of templates. **Templates** are a way for you to be able to create generic classes that can be extended to have the same functionality for different datatypes. It's another form of abstraction, letting you define a base set of behavior for a class without knowing what type of data will be used on it. If you've used the STL before, you've already been using templates, perhaps without knowing it. That's why the list class can contain any kind of object.

Here's an example of a simple templated class:

```
#include <iostream> // std::cout

template <class T>
class TemplateExample
{
public:
  // Constructor
  TemplateExample();
  // Destructor
```

```
    ~TemplateExample();
    // Function
    T TemplatedFunction(T);
};
```

In this case, we created our `TemplateExample` class and it has three functions. The constructor and deconstructor look normal, but then I have this `TemplateFunction` function which takes in an object of type `T`, and returns an object of type `T`. This `T` comes from the first line of our example code with the template `<class T>` section of our code. Anywhere that there is a `T` it will be replaced with whatever class we want to use this template with.

Now, unlike regular functions, we have to define templated functions within our `.h` file, so that, when we need to create an object using this template, it will know what the functions will do. In addition to this, the syntax is also a bit different:

```
template <class T> TemplateExample<T>::TemplateExample()
{
  printf("\nConstructor!");
}

template <class T> TemplateExample<T>::~TemplateExample()
{
  printf("\nDeconstructor!");
}

template <class T> T TemplateExample<T>::TemplatedFunction(T obj)
{
  std::cout << "\nValue: " << obj;
  return obj;
}
```

In this example, I'm just printing out text to display when a certain functionality is called, but I also want to point out the usage of `std::cout` and that using it will require you to add `#include <iostream>` to the top of your file.

We are using the standard library's `cout` function in this instance, instead of the `printf` that we have been using, because `cout` allows us to feed in `obj`--no matter what its type is-- to display something, which isn't possible with `printf` by default.

Once that's finished, we can go ahead and use this inside of our project:

```
TemplateExample<int> teInt;
teInt.TemplatedFunction(5);


TemplateExample<float> teFloat;
teFloat.TemplatedFunction(2.5);

TemplateExample<std::string> teString;
teString.TemplatedFunction("Testing");
```

As you can see, this will create three different kinds of `TemplateExample` class objects using different types. When we call the `TemplatedFunction` function, it will print out exactly the way we were hoping:

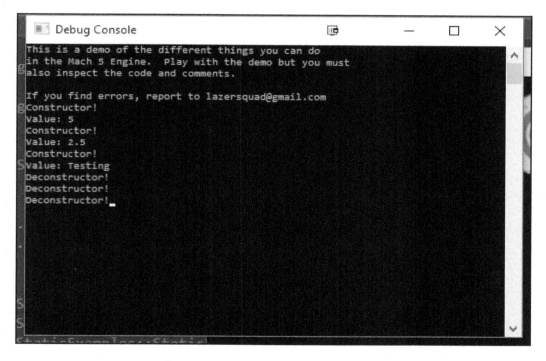

Later on, when we learn about abstract types, we can use templates with them to handle any kind of data. In our case right now, we are going to use this functionality to allow us to make as many Singletons as we'd like!

Templatizing Singletons

Now, assuming we get our Singleton working just the way that we want it to, you may wish to create more Singletons in the future. You could create them all from scratch, but a better thing to do is instead create a consistent approach, creating templates and inheritance to create a single implementation that you can use for any class. At the same time, we can also learn about an alternative way of creating a Singleton class, which will look something like the following:

```
template <typename T>
class Singleton
{
public:
  Singleton()
  {
    // Set our instance variable when we are created
    if (instance == nullptr)
    {
      instance = static_cast<T*>(this);
    }
    else
    {
      // If instance already exists, we have a problem
      printf("\nError: Trying to create more than one Singleton");
    }
  }

  // Once destroyed, remove access to instance
  virtual ~Singleton()
  {
    instance = nullptr;
  }

  // Get a reference to our instance
  static T & GetInstance()
  {
    return *instance;
  }

  // Creates an instance of our instance
  static void CreateInstance()
  {
    new T();
  }

  // Deletes the instance, needs to be called or resource leak
  static void RemoveInstance()
```

```
  {
    delete instance;
  }

private:
  // Note, needs to be a declaration
  static T * instance;

};


template <typename T> T * Singleton<T>::instance = nullptr;
```

You'll notice that most of the differences have to do with the class itself. The very first line in our code above uses the `template` keyword which tells the compiler that we are creating a template, and `typename T` tells the compiler that, when we create a new object using this, the type `T` will be replaced with whatever the class we want it to be based on is.

I also want to point out the use of a static cast to convert our Singleton pointer to a `T`. `static_cast` is used in code generally when you want to reverse an implicit conversion. It's important to note that `static_cast` performs no runtime checks for if it's correct or not. This should be used if you know that you refer to an object of a specific type, and thus a check would be unnecessary. In our case, it is safe because we will be casting from a Singleton object to the type that we've derived from it (`T`).

Of course, it may be useful to see an example of this being used, so let's create an example of a class that we could use as a Singleton, perhaps something to manage the high scores for our game:

```
class HighScoreManager : public Singleton<HighScoreManager>
{
public:
  void CheckHighScore(int score);

private:
  int highScore;
};
```

Notice here that, when we declare our `HighScoreManager` class, we say that it's derived from the `Singleton` class and, in turn, we pass the `HighScoreManager` class to the `Singleton` template. This pattern is known as the curiously recurring template pattern.

For more information on the curiously recurring template pattern, check out https://en.wikipedia.org/wiki/Curiously_recurring_template_patte rn.

After defining the class, let's go ahead and add in an example implementation for the function we've created for this class:

```
void HighScoreManager::CheckHighScore(int score)
{
  std::string toDisplay;

  if (highScore < score)
  {
    highScore = score;
    toDisplay = "\nNew High Score: " + std::to_string(score);
    printf(toDisplay.c_str());
  }
  else
  {
    toDisplay = "\nCurrent High Score: " + std::to_string(highScore);
    printf(toDisplay.c_str());
  }
}
```

By using the templatized version of our class, we don't need to create the same materials as in the preceding class. We can just focus on the stuff that is particular to what this class needs to do. In this case, it's checking our current high score, and setting it to whatever we pass in if we happen to beat it.

Of course, it's great to see our code in action, and in this case I used the `SplashStage` class, which is located in the Mach5 `EngineTest` project, under `SpaceShooter/Stages/SplashStage.cpp`. To do so, I added the following bolded lines to the `Init` function:

```
void SplashStage::Init(void)
{
  //This code will only show in the console if it is active and you
  //are in debug mode.
  M5DEBUG_PRINT("This is a demo of the different things you can do\n");
  M5DEBUG_PRINT("in the Mach 5 Engine.  Play with the demo but you
must\n");
  M5DEBUG_PRINT("also inspect the code and comments.\n\n");
  M5DEBUG_PRINT("If you find errors, report to lazersquad@gmail.com");

  HighScoreManager::CreateInstance();
```

```
HighScoreManager::GetInstance().CheckHighScore(10);
HighScoreManager::GetInstance().CheckHighScore(100);
HighScoreManager::GetInstance().CheckHighScore(50);

//Create ini reader and starting vars
M5IniFile iniFile;

// etc. etc.
```

In this case, our instance has been created by us creating a new `HighScoreManager`. If that is not done, then our project could potentially crash when calling `GetInstance`, so it's very important to call it. Then call our `CheckHighScore` functions a number of times to verify that the functionality works correctly. Then, in the `Shutdown` function, add the following bolded line to make sure the Singleton is removed correctly:

```
void SplashStage::Shutdown(void)
{
  HighScoreManager::RemoveInstance();

  M5ObjectManager::DestroyAllObjects();
}
```

With all of that gone, go ahead, save the file, and run the game. The output will be as follows:

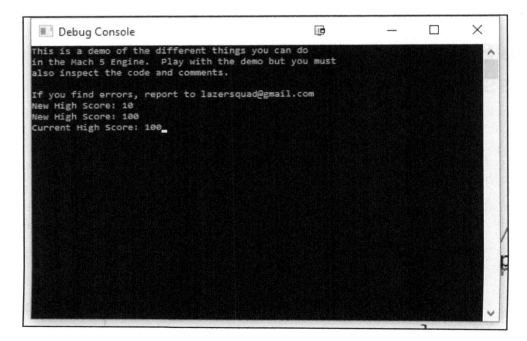

As you can see, our code works correctly!

Note that this has the same disadvantages we discussed with our initial version of the script, with the fact that we have to manually create the object and remove it; but it takes away a lot of the busy work when creating a number of Singletons in your project. If you're going to be creating a number of them in your project, this could be a good method to look into.

Advantages/disadvantages of using only one instance

There is the possibility that as you continue your project, something that looks at the time to be a thing that you'll only need one of will suddenly turn into something you need more of down the road. In games, one of the easiest examples would be that of a player. When starting the game, you may think you're only going to have one player, but maybe later you decide to add co-op. Depending on what you did before, that can be a small or huge change to the project.

Finally, one of the more common mistakes we see once programmers learn about Singletons, is to create managers for everything, and then make the managers all Singletons.

The Singleton in action - the Application class

The Singleton pattern achieves its ability to be accessible anywhere easily by having a special function that we use to get the `Singleton` object. When this function is called, we will check whether that object has been created yet. If it has, then we will simple return a reference to the object. If not, we will create it, and then return a reference to the newly created object.

Now, in addition to having this way to access it, we also want to block off our user from being able to create them, so we will need to define our class constructors to be private.

Now that we have an understanding of some implementations of the Singleton, we have one other version, which is what we actually used within the Mach5 engine.

In Mach5, the only Singletons that are included are aspects of the engine code. The engine code is designed to work with any game, meaning there is nothing gameplay-specific about it, which means that it doesn't need to have instances since they're just instructions. Building the engine in this way makes it much easier in the future to bring this to other games, since it's been removed from anything that's game-specific.

In this case, let's open up the M5App.h file which is in the EngineTest project under Core/Singletons/App and take a look at the class itself:

```
//! Singleton class to Control the Window
class M5App
{
public:
  friend class M5StageManager;

  /*Call These in Main*/

  /*This must be called first, before the game is started*/
  static void Init(const M5InitData& initStruct);
  /*Call this after you add your stages to start the game*/
  static void Update(void);
  /*Call this after Update is finished*/
  static void Shutdown(void);

  /*Call these to control or get info about the application*/

  /*Use this to change to fullscreen and back*/
  static void SetFullScreen(bool fullScreen);
  /*Use this to show and hide the window*/
  static void ShowWindow(bool show);
  /*Use this to show and hide the default window cursor*/
  static void ShowCursor(bool showCursor);
  /*Use this to change the resolution of the game*/
  static void SetResolution(int width, int height);
  /*Returns the width and height of the window (client area)*/
  static M5Vec2 GetResolution(void);

private:
  static LRESULT CALLBACK M5WinProc(HWND win, UINT msg, WPARAM wp, LPARAM
lp);
  static void ProcessMessages(void);

};//end M5APP
```

Now, the Mach5 engine follows the Singleton pattern. However, it is done in a different way from the others that we've looked at so far. You may notice in the class definition that every single function and variable that was created was made static.

This provides us with some unique benefits, namely that we don't need to worry about the user creating multiple versions of the class, because they'll only be restricted to using static properties and variables that are shared by everything. This means we don't need to worry about all of those fringe cases we mentioned in the previous examples that we've seen. This is possibly due to the fact that the Mach5 engine classes have no need to have child classes; there's no need for us to create a pointer or even call a GetInstance function.

You'll also notice the Init, Update, and Shutdown functions mentioned previously. We mentioned before that it was a disadvantage to manually have to create and destroy our singleton classes, but there are some distinct benefits to having this control. In the previous examples we had, the order in which classes were created was up to the compiler as we couldn't control the order. However, with our game engine it makes sense to create our Application (M5App) before we start up the graphics library (M5Gfx) and the only way we can make sure that happens is by telling our engine to do so, which you can look at if you open up the Main.cpp file and look at the WinMain function, which is what opens first when we create our project. I've gone ahead and bolded the uses of M5App:

```
int WINAPI WinMain(HINSTANCE instance,
                   HINSTANCE /*prev*/,
                   LPSTR /*commandLine*/,
                   int /*show*/)
{
   /*This should appear at the top of winmain to have windows find memory
leaks*/
   M5DEBUG_LEAK_CHECKS(-1);

   M5InitData initData;          /*Declare my InitStruct*/
   M5GameData gameData = { 0 };  /*Create my game data initial values*/
   M5IniFile iniFile;            /*To load my init data from file*/

   iniFile.ReadFile("GameData/InitData.ini");
   iniFile.SetToSection("InitData");

   /*Set up my InitStruct*/
   iniFile.GetValue("width", initData.width);
   iniFile.GetValue("height", initData.height);
   iniFile.GetValue("framesPerSecond", initData.fps);
   iniFile.GetValue("fullScreen", initData.fullScreen);

   initData.title      = "AstroShot";
   initData.instance   = instance;
```

```
/*Information about your specific gamedata */
initData.pGData      = &gameData;
initData.gameDataSize = sizeof(M5GameData);

/*Pass InitStruct to Function.  This function must be called first!!!*/
M5App::Init(initData);

/*Make sure to add what stage we will start in*/
M5StageManager::SetStartStage(ST_SplashStage);

/*Start running the game*/
M5App::Update();
/*This function must be called after the window has closed!!!*/
M5App::Shutdown();

return 0;
}
```

Afterwards, we can look at the `Init` function of `M5App` and see that it will initialize the other Singletons in our project:

```
void M5App::Init(const M5InitData& initData)
{
    // ...
        // Other init code above...

    M5StageManager::Init(initData.pGData, initData.gameDataSize,
initData.fps);
    M5ObjectManager::Init();
    M5Input::Init();
}
```

By having this control, our users have a much better idea as to the flow and order that things will be created. But, of course, with that great power comes great responsibility.

The Singleton pattern is used only for single-threaded applications. Should you be developing a multithreaded game, you'll want to use the Double-Checked Locking pattern instead, which was created by *Doug Schmidt* and *Tim Harrison*. If you're interested in learning more about it, check out `https://en.wikipedia.org/wiki/Double-checked_locking`.

Summary

In this chapter, we have demystified a lot of programming concepts in a quick refresher. We also started learning about our first design pattern, the Singleton, which is intended to allow us to always have access to a class's functions and variables due to the fact that there will only ever be one of these objects.

We discussed some of the typical downfalls of using the Singleton pattern, such as the possibility that objects could have multiple copies of them in the future, even if this is unlikely.

We learned about three different kinds of method for creating Singletons, starting off with the *Singleton*, then extending it and templating parts of it to create the curiously reoccurring template pattern, and then we saw a final all-static version of getting the same effect with minimal hassle.

Each of these methods has their own pros and cons, and we hope that you use them effectively, where they are relevant. Now that we've touched on the design pattern everyone is familiar with, we can move towards our next challenge: learning about how to deal with logic that is specific to each of our individual games.

3

Creating Flexibility with the Component Object Model

In the last chapter, we saw how the Singleton pattern can help us solve the problem of creating and using the big core engines of our game. The engine code is designed to work with any game, meaning there is nothing gameplay-specific about it. So as the game design evolves, we don't need to worry about changes in game design breaking our engine. The goal when writing code for a graphics or physics engine is to make it as reusable or game-agnostic as possible. This means that when you are done making the current game, you should be able to use the code in the next game with very little or no change. The way to do this is to separate the engine code from anything related to the specific game.

Game objects, on the other hand, are completely specific to our game. If the game changes, all our object types will need to change as well. If we are making a platformer and suddenly change to making a Space Shooter, our graphics and physics engine code probably doesn't need to change. However, every single game object and behavior will change. While this may be the most extreme example, the fact is that our game objects are likely to change a lot. So let's look at how we can use patterns to solve this small, but very important, piece of our game.

Chapter overview

In this chapter, we will be focusing on creating a game object that is flexible enough to adapt as our game design changes. We will do this by first looking at the two most common ways that new programmers create a game object, and the problems that arise when we use these approaches. Then we will discuss two design patterns that can help us solve our problem. Finally, we will arrive at our solution of creating a reusable, flexible game object. Since we know our game design and game objects are likely to change, the questions we are going to answer are the following:

- Is it possible to write game objects in a reusable way?
- How can we decouple our game objects from our core engine code?
- If we have a reusable game object, how can we make it flexible enough to use in different games or account for changes in our game design while the game is being developed?

Along the way, we will discuss a few important design principles that will come up again and again in this book that will help you write clean and solid code.

Your objectives

Over the course of this chapter, we will be focusing on a lot of important concepts and diving deep into some interesting code. Some of these concepts are about ways not to implement a game object. Learning the wrong way is often just as important as learning the right way. Here is an outline of the topics we will cover and your tasks for this chapter:

- Why a monolithic game object is a bad design
- Why inheritance hierarchies are inflexible
- Learning and implementing the Strategy pattern and the Decorator pattern
- Learning and implementing the Component Object Model

Why a monolithic game object is a bad design

When you break it down to the simplest terms, programming is about solving problems with code. Someone has an idea for a game or an app, and the problem that needs to be solved is how to describe that idea logically and correctly to the computer. Day to day, these problems usually come in the form of integrating code you wrote today with code written earlier by you or another programmer. When solving these problems, there is a constant struggle between doing things the *easy way* or doing them the *right way*.

The *easy way* to solve a problem means solving the immediate problem in the fastest way possible. Examples of this might be hardcoding a number or string literal instead of using a named constant, copying code instead of writing a function or refactoring code into a base class, or just writing code without thinking about how it can impact the rest of the code base.

On the other hand, solving a problem the *right way* means thinking about how the new code will interact with the old code. It also means thinking about how the new code will interact with future code if the design changes. The *right way* doesn't mean that there is only one correct solution to the problem. There are often many possible ways to reach the same result. The creativity involved in programming is one of the reasons programming is so much fun.

Veteran programmers know that in the long run, the *easy way* often turns out to be more difficult. This is often because a quick fix solves an immediate problem but doesn't consider the changes that will occur as the project evolves.

The monolithic game object

The *easy way* to do a game object is to have a single `struct` that contains all of the data a game object will need. This seems correct because everything in the game has the same basic data. For example, we know players and enemies all have a position, scale, and rotation. So our struct will look like this:

```
struct GameObject
{
  //using vectors from the Mach 5 Engine
  M5Vec2 pos;
  M5Vec2 scale;
  float rotation;
};
```

This game object works well in theory, but it is too basic. It is true that everything in our game probably needs a position, scale, and rotation. Even an invisible trigger region needs these properties. However, as it stands, we can't draw our object: we have no health, and no way to do damage. So, let's add a few things to make the game object a little more real:

```
struct Object
{
  //using vectors from the Mach 5 Engine
  M5Vec2 pos;
  M5Vec2 scale;
  float rotation;
  float damage;
  int health;
  int textureID;        //for drawing
  float textureCoords[4]; //for sprite animation
  unsignedchar color[4]; //the color of our image
};
```

Now we have added a few more basic elements to our game object. Most of our game object types will have health and damage, and we have added a texture ID so we can draw our game object, and some texture coordinates so we can use a sprite sheet for animation. Finally, we added a color so we can reuse the same texture and color it differently for different enemies (think about the different ghosts in Namco's *Pacman*).

This is not that bad yet but, unfortunately, this is just the beginning. Once we start making a real game instead of just brainstorming about a basic game object, our struct member count starts to explode.

Imagine we are making a Space Shooter. There are lots of things we will want to add:

- The player will have multiple types of weapons that all do different amounts of damage
- The player might have access to bombs and missiles that each have an ammo count
- The missile needs a target to seek
- The bomb needs an explosion radius
- There are two super enemies that each have a special ability with a cool-down time
- The player and one super enemy both have the ability to use a shield
- The UI buttons have some actions associated with clicking them
- We have power-ups that add health and add lives

- We need to add a lives count to all objects to account for the power up
- We should add velocity to objects and do time-based movement instead of just setting the position directly
- We need to add an enumeration for the type of the game object so we can update it properly

Here is what our game object looks like now:

```
struct GameObject
{
M5Vec2     pos;
M5Vec2     scale;
M5Vec2     vel;
float      rotation;
ObjectType type;       //Our object type enum
int        objectID;   //So the missile can target
int        lives;
int        shieldHealth; //For Player and SuperBomber
int        health;
float      playerLaserDamage;
float      playerIonDamage;
float      playerWaveCannonDamage;
float      superRaiderDamage;
float      superRaiderAbilityDamage;
float      superRaiderAbilityCoolDownTime;
float      superBomberDamage;
float      superBomberAbilityDamage;
float      superBomberAbilityCoolDownTime;
int        bombCount;
float      bombRadius;
int        missileCount;
int        missileTargetID;
int        textureID;    //the object image
float      textureCoords[4];//for sprite animation
unsigned   char color[4];    //the color of our image
Command*   command;      //The command to do
};
```

As you can see, this basic method of creating a game object doesn't scale very well. We already have more than 25 members in our struct and we haven't even talked about adding space stations that can spawn or repair units. We have only two boss types, we can make a few enemy types by allowing different enemies to use different player weapons such as the laser or missiles, but we are still limited.

The major problem with this approach is that, as the game gets bigger, our game object must also get very big. Some types, such as the player, will use many of these members, but other types, such as a UI button, will only use a small amount. This means if we have lots of game objects, we are very likely wasting a lot of memory per object.

The problem with object behavior

So far, we have only considered what members the game object has. We haven't considered how each object will have its behavior updated. Right now, the game object is just data. Since it has no functions, it can't update itself. We could easily add an `Update` function for the game object but, in order to update each type of object correctly, we would need a `switch` statement:

```
//Create our objects
Object gameObjects[MAX_COUNT];

//initialization code here
//...

//Update loop
for(int i = 0; i < objectInUse; ++i)
{
  switch(gameObjects[i].type)
  {
    case OT_PLAYER:
      //Update based on input
      break;
    case OT_SUPER_RAIDER:
      //Add intercept code here
      break;
    case OT_SUPER_BOMBER:
      //Add case code here
      break;
    case OT_MISSILE:
      //Add find target and chase code here
      break;
    case OT_BOMB:
      //add grow to max radius code here
      break;
    default:
      M5DEBUG_ASSERT(true, "Incorrect Object Type");
  }
}
```

Again, this approach doesn't scale well. As we add more object types, we need to add even more cases to our `switch` statement. Since we only have one `struct` type, we need to have a `switch` statement, whenever we need to do something object-type-specific.

If we are adding behaviors, we will also face the decision of adding data to our object or hardcoding a value into the `switch` statement. For example, if our bomb grows in size, how does it grow? We could hard code `scale.x *= 1.1f` into our `switch` statement or we can add member data float `bombScaleFactor` to our struct.

In the end, this approach just isn't that flexible. Changing our design is very difficult because there are `switch` statements and public members throughout our code. If we were to make a game like this, then our code base would be a complete mess after only a few months. The worst part would be that once the game was completed, we wouldn't be able to reuse any code. The game object and all behaviors would be so gameplay-specific that unless we make a sequel, we would need to remake a brand new game object.

The benefits of the monolithic game object

It is worth noting that even if you choose this approach, you can still have your core engines decoupled from the game object. When writing the graphics engine, for example, instead of passing in a game object as a parameter to a `Draw` function, we could pass in the members that the graphics engine needs:

```
void Graphics::SetTexture(int textureID);
void Graphics::SetTextureCoords(const float* coordArray);
void Graphics::Draw(const M5Mtx44& worldMtx);
vs
void Graphics::Draw(const Object& obj);
```

Another argument for creating objects like this is that we know exactly what is in our game object. Compared with other approaches, we never need to cast our object or search for properties within the object. These operations make the code more complicated and have a slight performance cost. By using a simple `struct`, we have direct access to the variables and the code is easier to understand.

The only time we might use this approach is if we know 100% that the number of object types won't be large, for example, if you are making a puzzle game and the only game objects are sheep and walls. Puzzle games are often very simple and use the same mechanics over and over. In this case, this is a good approach because it is easy and doesn't require any time building a complicated system.

Why inheritance hierarchies are inflexible

The idea that **Players, Enemies, Missiles,** and **Medics** should all derive from one base object is very common to programmers new to object-oriented programming. It makes a lot of sense on paper that if you have a Raider and a SuperRaider, one should inherit from the other. I believe this comes from how inheritance is taught. When you are first learning about inheritance, you will almost always see a picture similar to this:

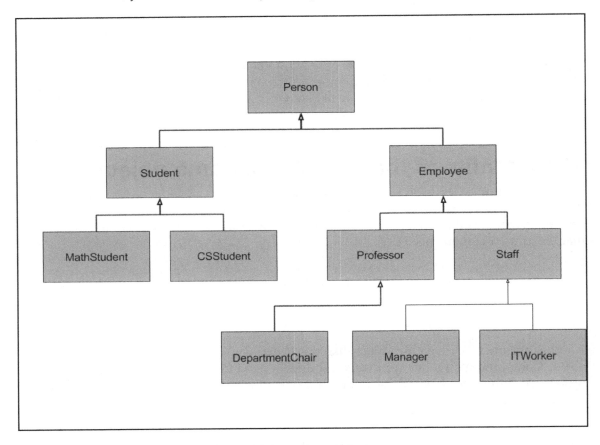

Figure 3.1 - A typical inheritance diagram when learning to program

Many introductory programming courses are so focused on the mechanics of inheritance that they forget to tell you how to use it properly. A picture like the one above makes it easy to understand that ITWorker is an Employee, which is a Person. However, once you go beyond the mechanics, it is time to learn how to use inheritance correctly. This is why books on design patterns exist.

Inheritance is a powerful tool that lets us extend classes by adding members and methods that are specific to the derived classes. It allows us to start with general code and create more specialized classes. This solves one of the original problems that we had with the extremely bloated object struct in the first section. Inheritance lets us take an existing class, such as a Raider, and add more members to create a SuperRaider:

```cpp
//Inheritance Based Object:
class Object
{
  public:
    Object(void);
    virtual ~Object(void);//virtual destructor is important
    virtual void Update(float dt);
    virtual void CollisionReaction(Object* pCollidedWith);
  protected:
    //We still need the basic data in all object
    M5Vec2 m_pos;
    M5Vec2 m_scale;
    float m_rotation;
    int m_textureID;
};

//Inheritance Based derived class
class Unit: public Object
{
  public:
    Unit(void);
    virtual ~Unit(void);
    virtual void Update(float dt);
    virtual void CollisionReaction(Object* pCollidedWith);
  protected:
    M5Vec2 m_vel;//So that Units can move
    float m_maxSpeed;
    float m_health;
    float m_damage;
};

class Enemy: public Unit
{
  public:
    Enemy(void);
```

```
        virtual ~Enemy(void);
        virtual void Update(float dt);
        virtual void CollisionReaction(Object* pCollidedWith);
    protected:
        unsigned char m_color[4];
        float m_textureCoords[4];//For animation
    };
```

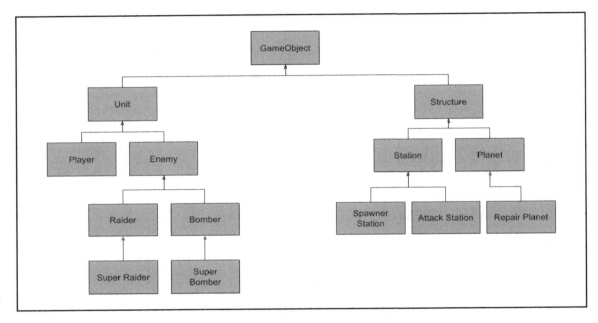

Figure 3.2 - An example of Space Shooter inheritance hierarchy

This hierarchy makes a lot of sense when first designing a space shooter. It allows us to separate the details of a `Raider` class or a `Bomber` class away from the `Player` class. Adding a game object is easy because we can extend a class to create what we need. Removing a game object is easy because all the code is contained within each derived class. In fact, now that we have separate classes, each one can be responsible for itself via class methods. This means we no longer need `switch` statements all over our code.

Best of all, we can use the power of virtual functions to decouple our derived classes from the core engines of our game. By using an array of base class pointers to the derived class instances, our core engines such as graphics or physics are only coupled to the object interface instead of derived classes, such as `Planet` or `SpawnerStation`.

Without inheritance hierarchy, the code would be as follows:

```
//Create our objects
Object gameObjects[MAX_COUNT];

//initialization code here
//...

for(int i = 0; i < objectsInUse; ++i)
{
 switch(gameObjects[i].type)
 {
  case OT_PLAYER:
   //Update based on input
  break;
  case OT_PLANET:
   //Add intercept code here
  break;
  case OT_ENEMY_SPAWNER:
   //Add case code here
  break;
  case OT_RAIDER:
   //Add find target and chase code here
  break;
  case OT_BOMBER:
   //Move slowly and do large damage code here
  break;
  default:
   M5DEBUG_ASSERT(true, "Incorrect Object Type");
 }
}
```

With inheritance and polymorphism, the code is as follows:

```
//Create our objects
Object* gameObjects[MAX_COUNT];//array of pointers

//initialization code here
//...

for(int i = 0; i < objectsInUse; ++i)
gameObjects[i]->Update(dt);
```

Organizing the code by what it does, not what it is

What is the difference between the Raider and the Bomber, really? How are a Raider and a SuperRaider different? Maybe they have a different speed, a different texture, and a different damage value? Do these changes in data really require a new class? Those are really just different values, not different behaviors. The problem is that we are creating extra classes because the concept of a Raider and SuperRaider is different, but there aren't differences in behavior.

Our class hierarchy actually violates three principles I teach, two of which I learned from the Gang of Four book:

> *"Keep your inheritance trees shallow"*

> *"Favor object composition over class inheritance" - Gang of Four, p20*

> *"Consider what should be variable in your design. This approach is the opposite of focusing on the cause of redesign. Instead of considering what might force a change to a design, consider what you want to be able to change without redesign. The focus here is on encapsulating the concept that varies, a theme of many design patterns" - Gang of Four, p29*

A different way to state the third principle is the following:

> *"Find what varies and encapsulate it"*

These principles exist to eliminate, or completely avoid, the problems that can and will arise when using inheritance.

The problem with our current design is that if we create a new class for every object type, we will end up with a lot of little classes that are mostly the same. Raider, SuperRaider, Bomber, and SuperBomber are mostly the same with just a few minor differences, some of which are only differences in `float` and `int` values. While this approach may seem like an improvement over the *easy way*, it becomes a problem because we will end up writing the same behavior code over and over again in many classes. If we have a lot of enemies, we might end up writing the same basic `ChasePlayerAI` code in every `Update` function. The only solution is moving the `ChasePlayerAI` up to a base class.

Let's take another look at our Space Shooter hierarchy but this time, let's add in some different behaviors to our classes:

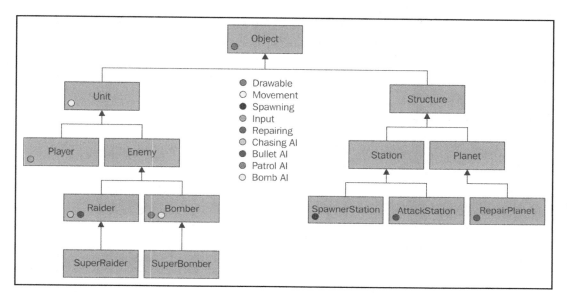

Figure 3.3 - After adding behavior to our objects (refer graphic bundle)

We have decided that our base `object` class will at least be drawable to make things simple. If an object such as a trigger region needs to be invisible, we can simply support disabling rendering by putting a `bool` in the drawable behavior so it won't get drawn. However, with this game object approach, I still have some duplicated code. Both the `Raider` class and the `AttackStation` class have some AI that targets and shoots bullets at the Player. We have only duplicated our code once so maybe it isn't a big deal.

Unfortunately, all game designs will change. What happens when our designer wants to add asteroids to our game? Technically, they are structures so they need some of the data inherited from that class, but they also move. Our designer also really liked the SpawnerStation class and wants to add that ability to a new SpawnerPlanet class, and to a new BossSpawner class. Should we rewrite the code two more times, or refactor the code into the base class? Our designer also wants to give the Station the ability to slowly patrol an area. This means the Station class needs the Patrol AI ability as well. Let's take a look at our hierarchy now:

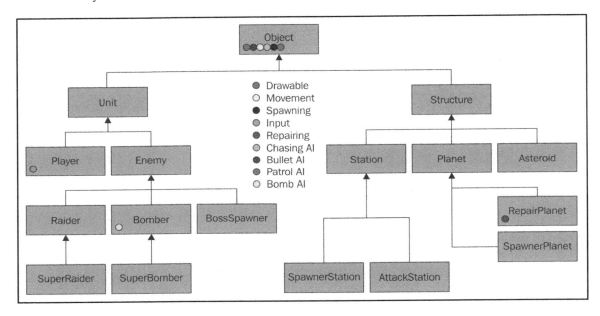

Figure 3 4 - After refactoring duplicate code to our base class (refer graphic bundle)

As it turns out, this approach isn't as flexible as it originally seemed. In order for our design to be really flexible, almost all of the behaviors need to be factored up into the base class. In the end, we aren't much better off than when we wrote our game object the *easy way*. And it is still possible that our designer will want to create the RepairHelper that chases the Player, meaning that everything will be in the base class.

This might sound like a contrived example but remember that games take years to develop and are likely to change. DMA Design's *Grand Theft Auto* was originally titled *Race'n'Chase*, but it was changed because a bug caused the police to try and run the Player off the road instead of pull them over. This ended up being way more fun. Another example is Blizzard's first-person shooter *Overwatch*, which was originally in development for 7 years as a massively multiplayer online game.

The purpose of object-oriented programming is to recognize that designs will change and to write code with that change in mind.

Another problem with our inheritance approach is that it isn't very easy to add or remove abilities at runtime. Let's say our game has a special power-up item that will let the Player use a shield for 1 minute. The shield will absorb 50% of the damage done to the Player for 1 minute then remove itself. We now have the problem of making sure that when a bullet collides with the shield, it will transfer some of the damage to the Player. The shield isn't just responsible for itself; it is responsible for the Player object too.

This same situation exists for all things that will affect another game object for some duration of time. Imagine if we want our Raider to be able to do acid damage to the Player over 5 seconds instead. We need a way to attach this acid damage to the Player, and to remember to remove it after 5 seconds. We could add new variables such as `bool hasAcid` and `float acidTime` in the `Player` class that we can use to know whether we should do acid damage in this frame. However, this still isn't a flexible solution, because each new type of damage caused over time will need new variables like this.

In addition, there is no way to stack the acid damage effect if three enemies are attacking the Player with acid damage. If we like this ability and want the Player to use it, we also need to give all game objects these extra time-based damage variables and behavior code. What we would really like to do is attach acid behavior (or any effect) onto a game object at runtime and have it automatically detach itself when the effect is over. We are going to talk about how to do that later in this chapter, but first we need to talk about one more problem related to inherence hierarchies in C++.

Avoiding the Diamond of Death

The final problem with our inheritance approach involves the situation where we take code reuse to the extreme. In our hierarchy, we have SuperRaider, which is very fast, weak, and shoots little bullets. We also have SuperBomber, which is slow, strong, and shoots big bombs. Someday, a clever designer will want to create SuperBomberRaider that is very fast, strong, and shoots both little bullets and big bombs. Here is our partial tree:

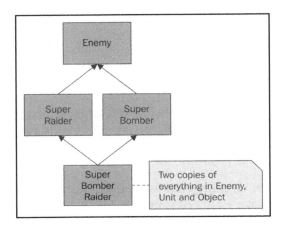

Figure 3.5 - Example of the Diamond of Death

This, of course, is the **Diamond of Death** (or **Dreaded Diamond of Death**), so named because the inheritance tree forms a diamond. The problem is that our SuperBomberRaider inherits from both the SuperBomber and SuperRaider. Those two classes each inherit from the Enemy, Unit, and object. That means SuperBomberRaider will have two copies of m_pos, m_scale, m_rotation, and every other member of object, Unit, and Enemy.

There will also be two copies of any functions that are contained in the `Object`, `Unit`, and `Enemy`. This means we need to specify which version of the functions we wish to use. This might sound good, since we get behavior from both classes, but remember that the individual base class function will only modify their version of variables. After calling `SuperRaider::Update` and `SuperBomber::Update`, we now need to figure out what version of `m_pos` (and `m_scale` and `m_rotation`) we want to use when we draw our object.

C++ has ways of solving this problem, but most programmers agree that the solution makes things more complicated to understand and more difficult to use. The rule of thumb is that we should just avoid using multiple inheritance. We have seen some of the problems that it can cause and we haven't even talked about bugs related to using `new` and `delete` in a situation like this.

The Strategy pattern and the Decorator pattern

We saw that in trying to be more flexible with our game object, a lot of behavior was factored into the base class. We also said that it would be nice to attach a behavior at runtime and have it detach itself when we are done with it.

There are actually two design patterns that have the potential to help our design, the Strategy pattern and the Decorator pattern. The Strategy pattern is all about encapsulating sets of behaviors instead of inheriting. The Decorator pattern is all about dynamically adding responsibilities as needed.

The Strategy pattern explained

The Strategy pattern is about encapsulating a set of behaviors and having the client control the behavior through an interface, instead of hardcoding the behavior into the client function itself. What this means is that we want the game object to be completely independent of the behavior it uses. Imagine that we want to give each enemy a different attack and flight AI. We could use the Strategy pattern instead of creating an inheritance tree:

```
class Enemy: public Unit
{
  public:
    Enemy(void);
    virtual ~Enemy(void);
    virtual void Update(float dt);
    virtual void CollisionReaction(Object* pCollidedWith);
  protected:
    unsigned char m_color[4];
    FlightAI*    m_flight;
    AttackAI*    m_attack;
};
```

In this case, our client is the `Enemy` class and the interfaces that the client controls are the `AttackAI` and `FlightAI`. This is a much better solution than inheriting from the `Enemy` because we are only encapsulating what varies: the behavior. This pattern allows us to create as many `FlightAI` derived classes as we need and to reuse them to create different kinds of game object types, without needing to expand our inheritance tree. Since we can mix different strategy combinations, we can get a large number of different overall behaviors.

We are going to share the same strategies for both units and structures, so we should actually remove our inheritance tree altogether and just use the `Object` as our client. This way, the `Object` class becomes a collection of strategies, and our design is simpler. Plus, we are following some great programming principles:

- Programing to an interface means that our client depends on behavior in an abstract class instead putting behavior in the client itself.
- Our interfaces are opened for extension so we can easily add as many behaviors as we need. The interface is simple so it won't need to be changed, which might break code.
- Our inheritance trees are shallow so we don't need to worry about the Diamond of Death.

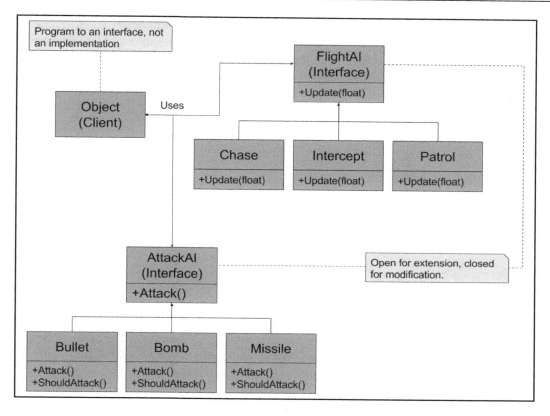

Figure 3.6 - Example of our Object using the Strategy pattern

The Strategy pattern allows our game object to be very flexible without the need for an inheritance tree. With these six small classes shown in the preceding diagram, we can have a total of nine different game object behaviors. If we add a new **FlightAI**, we have 12 possible game object behaviors. Creating brand new strategies allows for an amazing amount of mixed behaviors. However, if we only extend just the two strategies, we don't need to modify the **Object** at all. This works for the Player as well, if we make an **AttackAI** and **FlightAI** that have access to input.

Staying with only two strategies is unlikely, which means that whenever we add a new strategy, we will need to change the **Object** by adding a new member and modifying the `Update` function. This means that while the pattern is flexible enough to let us change strategies at runtime, we can't add behaviors dynamically. If we need to add acid damage as a debuff in our game, we would need a `Damage` base class, and to give a `Damage` base class pointer to the `object`:

```
class Object
{
  public:
    //Same as before...
  protected:
    //Other Object Strategies
    //...
    Damage* m_damage.
};
```

This doesn't seem like a great solution because most damage will be instantaneous and, most of the time, the player isn't even taking damage. That means this will be either null or an empty strategy class, such as using a `NoDamage` derived class, that will be updated every frame but will do nothing. This is also no way to stack corrosive effects or to have two types of damage affecting the Player, such as corrosive damage and ice damage, which might cause the Player to move slower for 10 seconds. We really need a way to dynamically add and remove these abilities. Luckily, there is a pattern for that.

The Decorator pattern explained

The purpose of the Decorator pattern is to dynamically add responsibilities to an object at runtime. The goal is to be a flexible alternative to creating derived classes while still allowing for extended behavior. What this means is that we can take our `object` and add decorations or, in our case, behaviors at runtime.

This pattern requires that the `Decorator` and our `object` are derived from a common base class so they share the same interface. Each `Decorator` will then layer itself on top of an `object` or another `Decorator` to create more interesting object types and effects. When a function gets called on a `Decorator`, it will call the corresponding function on the next layer down, eventually calling the function of the `object`. It is similar in concept to the *Russian Matryoshka* dolls, the dolls that contain smaller and smaller versions inside of themselves. The final, most nested object is always the object with the core functionality:

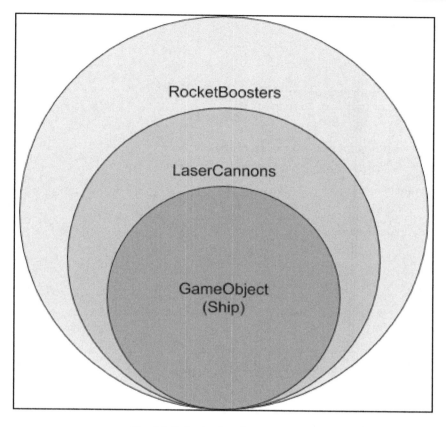

Figure 3.7 - The layering effects of the Decorator pattern

Here is a simplified version in code:

```
class Component //Our base interface
{
  public:
    virtual ~Component(void) {}
    virtual std::string Describe(void) const = 0;
};

class Object: public Component //Our core class to decorate
{
  public:
    Object(const std::string& name) :m_name(name){}
    virtual std::string Describe(void) const
  {
    return m_name;
```

```
    }
  private:
    std::string m_name;
};

//Our base and derived Decorators
class Decorator: public Component
{
  public:
    Decorator(Component* comp):m_comp(comp){}
    virtual ~Decorator(void) { delete m_comp; }
  protected:
    Component* m_comp;
};

class RocketBoosters: public Decorator
{
  public:
    RocketBoosters(Component* comp) : Decorator(comp) {}
    virtual std::string Describe(void) const
  {
    return m_comp->Describe() + " with RocketBoosters";
  }
};

class LaserCannons: public Decorator
{
  public:
    LaserCannons(Component* comp) : Decorator(comp) {}
    virtual std::string Describe(void) const
  {
    return m_comp->Describe() + " with LaserCannons";
  }
};
```

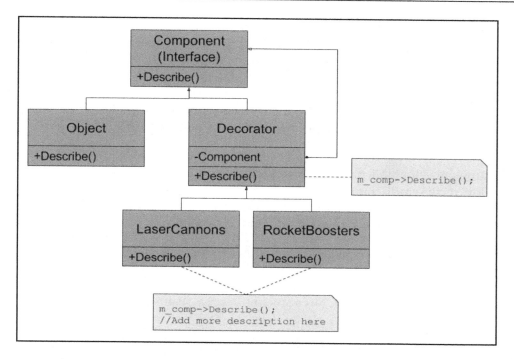

Figure 3.8 - The Decorator pattern using our Object

```cpp
//Using this code:
int main(void)
{
  Component* ship = new Object("Player");
  std::cout << ship->Describe() << std::endl;
  delete ship;

  Component* rocketShip = new RocketBoosters(new
      GameObject("Enemy"));
  std::cout << rocketShip->Describe() << std::endl;
  delete rocketShip;

  Component* laserRocketShip = new LaserCannons(new
      RocketBoosters(new GameObject("Boss")));
  std::cout << laserRocketShip->Describe() << std::endl;
  delete laserRocketShip;
}
```

The `Decorator` classes layer our concrete `object` class and add more information on top of the `object`. However, right now, all we are doing is adding superficial decorations. Since the `Decorator` class doesn't know whether it has a pointer to the `object` class or another `Decorator`, it can't modify the `object`. A good analogy is that the Strategy pattern changes the guts of the object, while the Decorator pattern changes the skin. This can be useful but doesn't help us with our buff/debuff problem. To solve this problem, we would need to add a method to find the `object` down the chain, or give a pointer to the `object` in the constructor of a `Decorator`.

Another problem is that this pattern was designed to add a `Decorator` dynamically, but doesn't allow us to remove one. In the case of using a corrosive damage `Decorator`, we would only want it to exist for a set time, and then automatically detach itself. This can't be done, since a `Decorator` doesn't have a pointer to its parent.

The final problem for games is that our `Decorators` can't live in a vacuum. Sometimes, different gameplay behaviors may need to interact with each other. For example, the corrosive damage `Decorator` may affect the health of an `object`; however, it may first need to check whether the `object` has a shield `Decorator` and remove health from the shield.

Unfortunately, neither the Decorator nor the Strategy pattern will work perfectly for us. What we really need is a new pattern that is a combination of the Strategy and Decorator patterns that does the following:

- Encapsulates specific behavior into components so we avoid `Object` inheritance trees
- Allows for a flexible number of components so we don't need to modify the `Object` each time we create a new component type
- Lets us add and remove components at runtime
- Gives components direct access to the `Object` so it can be modified
- Allows components to be searchable by other components so they can interact

The Component Object Model explained

The alternative can be found by many names, though none are definitive yet. In this book, we will call it the **Component Object Model**, but others have called the **Entity Component System** or just **Component System**. No matter what you call it, the concept is surprisingly simple to learn and easy to implement.

The Component Object Model inverts the concept of the Decorator pattern, where each `Decorator` added a new layer on top of the game object. Instead of layering our `object`, which we have already seen problems with, we will put the decorations inside of it. Since we don't know how many we will need, our `object` will hold a container of decorations, as opposed to a single pointer. In the simplest form, our `object` is nothing more than a container for these components.

If you search for Component Object Model (or Component Based object Model) on the Internet, you will get results that are similar to what we saw in the Strategy pattern. The object contains hardcoded pointers to each possible strategy. While using this approach alone is much better than a monolithic object or an inheritance-based object, we are stuck checking for null pointers or constantly modifying what strategies exists in our `object`.

In this alternative method, every strategy type will derive from a common interface. This way, our `object` can contain an array, or in our case an STL vector of base class `Component` pointers. This is like the `Decorator`, except our `object` is a separate class; it doesn't derive from the `Component` interface. Instead, a `Component` will have a pointer to its parent `object` class. This solves the problem in which a `Decorator` didn't know whether it held a pointer to another `Decorator`, or to the actual `object`. Here we avoid that problem by always giving our `Component` a pointer to the `object` it controls:

```
//Using only Strategy Pattern
class Object
{
  public:
    void Update(float dt);//Non virtual function to update
        Strategies
 //Other interface here
 //...
  private://Lots of different Strategies
    GfxComp*    m_gfx;
    BehaviorComp* m_behavior;
    ColliderComp* m_collider;
};

//Using Flexible Component Object Model
class Object
{
  public:
    void Update(float dt);//Non virtual function to update
        Components
    //Other interface here
 //...
  private:
    std::vector<Component*> m_components.
```

```
};

//Our Base Component
class Component
{
  public:
    virtual void Update(float dt) = 0;
  protected:
    Object* m_obj;
};
```

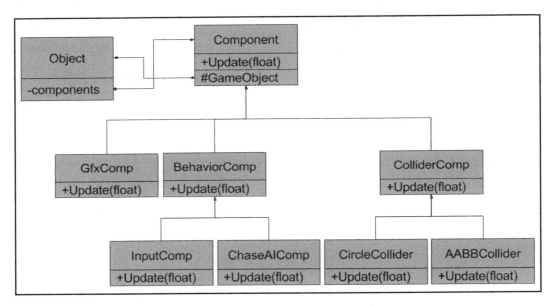

Figure 3.9 - The Component Object Model

This approach allows us to be very flexible because our **object** is nothing more than components. There is nothing in it that is specific to any type. There is no code that is strictly for the Player or SuperRaider. We are free to add, change, or remove anything at runtime. This is important because in the early stages of development, the game design and game objects will change a lot. If we were to hardcode pointers to different base class `Strategies`, we would spend a lot of time changing those pointer types in the game object.

Using the Component Object Model makes our code almost completely reusable as well. The game object itself is just an empty container of Components, and they are often so simple that most of them, such as a **CircleCollider**, can be used in any game. This means that a behavior component, originally meant only for the Player or SpawnerStation, can be easily used for any game object.

Implementing the Component Object Model

Now that we have seen a basic version in code as well as a diagram, let's look at exactly how the Mach5 Engine implements this system. As you will see, the M5object, as it is called, contains a position, rotation, scale, and velocity. Of course, these elements could be contained in a transform component; however, these are so common that most other components will need access to this information. This is different to data such as texture coordinates or a circle collider's radius, which might not need to be shared at all:

```
//Component based Game object used in the Mach 5 Engine
class M5Object
{
  public:
    M5Object(M5ArcheTypes type);
    ~M5Object(void);

    //Public interface
    void      Update(float dt);
    void      AddComponent(M5Component* pComponent);
    void      RemoveComponent(M5Component* pComponent);
    void      RemoveAllComponents(void);
    void      RemoveAllComponents(M5ComponentTypes type);
    int       GetID(void) const;
    M5ArcheTypes GetType(void) const;
    M5Object*  Clone(void) const;
    template<typename T>
    void GetComponent(M5ComponentTypes type, T*& pComp);
    template<typename T>
    void GetAllComponents(M5ComponentTypes type,
        std::vector<T*>& comps);

    M5Vec2    pos;
    M5Vec2    scale;
    M5Vec2    vel;
    float     rotation;
    float     rotationVel;
    bool      isDead;
  private:
    //Shorter name for my vector
```

```
        typedef std::vector<M5Component*> ComponentVec;
        //Shorter name for my iterator
        typedef ComponentVec::iterator   VecItor;

        ComponentVec m_components;
        M5ArcheTypes m_type;
        int       m_id;
        static int   s_objectIDCounter;
    };
```

The first thing you will notice is that there are two enumerations in this code, `M5ArcheTypes` and `M5ComponentTypes`. These will become more useful later when we talk about creating Factories. However, for now, it is enough to understand that these will allow us to search through a collection of `M5objects` and get the components we need. For example, if we have a collection of `M5objects` but we need to find the Player, the `M5ArcheTypes` enum will allow us to do that.

The next thing you will notice is the `M5object` is more than just a container of components. It has some public and private data. The public data is unlikely to need validating or protecting. We could create getters and setters but they would really just simply get and set the data, so it isn't 100% necessary. Since they are public, we are locked into keeping them public forever. If you wish to make them `private` and create `accessor` methods, that is fine. There are some very important variables that we want to be private. The ID and the type are set once and can't be changed, and the array of components is accessed through functions to add, remove, and clear all components. Let's discuss the purpose of the public variables first:

- `pos`: The position of the `M5Object`. This is the rotational center, or pivot point, of the object.
- `scale`: The height and width of the `M5Object`, before rotation.
- `vel`: The velocity of the `M5Object`. This is used to do time-based movement instead of simply setting the position to plus or minus some value.
- `rotation`: The rotation in radians. Positive rotations are counterclockwise.
- `rotationalVel`: The rotational velocity of the `M5Object`, used to do time-based rotations.
- `isDead`: This allows the `M5Object` to mark itself for deletion. Other objects or components are free to call one of the `DestroyObject` functions found in the `M5ObjectManager`; however, it isn't a good idea for an object to delete itself in the middle of its own `Update` function.

We are keeping these as part of the `M5object` because they are so common that all or almost all components will need access to them. We are marking these as public because there is no validation or protecting that we need to do on the data.

The private section starts with two type `def`s. They let us create shorter names for templated types. This is simply a style choice. Another style choice is to have an `m_` in front of all of the private member variable names. This or something similar is a common practice for class members. We didn't do this with our public members because we are treating them more like properties. Now let's look at the rest of the private data:

- `m_components`: This is the array of `M5Component` pointers. Each component in the vector will get updated in the `Update` function.
- `m_type`: The type of object. It will get set in the constructor and never change. It allows the user to use the `M5ObjectManager` to search or remove objects based on type.
- `m_id`: This is a unique ID among `M5Objects`. It can be useful in cases such as a missile needing to target a specific instance of an object. If the missile contains a pointer to the target object, it can't know whether the object has been destroyed. If we instead know the ID, we can search to see whether the target still exists.
- `s_objectIDCounter`: This is the shared ID counter for all `M5Objects`. This guarantees that each object will get a unique value because they are all using the same shared variable. Notice that this is marked with an `s_` to indicate that it is static.

That is all of the data in the `object`. Now, let's look at the functions.

`M5object` is the constructor for the class. It sets starting values for the variables as well as setting the type and giving a unique ID. Notice that we reserve an amount of starting space for the vector. A game object can have as many components as it needs, but in an actual game, we don't expect them to have more than a few on average. By pre-allocating, we may avoid any additional calls to new (we will be a doing a lot anyway):

```
M5Object::M5Object(M5ArcheTypes type) :
pos(0, 0),
   scale(1, 1),
   vel(0, 0),
   rotation(0),
   rotationVel(0),
   isDead(false),
   m_components(),
   m_type(type),
   m_id(++s_objectIDCounter)
{
```

```
    m_components.reserve(START_SIZE);
  }
```

~M5object is the destructor for our game object. Here we want to make sure that we delete all of the components in our game object, so we make use of one of our public functions to help us:

```
M5Object::~M5Object(void)
{
  RemoveAllComponents();
}
```

AddComponent adds the given component pointer to this object vector. You will notice that before the component is added, you will need to first check to make sure the same pointer isn't already in the list. While this isn't very likely to happen, it could be a hard bug to find later so it is worth the check. It is also important when given a component to use the SetParent method of M5Component to make sure this object will be controlled by the component:

```
void M5Object::AddComponent(M5Component* pToAdd)
{
  //Make sure this component doesn't already exist
  VecItor found = std::find(m_components.begin(),
    m_components.end(), pComponent);

  if (found != m_components.end())
    return;

  //Set this object as the parent
  pComponent->SetParent(this);
  m_components.push_back(pComponent);
}
```

Update is the most used function in the M5object. This will get called automatically by the M5ObjectManager every frame. It is used to update every component as well as update position and rotation based on their velocities. The other important role of the Update function is that it deletes any dead components. Except for the RemoveAllComponents function, this is the only place where components are deleted:

```
void M5Object::Update(float dt)
{
  int endIndex = m_components.size() - 1;
  for (; endIndex >= 0; --endIndex)
  {
    if (m_components[endIndex]->isDead)
    {
```

```
        delete m_components[endIndex];
        m_components[endIndex] = m_components[m_components.size()
            - 1];
        m_components.pop_back();
    }
    else
    {
        m_components[endIndex]->Update(dt);
    }
  }
//Update object data
  pos.x   += vel.x * dt;
  pos.y   += vel.y * dt;
  rotation += rotationVel * dt;
}
```

RemoveComponent is used for cases such as when you have buffs or debuffs on an object and you want the stage, or some other object, to delete it. For example, the Player may be using a shield but, after being hit with ion damage, the physics collider finds the shield and immediately removes it. Instead of using this method, it would also be fine to simply mark the component as dead and it will be cleaned up in the next update loop.

This code follows a similar pattern to the AddComponent function. First, we test to make sure the component exists. If it does exist, we swap places with the last item in the vector and pop back the vector. After that, we use the SetParent method to remove this object as the parent pointer before deleting it. This is a small precaution as, in case another pointer to this component exists, the program will crash instead of causing an undefined error:

```
void M5Object::RemoveComponent(M5Component* pComponent)
{
   //Make the sure the instance exists in this object
   VecItor end = m_components.end();
   VecItor itor = std::find(m_components.begin(), end, pToRemove);

   if (itor != end)
     return;

   (*itor)->isDead = true;
}
```

RemoveAllComponents is the helper function used in the destructor. It deletes all components in the object. Except for the destructor, there probably isn't much use for it. However, it was made public for those rare occasions where this is the behavior you need. This function simply loops through the vector and deletes every component, then finally clears the vector:

```
void M5Object::RemoveAllComponents(void)
  {
  VecItor itor = m_components.begin();
  VecItor end = m_components.end();
  while (itor != end)
  {
    delete (*itor);
    ++itor;
  }
  m_components.clear();
}
```

The second version of RemoveAllComponents removes all components of a specific type. This is another situation where external code, such as a stage, object, or even another component needs to remove a group of the same component type. This could be used to remove all corrosive damage effects on the Player, for example.

In this code, we are searching for the correct type, so we cannot use the std::vector::find method. Instead, we use a for loop and check the type of each component. If we find the correct type, we delete the current one, swap with the end and pop back. Since we are doing a swap, but continue searching, we must make sure to check the current index again to see whether it matches as well:

```
void M5Object::RemoveAllComponents(M5ComponentTypes type)
{
    for (size_t i = 0; i < m_components.size(); ++i)
    {
      if (m_components[i]->GetType() == type)
        m_components[i]->isDead = true;
    }
}
```

`GetComponent` and `GetAllComponents` are helper functions to find and cast specific component types in an `M5object`, if they exist. As I said before, sometimes it is necessary that components interact. In that case, we need a way to search for a specific component and to convert it to the correct type. These two functions are almost the same. The first one finds the first instance of the correct component type and assigns it to the pointer parameter. If one doesn't exist, we make sure to set the parameter to 0. The second one finds all components of the correct type and saves them in the vector parameter. These are template functions so the component can be cast to the correct type supplied by the user:

```
template<typename T>
void M5Object::GetComponent(M5ComponentTypes type, T*& pComp)
{
  size_t size = m_components.size();
  for (size_t i = 0; i < size; ++i)
  {
    //if we found the correct type, set and return
    if (m_components[i]->GetType() == type)
    {
      pComp = static_cast<T*>(m_components[i]);
      return;
    }
  }
  pComp = 0;
}

template<typename T>
void GetAllComponent(M5ComponentTypes type, std::vector<T*>& comps)
{
  size_t size = m_components.size();
  for (size_t i = 0; i < size; ++i)
  {
    //if we found the correct type, add to vector
    if (m_components[i]->GetType() == type)
    comps.push_back(static_cast<T*>(m_components[i]));
  }
}
```

The `GetID` and `GetType` functions just return the private class data. The `Clone` method is more interesting but we will go into more detail about it when we discuss the Prototype pattern.

Implementing components

Now that you have seen the M5object, let's take a look at how the Mach5 Engine creates and uses the component hierarchy. Since this is an abstract class, there is no way to create an instance of an M5Component. It is only an interface.

As you will see, the base component contains some of the same members as the M5object. Since we will have a lot of components, it is important to give each one a type, so they can be searchable. It is important to give each a unique ID. Since these components can be deleted at any time, it is important to save an ID instead of a pointer, which can become invalid:

```
class M5Component
{
  public:
    M5Component(M5ComponentTypes type);
    virtual ~M5Component(void);
    virtual M5Component* Clone(void) = 0;
    virtual void Update(float dt)= 0;
    virtual void FromFile(M5IniFile&);
    void SetParent(M5Object* pParent);
    M5ComponentTypes GetType(void) const;
    int GetID(void) const;
  //public data
    bool isDead;
  protected:
    M5Object* m_pObj;
  private:
    int m_id;
    M5ComponentTypes m_type;
    staticint     s_compIDCounter;
};
```

The data section doesn't contain as much as the M5object, but now it is split into three sections which are public, private, and protected:

- isDead: This is the only public data and it serves a similar function to the member in the game object. This allows the component to mark itself for deletion. It isn't a good idea for a component to call RemoveComponent on itself during its own Update function.
- m_pObj: This is a pointer to the M5Object that owns this component.
- m_id: The unique ID of this component. This allows users to get access to this specific component again, without the risk of saving a pointer which may become invalid.

- `m_type`: The type of this component. This allows users to search for a specific component within a game object.
- `s_compIDCounter`: This is used to create a unique ID for each component.

The functions of the `M5Component` are not that interesting because they are mostly virtual. However, it is worth going over their purpose.

`M5Component` is the non-default constructor for the component. This takes an argument of type `M5ComponentTypes` so that the private data `m_type` is guaranteed to be set by a derived type:

```
M5Component::M5Component(M5ComponentTypes type):
  isDead(false),
  m_pObj(0),
  m_type(type),
  m_id(++s_componentID)
{
}
```

`~M5Component` is the destructor for the class. Since this is meant to be a base class, it is important that a virtual destructor exists so that the correct method will be called when using polymorphism:

```
M5Component::~M5Component(void)
{
  //Empty Base Class virtual destructor
}
```

`Update` is where the component does the action. This method will be called every frame and its intended purpose is to add a behavior and/or data to the `M5object`. It is marked as pure virtual (= 0) so that the base class is forced to override it. That also means there is no body to the base class version.

`FromFile` is a virtual function that allows the component to read data from a preloaded INI file. It is not marked as pure virtual, meaning that a component doesn't need to override this function. This might be the case if the derived component has no data to be loaded from a file:

```
void M5Component::FromFile(M5IniFile&)
{
  //Empty for the base class
}
```

The `SetParent` method is simply a setter for `m_pObj`. Recall the `AddComponent` function of `M5object`. When a component is added to an object, the object uses this function so the component knows which object to control.

The `GetType` and `GetID` functions are similar to the functions in `M5object`. They allow the component to be searchable and saved without needing to use pointers that may become invalid. The `M5Component` also has a pure virtual `Clone` method. There is no function body in the base class. We will discuss the `Clone` method of both `M5Component` and `M5object` when we discuss the Prototype pattern.

To add a behavior to an object, we must derive from the `M5Component` base class, overload the necessary methods, add a value to the `M5ComponentTypes` enumeration, then finally register the class and the associated builder with the object manager. Of course, these steps are prone to error and doing them repeatedly would be very tedious.

For this reason, the Mach5 engine has included a batch file to do these steps automatically. By adding components to the `Source` folder within the file hierarchy, the batch file will find all files named `*Component.h`, where the asterisk is a wildcard character that includes any valid C++ identifier.

For example, if a component named `LazerComponent` is located within a file named `LazerComponent.h`, an enumeration value named `CT_LazerComponent` will be automatically created along with the correct class builder, and both will be registered with the `M5ObjectManager`.

Creating and removing objects and components

In order to use the Component Object Model, first create a game object, then add some components, then finally add it to the `M5ObjectManager` which calls an update on the game object every frame. Let's look at some code for creating objects and components.

If we wanted to create a `Player` object to fly around on screen, but stay within the bounds of the screen, we could do this inside the `Init` method of a stage:

```
M5Object* pObj = new M5Object(AT_Player);
GfxComponent* pGfxComp = new GfxComponent;
PlayerInputComponent* pInput = new PlayerInputComponent;
ClampComponent* pClamp = new ClampComponent;
pObj->AddComponent(pGfxComp);
pObj->AddComponent(pInput);
pObj->AddComponent(pClamp );
//Set position, rotation, scale here
//...
M5ObjectManager::AddObject(pObj);
```

This code works fine, but there are a few problems. First, we didn't specify what texture we want. However, we could easily add a `textureID` or filename as a parameter to the `GfxComponent` constructor. The larger problem is that this code was tedious to write and we don't want to write it again and again. If we are creating a Player in another stage, it will likely contain the exact same code. So a better approach is to factor this code into the `M5ObjectManager`:

```
M5Object* M5ObjectManager::CreateObject(M5ArcheTypes type)
{
  switch(type)
  {
    case AT_Player:
    M5Object* pObj = new M5Object(AT_Player);
    GfxComponent* pGfxComp = new GfxComponent;
    PlayerInputComponent* pInput = new PlayerInputComponent;
    ClampComponent* pClamp = new ClampComponent;
    pObj->AddComponent(pGfxComp);
    pObj->AddComponent(pInput);
    pObj->AddComponent(pClamp );
    AddObject(pObj);
    //Set position, rotation, scale here
    //...
    return pObj;
    break;
    case AT_Bullet:
     //...More Code here
```

Now in our stage `Init` function, we can simply write the following:

```
M5Object* pObj = M5ObjectManager::CreateObject(AT_Splash);
//Set additional data here if needed
```

However, this is pretty hardcoded. This explicitly creates all of the components that a Player (and every type) needs, which means that our `M5ObjectManager` now contains game-specific code. The benefit of using the Component Object Model is that it is flexible, but we have lost some of that flexibility by having a hardcoded `switch` statement. We really want our designers, not programmers, to choose what goes into a Player, Raider, or SuperRaider. That means loading our object types from a file. In our case, we will use INI files because they are simple to use and simple to understand. They consist of global or labeled sections of key/value pairs. Here is an example Player archetype found in `Player.ini`:

```
posX  = 0
posY  = 0
velX  = 0
velY  = 0
scaleX = 10
scaleY = 10
rot  = 0
rotVel = 0
components = GfxComponent PlayerInputComponent ClampComponent

[GfxComponent]
texture = playerShip.tga

[PlayerInputComponent]
forwardSpeed = 100
bulletSpeed = 7000
rotationSpeed = 10
```

Notice that the first (global) section of the INI file contains all data found in the `M5object`. Since we know that those variables always exist in the object, they are placed at the top. This includes a list of components that this archetype will use. Here we have `GfxComponent`, `PlayerInputComponent`, and `ClampComponent`. The next sections are data associated with each component, for example, with the `GfxComponent` we can specify our texture to load. The `ClampComponent` doesn't need any data loaded so we didn't need to add a section for it.

Comparing the Component Object Model with the monolithic object or the inheritance tree, we can see that the component-based approach is vastly more flexible and reusable. With this method, we can write as many different components as we want and let the designer choose what behaviors each object uses. The best part is that everything but the most game-specific components can be reused in another game.

That means that the `PlayerInputComponent` probably can't be reused in another game, but the `ClampComponent` and `GfxComponent` can be used whether we are making another Space Shooter, Platformer, or Racer.

One note about components used for graphics and physics, such as `GfxComponent` and `CircleColliderComponent`: these are special in the sense that they need to interact with core engines in a way that other components may not need to. For example, the Graphics engine might want to organize these components based on whether they are world space objects or screen space objects (referred to as HUD space, since these would be things such as buttons and health bars). The Physics engine might want to use a special partition data structure to minimize the number of collision tests that need to be performed. For this reason, these components are automatically registered to their respective core engines when created through the object Manager and they automatically unregister when they are deleted.

Performance concerns

There are a lot of benefits to using the Component Object Model. These days, many engines use this approach because of the flexibility it provides. However, that flexibility comes at a cost to performance. The biggest performance costs are calls to new/delete, cache coherency, and virtual methods.

Our `M5ObjectManager` uses pointers to `M5objects` which uses an STL vector of pointers to components. This means that as we create `Bullets`, `Asteroids`, `Raiders`, and `Planets`, we are constantly calling new and delete. These are slow functions and have the chance to fragment our memory. In a later chapter, we will see how object pools can help us solve both of these problems.

However, even with object pools, we still have problems with cache misses. The fact is that iterating over an array of contiguous data is much faster than iterating over an array of pointers to data. When using the Component object Model, the CPU will be spending a lot more time chasing pointers and loading that data into the cache than if we just used arrays. Unfortunately, this is the price we pay for flexibility. Depending on the game, this may or may not cause a problem.

Virtual methods are also a source of potential performance problems because the function to call must always be looked up at runtime and they cannot be inlined by the compiler. Again, this is the price we pay for flexibility. We have an approach that allows our designer to load a behavior from a file and change that behavior at runtime. In my opinion, that outweighs the performance issues, at least at the beginning of the development cycle.

You may have heard *premature optimization is the root of all evil*. It is more important to focus on making a fun game and to solve the performance problems later. You always have the option of hardcoding specific behaviors or data in the game object much later in the development cycle. If possible, you might merge two or more components that always get used together once you are in the polish stage. However, by limiting your flexibility early on, you may never discover a fun feature that comes from mixing two components in a way that wasn't originally planned.

My advice is to focus first on algorithmic optimizations, then macro optimizations, then finally micro optimizations. What I mean is that it is better to worry about the time complexity of your physics engine and how many draw calls or collision tests you are performing, before worrying about what is in the CPU cache or the performance cost of virtual functions. While they can be a problem, these things fall under the category of micro optimizations.

However, before starting the long process of creating a game using an unfamiliar game engine, it can be a good idea to do some simple prototype tests to make sure the engine can meet the needs of the game. For example, a programmer could approximate the number of objects, and components, and test for performance to see whether the engine will work.

Summary

In this chapter, we have explored many different ways to create a game object. We have seen the problems with using monolithic objects or large inheritance trees. We now know that neither of those approaches scale when creating a large game. They both suffer from the problem of giant bloated classes and dependencies in our code.

We have also seen the flexibility that using the Component Object Model can bring to our games. It lets programmers focus on writing new code, while allowing designers to use that code to create new object types, even at runtime. Since we can now define objects completely in a file, we can create a tool that will let our designer, or even players, make completely new objects, or possibly a new game.

We also briefly touched on the performance issues related to using the Component Object Model. While these can be a problem, it is much better to focus on algorithmic optimizations then very low-level CPU instruction optimizations. We will revisit these problems in later chapters.

For now, let's move on to a design pattern that can help us implement one of the big core engines of our game, as well as a small but important type of component. In the next chapter, we will discover how the State pattern can help decouple our code and can give us a great way to implement artificial intelligence in our game.

4

Artificial Intelligence Using the State Pattern

In the last chapter, we discussed the Component Object Model. Giving an entity a behavior is now as simple as just creating a new component and having that control the game object.

Whenever someone starts to make a game, they begin by writing gameplay code. That is the fun stuff. Everyone wants to see graphics and physics take effect on screen. Things such as a pause screen, options menu, or even a second level are an afterthought. The same happens for organizing the behaviors of a player. Programmers are excited to make a player jump and make a player dash, but with each new ability a player has, there are combinations that you may want to disallow. For example, the player might not be allowed to dash while jumping, or may only be able to dash every 3 seconds. The State pattern solves these problems.

By coding the Game State Manager first, the problem of switching to a menu or pausing is solved. By coding finite State Machines as a component for the game object, the problem of complex behavior or a player or enemy is solved. By adding multiple State Machines to the same game object, complex behavior can be created with very simple code, as is seen in many games, and is a widely used feature built into the Unreal Engine and given visual editors in Unity using Hutong Games LLC's popular Playmaker extension.

Chapter overview

In this chapter, we will create a simple State Machine to control the player via input, as well as create an enemy State Machine which will detect when the player gets close to it and will follow them when in range. We will also look at the base `StateMachineComponent` class in the Mach5 Engine and show that, by writing code for a few states, we can create a more complex behavior quite easily. We will also show that adding more than one State Machine to an object can create multiple behaviors to run at the same time, avoiding duplicated state code.

Your objectives

This chapter will be split into a number of topics. It will contain a simple step-by-step process from beginning to end. Here is the outline of our tasks:

- The State pattern explained
- Introduction to State Machines
- An overview of enumerations
- Doing things based on our states
- Why if statements could get you fired
- Expanding on the State Machine
- The State pattern in action--M5StateMachine
- The State pattern in action--StageManager
- Issues with FSMs

The State pattern explained

The State pattern is a way to allow a game object to change its behavior and functionality in response to different stimuli within the game, especially when a variable or a condition within that object changes, as those changes may trigger a change in state. The state of an object is managed by some context (commonly referred to in the game industry as a machine), but the states tell the machine when to change states and thereby functionality. The State pattern contains two parts: the state and the context. The context object holds the current state and can be used by the state class to change what state should be run, whereas the state object holds the actual functionality:

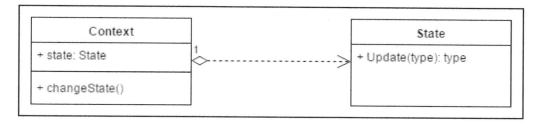

In the Mach5 Engine, there is a class that already uses the State pattern (M5StateMachine) but, before we dive into a completed version, let's actually build one from scratch.

There are multiple ways to implement the State pattern or to get a State-like behavior. We'll go over some of the commonly seen versions and the pros and cons of using them before moving to our final version.

Introduction to State Machines

We often write code to react to things happening within the game environment based on the expectations of us, as well as our players. For instance, if we are creating a 2D side-scrolling platformer game, when the player presses one of the arrow keys, we're expecting the player's character to move and, whenever we press the spacebar, we expect the sprite to jump into the air. Or perhaps in a 3D game, when our player sees a panel with a large button, they expect to be able to press it.

Tons of things in our ordinary lives act this way as well, reactive to certain stimuli. For instance, when you use your television remote, you expect certain things to happen, or even when swiping or tapping on your mobile phone. Based on the stimuli provided, the *state* of our object may change. We call something that can be in one of multiple states at a time a State Machine.

Almost every program you write can be considered a State Machine of some sort. The second that you add in an if statement to your project, you have developed code that can be in at least one of those states. That being said, you don't want to have a bunch of switch and/or if statements inside of your code as it can quickly get out of hand and make it difficult to understand exactly what it is that your code is doing.

As programmers, we often want to take our problems and break them down over and over again until they're in their simplest form, so let's see a possible way to do that. In game development, you'll hear references to an **FSM** which stands for **Finite State Machine**. Finite means that there are only a certain number of states and that they are all clearly defined for what they can do and how they will change between states.

An overview of enumerations

Let's say we're going to create a simple enemy. This enemy will not do anything by default, but if the player is nearby, it will move toward them. However, if the player gets too far away from them, then they will stop their pursuit. Finally, if the player shoots the enemy, it will die. So, keeping that in mind, we can extract the states that we'll need. They are as follows:

- Idle
- Follow
- Death

While we are creating our State Machine, we need some way to keep track of what state our objects are going to be in. One may think a way to do this would be to have a `bool` (Boolean value of true or false) for each possible state there is and then set them all to `false`, except for the state that we're in. This is a very bad idea.

Another thought could be to just have an integer and then set a value for each one that there is. This is also a bad idea, as using numbers in this way is basically the same thing as using magic numbers in our code, since the numbers have no logic to them for people to read. Alternatively, you could have `#defines` for each possible value, but that will allow people to put in whatever number they want without any protections at all. Instead, whenever we see a series of things where only one of them is true at a time, we can make use of the programming feature of enumerations, called enums for short.

The basic concept of using enumerations is that you get to create your own custom data types which are restricted to only have a certain list of values. Unlike integers or `#defines`, these numbers are expressed using constants and allow us to have all of the advantages of having a value, such as being able to compare values. In our case, an `enum` for our states would look something like the following:

```
enum State
{
    Idle,
    Follow,
    Death
};
```

Acting on states

Now that we have our states defined, let's now make it so that we can actually do something in our code based on what state our object is in. For this first example, I'm going to update the ChasePlayerComponent class that already exists in the EngineTest project.

From the **Solution Explorer** tab on the right-hand side, open up the SpaceShooter/Components/ChasePlayerComp folder and access the ChasePlayerComponent.h file. From there, replace the class with the following changes in bold:

```
enum State{
  Idle,
  Follow,
  Death
};

//!< Simple AI to Chase the Player
class ChasePlayerComponent : public M5Component
{
public:
  ChasePlayerComponent(void);
  virtual void Update(float dt);
  virtual void FromFile(M5IniFile& iniFile);
  virtual ChasePlayerComponent* Clone(void);
private:
  float m_speed;
  float m_followDistance;
  float m_loseDistance;

  void FollowPlayer();
  float GetDistanceFromPlayer();
  State m_currentState;

};
```

The FollowPlayer and GetDistanceFromPlayer functions are going to be helper functions for our functionality. We've added our state enum to store each of the possible states we can be in, and we added the m_currentState variable to hold the current state we are in. To determine when we should switch states, we have two other values, m_followDistance and m_loseDistance, which are the distance in pixels that our player needs to be from the enemy to follow them, and then how far the player needs to get away to escape, respectively.

Now that we have that finished, let's first go ahead and add in the helper functions at the bottom of the `ChasePlayerComponent.cpp` file so that we can have the proper functionality, once we update our other functions:

```
/*********************************************************************/
/*!
Makes it so the enemy will move in the direction of the player
*/
/*********************************************************************/
void ChasePlayerComponent::FollowPlayer()
{
  std::vector<M5Object*> players;
  M5ObjectManager::GetAllObjectsByType(AT_Player, players);
  M5Vec2 dir;
  M5Vec2::Sub(dir, players[0]->pos, m_pObj->pos);
  m_pObj->rotation = std::atan2f(dir.y, dir.x);
  dir.Normalize();
  dir *= m_speed;
  m_pObj->vel = dir;
}


/*********************************************************************/
/*!
Returns the distance of the object this is attached to the player
*/
/*********************************************************************/
float ChasePlayerComponent::GetDistanceFromPlayer()
{
  std::vector<M5Object*> players;
  M5ObjectManager::GetAllObjectsByType(AT_Player, players);

  return M5Vec2::Distance(m_pObj->pos, players[0]->pos);
}
```

These functions use some basic linear algebra in order to move our object toward the player and to get the distance between two positions.

Diving into the mathematics behind it is out of the scope of this book, but if you're interested in learning more, I highly suggest you check out the following link. The code is written for Cocos2D so it will not be exactly the same as what Mach5 would use, but the concepts are explained very well: https://www.raywenderlich.com/35866/trigonometry-for-game-progra mming-part-1.

Now that we have that functionality in, we need to update a couple of things. First of all, we will use the constructor to set the initial value of our currentState variable:

```
/*******************************************************************/
/*!
Sets component type and starting values for player
*/
/*******************************************************************/
ChasePlayerComponent::ChasePlayerComponent(void) :
  M5Component(CT_ChasePlayerComponent),
  m_speed(1)
  {
m_currentState = Idle;
  }
```

Next, we need to tell our object to read in the values of our object through its INI file:

```
void ChasePlayerComponent::FromFile(M5IniFile& iniFile)
{
  iniFile.SetToSection("ChasePlayerComponent");
  iniFile.GetValue("speed", m_speed);
 iniFile.GetValue("followDistance", m_followDistance);
  iniFile.GetValue("loseDistance", m_loseDistance);

}
```

FromFile is only called once on the first object that gets created in initialization. In order to make it easy to tweak values without having to recompile the project, Mach 5 reads in information from a file to set variables. We haven't modified the .ini file yet, but we will once we finish all of these modifications:

```
M5Component* ChasePlayerComponent::Clone(void)
{
  ChasePlayerComponent* pNew = new ChasePlayerComponent;
  pNew->m_speed = m_speed;
pNew->m_followDistance = m_followDistance;
  pNew->m_loseDistance = m_loseDistance;
  return pNew;
}
```

We then need to go to Windows Explorer and move to the project's `EngineTest/EngineTest/ArcheTypes` folder, and then access the `Raider.ini` file and add the new properties to the object:

```
posX    = 0
posY    = 0
velX    = 0
velY    = 0
scaleX = 10
scaleY = 10
rot     = 0
rotVel = 0
components = GfxComponent ColliderComponent ChasePlayerComponent

[GfxComponent]
texture = enemyBlack3.tga
drawSpace = world

[ColliderComponent]
radius = 5
isResizeable = 0

[ChasePlayerComponent]
speed = 40
followDistance = 50
loseDistance = 75
```

If a text editor doesn't open for you, feel free to use Notepad. In this case, we are adding in two new properties which represent the values we created earlier.

Then, we need to update our stage so it's a little easier for us to do some testing. Back in Windows Explorer, open up the `EngineTest/EngineTest/Stages` folder and then open up the `Level01.ini` file and set it to the following:

```
ArcheTypes = Player Raider

[Player]
count = 1
pos = 0 0

[Raider]
count = 1
pos = 100 10
```

With this, our level will just have our player in the center of the world and an enemy Raider positioned at (100, 10). With all of that accomplished, save the files and dive back into our ChasePlayerComponent.cpp file and replace the Update function with the following:

```cpp
void ChasePlayerComponent::Update(float)
{
  // Depending on  what state we are in,  do different things
  switch (m_currentState)
  {
  case Idle:
    // No longer move if we were
    m_pObj->vel = M5Vec2(0, 0);

    // If the player gets too close, the enemy notices them
    if (GetDistanceFromPlayer() < m_followDistance)
    {
      // And will begin to give chase
      m_currentState = Follow;
    }

    return;
  case Follow:
    // Follow the player
    FollowPlayer();

    // If the player manages to get away from the enemy
    if (GetDistanceFromPlayer() > m_loseDistance)
    {
      // Stop in your tracks
      m_currentState = Idle;
    }
    break;
  case Death:
    // Set object for deletion
    m_pObj->isDead = true;
    break;
  }

}
```

Save everything and go ahead and run the project. If all goes well, you should see a scene like this:

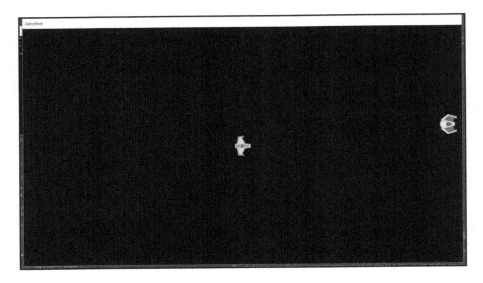

Notice that our enemy is not moving at the beginning due to it being in the Idle state. However, if we move closer to it, it would look something like this:

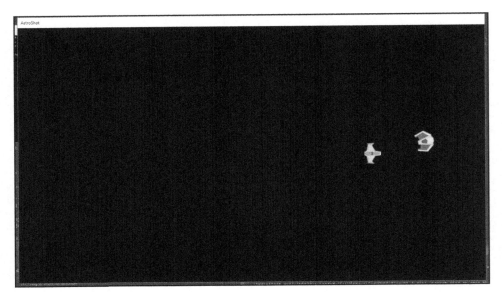

You'll see that it now follows us without stopping. If we manage to move far enough away from the enemy though, they'll stop:

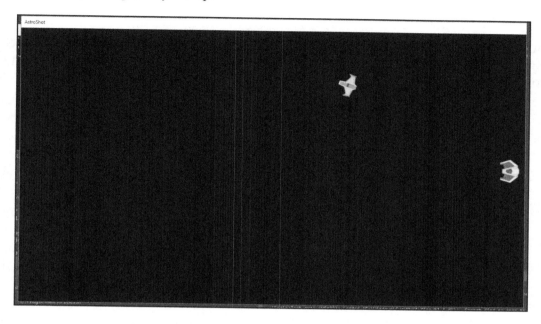

This clearly shows the basic principles of the State pattern in use, though there are a number of things we can do to improve this, which we will talk about soon.

Issues with conditionals

The next thing we need to consider is how we should do something based on what state we are in. When writing programs, conditional clauses such as the `if` and `switch` statements that we learned about earlier may make your code more difficult to manage. Sometimes, when writing code for specific functionality, writing if statements is completely understandable, especially if it makes sense when you are writing it. For example, the following code makes perfect sense:

```
void MinValue(int a, int b)
{
  if (a < b)
    return a;
  else
    return b;
}

// Could also be written in the following way:
```

```
void MinValue(int a, int b)
{
   return (a < b) ? a : b;
}
```

However, if you are writing something where you are checking what the type of an object is, or whether a variable is of a certain type, that is a bit of an issue. For instance, look at the following function:

```
void AttackPlayer(Weapon * weapon)
  {
    if (weapon.name == "Bow")
    {
      ShootArrow(weapon);
    }
    else if (weapon.name == "Sword")
    {
      MeleeAttack(weapon);
    }
    else
    {
      IdleAnimation(weapon);
    }
  }
```

As you can see, if we start going down this path, we will need to add many different checks throughout our project, which will make our code hard to change if we ever decide to add more things to support here. First of all, instead of a bunch of if/else statements, when we see something that's comparing the same value and doing something based off of that value, we should be using a switch statement, like we did earlier, with a few modifications:

```
void AttackPlayer(Weapon * weapon)
{
// C++ doesn't support using string literals in switch
// statements so we have to use a different variable
// type, such as an integer
  switch (weapon.type)
  {
  case 0:
    ShootArrow(weapon);
    break;

  case 1:
    MeleeAttack(weapon);
    break;
```

```
    default:
      IdleAnimation(weapon);

  }

}
```

But in this particular case, we are just calling a different function based on the value, with each of the functions being some kind of attack. Instead, we should make use of polymorphism and have the code automatically do the correct thing:

```
class Weapon
{
public:
  virtual void Attack()
  {
    // Do nothing
  };
};

class Bow : Weapon
{
public:
  virtual void Attack()
  {
    // Attack with Bow
  };
};

void AttackPlayer(Weapon * weapon)
{
  weapon->Attack();
}
```

Now whenever we call `AttackPlayer`, it will do the correct thing automatically.

Just remember that creating complex behavior leads to ugly code being written and increases the likelihood of bugs. If you forget about a condition that needs to be there, your game hopefully would break, letting you know there is a problem, but it could not do anything. Then, when you find your game crashes down the road, your life becomes a lot more complex and your game could become unplayable or just plainly not fun.

Robert Elder has a link of the subject which I think explains the kind of crazy things that you can do with conditional statements, which would almost certainly get you fired: http://blog.robertelder.org/switch-statements-statement-expressions/.

Don't lose sleep over having conditionals in your code, but make sure that you only include them when you actually need them there. As you continue coding, you'll have a better idea as to when it's a good idea or not, but it is something to keep in mind.

Expanding on the State Machine

So currently, you'll notice that in the Idle state we are setting our velocity to 0, 0 every single frame. In this simple example, it's not a terribly big deal, but this overdoing of calculations is something that we'd like to avoid in the future. We only really need to do it once, right when we enter the state. We may also want to do certain actions when we leave the state, but we won't be able to do that in the current form of our State Machine, so we are going to need to redo some stuff.

First, let's go back to the ChasePlayerComponent.h file and add the following bold function definitions:

```
class ChasePlayerComponent : public M5Component
{
public:
  ChasePlayerComponent(void);
  virtual void Update(float dt);
  virtual void FromFile(M5IniFile& iniFile);
  virtual M5Component* Clone(void);
  virtual void EnterState(State state);
  virtual void UpdateState(State state, float dt);
  virtual void ExitState(State state);
  virtual void SetNewState(State state, bool initialState = false);
private:
  float m_speed;
  float m_followDistance;
  float m_loseDistance;

  void FollowPlayer();
  float GetDistanceFromPlayer();
  State m_currentState;

};
```

So instead of having our `Update` function handle everything, we've now created three functions for each of the different times that our state can be in: entering a new state, updating based on that state, and then what to do when we leave the state. Aside from that, we also have a `SetNewState` function which will take care of changing the state to something else. All of the functions take in a `State` enum to choose how to execute, with the `Update` state also having the time that passed this frame, and the `SetNewState` having an option for saying it's the first time you've set a state so you don't need to leave the previous one. After that, we need to actually add in the functionality for these new functions:

```cpp
void ChasePlayerComponent::EnterState(State state)
{
  // Depending on what state we are in, do different things
  switch (state)
  {
  case Idle:
    // No longer move if we were
    if (m_pObj)
    {
      m_pObj->vel = M5Vec2(0, 0);
    }

    M5DEBUG_PRINT("\nIdle: Enter");
    break;

  case Follow:
    M5DEBUG_PRINT("\nFollow: Enter");
    break;

  case Death:
    m_pObj->isDead = true;
    M5DEBUG_PRINT("\nDeath: Enter");
    break;
  }
}

void ChasePlayerComponent::UpdateState(State state, float)
{
  // Depending on what state we are in, do different things
  switch (state)
  {
  case Idle:
    //M5DEBUG_PRINT("\nIdle: Update");
    // If the player gets too close, the enemy notices them
    if (GetDistanceFromPlayer() < m_followDistance)
    {
```

```
      // And will begin to give chase
      SetNewState(Follow);
    }

  break;

  case Follow:
    //M5DEBUG_PRINT("\nFollow: Update");

    // Follow the player
    FollowPlayer();

    // If the player manages to get away from the enemy
    if (GetDistanceFromPlayer() > m_loseDistance)
    {
      // Stop in your tracks
      SetNewState(Idle);
    }
    break;
  }
}

void ChasePlayerComponent::ExitState(State state)
{
  // Depending on what state we are in, do different things
  switch (state)
  {
  case Idle:
    M5DEBUG_PRINT("\nIdle: Exit");
    break;

  case Follow:
    M5DEBUG_PRINT("\nFollow: Exit");
    break;
  }
}

// initialState by default is false, so will only need to give
// second parameter the first time it is called
void ChasePlayerComponent::SetNewState(State state, bool initialState)
{
  if (!initialState)
  {
    // Exit of our old state
    ExitState(currentState);
  }

  // Then start up our new one
```

```
    m_currentState = state;
    EnterState(m_currentState);
  }
```

And then, we need to update our `Update` function to just call our correct function:

```
void ChasePlayerComponent::Update(float dt)
{
  UpdateState(m_currentState, dt);
}
```

We also need to change our constructor so that instead of setting the current state, we set it ourselves:

```
/*****************************************************************/
/*!
Sets component type and starting values for player
*/
/*****************************************************************/
ChasePlayerComponent::ChasePlayerComponent(void):
  M5Component(CT_ChasePlayerComponent),
  m_speed(1)
{
  SetNewState(Idle, true);
}
```

First of all, note that I am calling the `M5DEBUG_PRINT` function. This is to make it easy to tell that we are changing between different states. For the purposes of this demonstration, I commented out the `Update` function's version, but it could be useful for you to check it out. Note in this version, we have a `switch` statement for each of the functions and do something differently based on the state that is set in there.

In my version of the editor, by default the text will not be displayed on the screen. To fix this issue, go to the `SplashStage.cpp` file and comment out the following bold code:

```
SplashStage::~SplashStage(void)
{
  //We are done this with ArcheType so lets get rid of it.
  M5ObjectManager::RemoveArcheType(AT_Splash);
  //M5DEBUG_DESTROY_CONSOLE();
}
```

Now let's run our project!

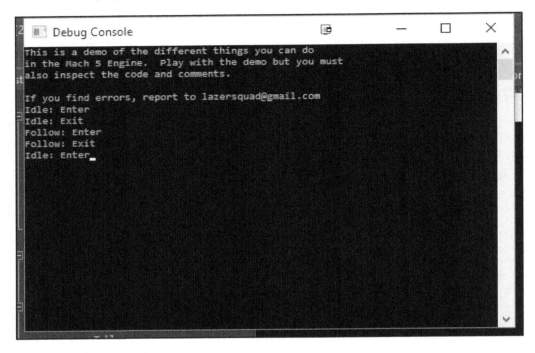

```
Debug Console

This is a demo of the different things you can do
in the Mach 5 Engine.  Play with the demo but you must
also inspect the code and comments.

If you find errors, report to lazersquad@gmail.com
Idle: Enter
Idle: Exit
Follow: Enter
Follow: Exit
Idle: Enter
```

You can tell from the editor when we are switching our states and that the code is being called correctly!

This version works pretty well, but there are some issues with it; namely that it involves a lot of rewriting, and we will need to copy/paste this functionality and make changes anytime we want to make a new version. Next, we will take a look at the State Machine included in the Mach5 Engine and the advantages that it has over what we've been talking about so far.

The State pattern in action - the M5StateMachine class

The Mach5 Engine itself also has its own implementation of a State Machine, using inheritance to allow users to not have to rewrite the base functionality over and over again and using function pointers instead of having one function for each state. A function pointer is what it sounds like--a pointer to the address in memory where the function is-- and we can call it from that information.

To learn more about function pointers and how they are used, check out h ttp://www.cprogramming.com/tutorial/function-pointers.html.

You can take a look at the base version of one here, starting with the `Header` file:

```
#ifndef M5STATEMACNINE_H
#define M5STATEMACNINE_H

#include "M5Component.h"
#include "M5Vec2.h"

//! Base State for M5StateMachines
class M5State
{
public:
  //! Empty virtual destructor
  virtual ~M5State(void) {}
  //! Called when we first enter a state
  virtual void Enter(float dt)  = 0;
  //! called once per frame
  virtual void Update(float dt) = 0;
  //! called before we exit a state
  virtual void Exit(float dt)   = 0;
};

//! Base class for Finite statemanchine component for AstroShot
class M5StateMachine : public M5Component
{
public:
  M5StateMachine(M5ComponentTypes type);
  virtual ~M5StateMachine(void);
  virtual void Update(float dt);
  void SetNextState(M5State* pNext);
private:
  M5State* m_pCurr; //!< a pointer to our current state to be updated
};

#endif //M5STATEMACNINE_H
```

In the preceding code, note that we finally broke apart the `StateMachine` and the `State` object into their own classes, with the state function having its own `Enter`, `Update`, and `Exit` functions. The State Machine keeps track of the current state that we are in and updates appropriately using the `Update` and `SetNextState` functions, and a `SetStateState` function is used to dictate what state we should start from. The implementation for the class looks a little something like this:

```
#include "M5StateMachine.h"

M5StateMachine::M5StateMachine(M5ComponentTypes type):
 M5Component(type),
 m_pCurr(nullptr)
{
}

M5StateMachine::~M5StateMachine(void)
{
}

void M5StateMachine::Update(float dt)
{
 m_pCurr->Update(dt);
}

void M5StateMachine::SetNextState(M5State* pNext)
{
 if(m_pCurr)
 m_pCurr->Exit();

 m_pCurr = pNext;
 m_pCurr->Enter();
}
```

This system provides a template that we can expand upon, in order to create more interesting behavior that does something a bit more complex. Take, for example, the `RandomGoComponent` class, whose header looks like this:

```
#ifndef RANDOM_LOCATION_COMPONENT_H
#define RANDOM_LOCATION_COMPONENT_H

#include "Core\M5Component.h"
#include "Core\M5StateMachine.h"
#include "Core\M5Vec2.h"

//Forward declation
class RandomGoComponent;
```

```
class RLCFindState : public M5State
{
public:
  RLCFindState(RandomGoComponent* parent);
  void Enter(float dt);
  void Update(float dt);
  void Exit(float dt);
private:
  RandomGoComponent* m_parent;
};
class RLCRotateState : public M5State
{
public:
  RLCRotateState(RandomGoComponent* parent);
  void Enter(float dt);
  void Update(float dt);
  void Exit(float dt);
private:
  float m_targetRot;
  M5Vec2 m_dir;
  RandomGoComponent* m_parent;
};
class RLCGoState : public M5State
{
public:
  RLCGoState(RandomGoComponent* parent);
  void Enter(float dt);
  void Update(float dt);
  void Exit(float dt);
private:
  RandomGoComponent* m_parent;
};


class RandomGoComponent : public M5StateMachine
{
public:
  RandomGoComponent(void);
  virtual void FromFile(M5IniFile&);
  virtual M5Component* Clone(void);
private:
  friend RLCFindState;
  friend RLCGoState;
  friend RLCRotateState;

  float           m_speed;
  float           m_rotateSpeed;
  M5Vec2          m_target;
```

```
      RLCFindState    m_findState;
      RLCRotateState m_rotateState;
      RLCGoState      m_goState;
   };


   #endif // !RANDOM_LOCATION_COMPONENT_H
```

This class contains three states, `Find`, `Rotate`, and `Go`, which have been added as objects in the `RandomGoComponent`. Each of the states has their own `Enter`, `Update`, and `Exit` functionality, in addition to the constructor and a reference to their parent. The implementation for the classes looks something like this:

```cpp
#include "RandomGoStates.h"
#include "RandomGoComponent.h"

#include "Core\M5Random.h"
#include "Core\M5Object.h"
#include "Core\M5Intersect.h"
#include "Core\M5Gfx.h"
#include "Core\M5Math.h"
#include <cmath>

FindState::FindState(RandomGoComponent* parent): m_parent(parent)
{
}
void FindState::Enter()
{
 M5Vec2 botLeft;
 M5Vec2 topRight;
 M5Gfx::GetWorldBotLeft(botLeft);
 M5Gfx::GetWorldTopRight(topRight);

 M5Vec2 target;
 target.x = M5Random::GetFloat(botLeft.x, topRight.x);
 target.y = M5Random::GetFloat(botLeft.y, topRight.y);

 m_parent->SetTarget(target);

}
void FindState::Update(float)
{
 m_parent->SetNextState(m_parent->GetState(RGS_ROTATE_STATE));
}
void FindState::Exit()
{
}
```

This class will just tell our main State Machine where its intended location is. This only needs to be done once, so it is done in the `Enter` state. The `Update` state just states that after this is done, we want to move to the `Rotate` state, and `Exit` does nothing. Technically, we could not create it, and that would be fine as well since the base class doesn't do anything as well, but it is here if you wish to expand upon it:

```
RotateState::RotateState(RandomGoComponent* parent): m_parent(parent)
{
}
void RotateState::Enter()
{
 M5Vec2 target = m_parent->GetTarget();

 M5Vec2::Sub(m_dir, target, m_parent->GetM5Object()->pos);

 m_targetRot = std::atan2f(m_dir.y, m_dir.x);
 m_targetRot = M5Math::Wrap(m_targetRot, 0.f, M5Math::TWO_PI);

 m_parent->GetM5Object()->rotationVel = m_parent->GetRotationSpeed();
}
void RotateState::Update(float)
{
 m_parent->GetM5Object()->rotation =
M5Math::Wrap(m_parent->GetM5Object()->rotation, 0.f, M5Math::TWO_PI);

 if (M5Math::IsInRange(m_parent->GetM5Object()->rotation, m_targetRot -
.1f, m_targetRot + .1f))
 m_parent->SetNextState(m_parent->GetState(RGS_GO_STATE));
}
void RotateState::Exit()
{
 m_parent->GetM5Object()->rotationVel = 0;

 m_dir.Normalize();
 M5Vec2::Scale(m_dir, m_dir, m_parent->GetSpeed());

 m_parent->GetM5Object()->vel = m_dir;
}
```

The `Rotate` state will just rotate the character till it is facing the location that it wants to go to. If it is within the range of the rotation, it will then switch to the `Go` state. Before leaving though, it will set the velocity of our parent to the appropriate direction in the `Exit` function:

```
GoState::GoState(RandomGoComponent* parent): m_parent(parent)
{
}
void GoState::Enter()
{
}
void GoState::Update(float)
{
  M5Vec2 target = m_parent->GetTarget();
  if (M5Intersect::PointCircle(target, m_parent->GetM5Object()->pos,
m_parent->GetM5Object()->scale.x))
  m_parent->SetNextState(m_parent->GetState(RGS_FIND_STATE));
}
void GoState::Exit()
{
  m_parent->GetM5Object()->vel.Set(0, 0);
}
```

The `Go` state merely checks whether the enemy intersects with the target that we are set to go to. If it does, we then set our state to move back to the `Find` state and start everything over again, and also stop the player from moving in the `Exit` function:

```
RandomGoComponent::RandomGoComponent():
  M5StateMachine(CT_RandomGoComponent),
  m_speed(1),
  m_rotateSpeed(1),
  m_findState(this),
  m_rotateState(this),
  m_goState(this)
{
  SetNextState(&m_findState);
}
void RandomGoComponent::FromFile(M5IniFile& iniFile)
{
  iniFile.SetToSection("RandomGoComponent");
  iniFile.GetValue("speed", m_speed);
  iniFile.GetValue("rotationSpeed", m_speed);
}
RandomGoComponent* RandomGoComponent::Clone(void) const
{
  RandomGoComponent* pNew = new RandomGoComponent;
  pNew->m_speed = m_speed;
```

```
  pNew->m_rotateSpeed = m_rotateSpeed;
  return pNew;
}

M5State* RandomGoComponent::GetState(RandomGoStates state)
{
  switch (state)
  {
  case RGS_FIND_STATE:
  return &m_findState;
  break;
  case RGS_ROTATE_STATE:
  return &m_rotateState;
  break;
  case RGS_GO_STATE:
  return &m_goState;
  break;
  }

  //In case somethings goes wrong
  return &m_findState;
}
```

As you can see, this works in a very similar way to what we have done before--setting our first state, getting the initial values from the INI file, and then setting things properly when cloned. Finally, we also have a `GetState` function which will return the current state that the player has using a switch like we talked about previously.

To see this in action, go ahead and go to the `Raider.ini` file and modify the code to fit the following:

```
posX   = 0
posY   = 0
velX   = 0
velY   = 0
scaleX = 10
scaleY = 10
rot    = 0
rotVel = 0
components = GfxComponent ColliderComponent RandomGoComponent

[GfxComponent]
texture = enemyBlack3.tga
drawSpace = world

[ColliderComponent]
radius = 5
```

```
isResizeable = 0

[RandomGoComponent]
speed = 40
rotationSpeed = 40
```

If all went well, save the file and then run the project!

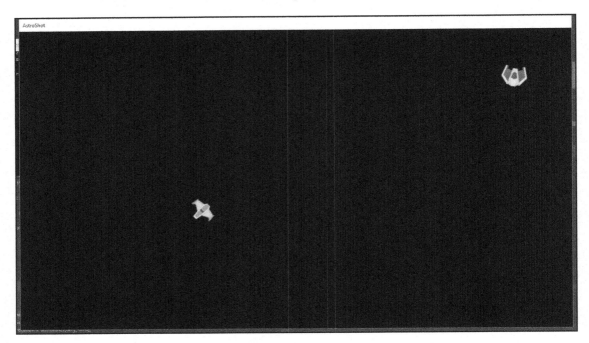

Now we will see the enemy continually move into new areas, rotating before going there!

The State pattern in action - StageManager

Another aspect of the Mach5 Engine that uses the State pattern is the M5StageManager class:

```
class M5StageManager
{
public:
  friend class M5App;

  //Registers a GameStage and a builder with the the StageManger
  static void AddStage(M5StageTypes type, M5StageBuilder* builder);
```

```
    //Removes a Stage Builder from the Manager
    static void RemoveStage(M5StageTypes type);
    //Clears all stages from the StageManager
    static void ClearStages(void);
    //Sets the given stage ID to the starting stage of the game
    static void SetStartStage(M5StageTypes startStage);
    //Test if the game is quitting
    static bool IsQuitting(void);
    //Test stage is restarting
    static bool IsRestarting(void);
    //Gets the pointer to the users game specific data
    static M5GameData& GetGameData(void);
    //Sets the next stage for the game
    static void SetNextStage(M5StageTypes nextStage);
    // Pauses the current stage, so it can be resumed but changes stages
    static void PauseAndSetNextStage(M5StageTypes nextStage);
    // Resumes the previous stage
    static void Resume(void);
    //Tells the game to quit
    static void Quit(void);
    //Tells the stage to restart
    static void Restart(void);
  private:
    static void Init(const M5GameData& gameData, int framesPerSecond);
    static void Update(void);
    static void Shutdown(void);
    static void InitStage(void);
    static void ChangeStage(void);

};//end M5StageManager
```

Since there will only be one of these in the game, all of the functionality has been made static similarly to a Singleton but, depending on the state that the project is in, it will do different things. Take, for example, changing what stage we are in. I'm sure you'll find that it looks very similar to how we changed states earlier:

```
void M5StageManager::ChangeStage(void)
{
 /*Only unload if we are not restarting*/
 if (s_isPausing)
 {
   M5ObjectManager::Pause();
   M5Phy::Pause();
   M5Gfx::Pause(s_drawPaused);
   PauseInfo pi(s_pStage, s_currStage);
   s_pauseStack.push(pi);
   s_isPausing = false;
 }
```

```
  else if (s_isResuming)
  {
    /*Make sure to shutdown the stage*/
    s_pStage->Shutdown();
    delete s_pStage;
    s_pStage = nullptr;
  }
  else if (!s_isRestarting) //Just changine the stage
  {
    /*Make sure to shutdown the stage*/
    s_pStage->Shutdown();
    delete s_pStage;
    s_pStage = nullptr;

    //If we are setting the next state, that means we are ignore all
    //paused states, so lets clear the pause stack
    while (!s_pauseStack.empty())
    {
      M5Gfx::Resume();
      M5Phy::Resume();
      M5ObjectManager::Resume();
      PauseInfo pi = s_pauseStack.top();
      pi.pStage->Shutdown();
      delete pi.pStage;
      s_pauseStack.pop();
    }

  }
  else if (s_isRestarting)
  {
    /*Make sure to shutdown the stage*/
    s_pStage->Shutdown();
  }

  s_currStage = s_nextStage;
}
```

I highly advise taking a closer look at the file and going through each function to see how they interact with each other.

Issues with FSMs

We've seen some of the ways in which FSMs can be valuable things to add to your projects and how they can make simple AI behaviors much easier, but there are some issues with them.

Traditional FSMs such as the ones we've displayed here can, over time, become unmanageable as you continue to add many different states to them. The difficult part is keeping the number of states to a minimum while also adding complexity by adding new contexts in which your characters can respond.

You'll also have a lot of similar code being written as you'll be rebuilding different behaviors that have pieces of others, which can also be time-consuming. Another thing that's been going on recently in the game industry is AI programmers moving on to more complex ways of handing AI, such as behavior trees.

 If you're interested in why some people believe that the age of Finite State Machines is over, check out `http://aigamedev.com/open/article/fsm-age-is-over/`. A look at the issues with FSMs, as well as some potential solutions to fix those issues, can be found here: `http://aigamedev.com/open/article/hfsm-gist/`.

Summary

In this chapter, we learned about the State pattern, which is a way to allow a game object to change its behavior and functionality in response to different stimuli within the game. We learned about the State and the Context (Machine) and how they are used together. We then learned how we can use the State pattern to gain some exposure toward AI programming, as well as how our project's Game State Manager works and why it's important. Of course, FSMs are most popular in being used for AI, but can also be used in UI as well as dealing with user input, making them another useful tool to have in your arsenal.

5
Decoupling Code via the Factory Method Pattern

Every project and every game design is going to change. One of the goals of object-oriented programming is to program with that change in mind. This means writing flexible and reusable code so that, when changes happen, the project doesn't fall apart. Unfortunately, the requirements are never fully known and the vision of the designer is never 100% complete. The good news is that newly added features may interact with old features in unexpectedly fun ways, leading to unplanned features being created, which can make for a completely different, and more enjoyable, game.

In the worst-case scenario, the game design may not be fun at all, which can lead to drastic changes in game object types, object behaviors, and even the design of the entire game. In this case, we want to be able to rework our game to try new possibilities with the least amount of change to code. Changing code takes time to write, test, and debug, and any time new code is added, it has the possibility of causing bugs in older code.

Since we know that our design will change, we must plan for that change by following good design principles and utilizing design patterns to solve common problems. This includes using flexible designs such as the Component Object Model to avoid inheritance hierarchies. This includes using the State pattern and finite state machines to avoid complex `if` statements and cascading `if else` chains that lead to bugs any time a change occurs. This also includes things such as striving for low coupling and avoiding *hardcoding* anything.

We all know that as programmers, we should avoid *magic numbers*. We don't want to see seemingly random or odd numbers in our code. A hardcoded number isn't descriptive enough, which makes the code hard to read, maintain, and debug. If we need to change a magic number, we have to spend time searching our code for every time it appears. Unfortunately, these hardcoded values tend to change a lot during development. In the real world, gravity may be 9.8 m/s^2, but in the game world, we may need to adjust it so the game is more fun, or possibly change it at runtime so the player can walk on the ceiling.

When we think about hard coding, we usually think about magic numbers. However, a call to the `new` operator using a concrete class type such as a new `ChaseAIComponent` may be readable, but it is just as likely to change as the value of gravity or the size of an array.

Chapter overview

In this chapter, you will be focusing on a common interface to create new objects without the need to call constructors directly. First, we will look at reasons why a `switch` statement can be harmful. Next we will look at a design principle that leads us to our final solution, a factory. Then we will look at few different ways to design our factories to make them flexible and reusable.

Your objective

Over the course of this chapter, we will be looking at a few more important concepts and principles that can make our programs better. Here is an outline of what we will cover and your tasks for this chapter:

- Learning why using `switch` statements can be bad
- Learning the Dependency Inversion Principle
- Learning the Factory Method pattern
- Building a Component, Stage, and Object Factory
- Improve your Factories by using templates

The trouble with switch statements

When first learning to program, simply understanding the grammar of the language is very difficult. Often, new programmers focus on the syntax of a function call or `for` loop and they don't even think about making reusable, maintainable code. This is partly because they jump into the coding without planning anything out. This is true for games as well. Often, new programmers want to get straight to writing the game and they forget about things such as user interface and pause menus. Things such as the window resolution, enemy placement in the stages, and even where the mouse should be when clicking buttons will be hardcoded. Here is code from one of the authors' first games. This was a section in the `MainMenu` function that would switch the game into the Load state when the button was clicked. The variable p is the location of the mouse:

```
if ((p.x > .15 * GetSystemMetrics(SM_CXSCREEN)) &&
    (p.x < .42 * GetSystemMetrics(SM_CXSCREEN)) &&
    (p.y > .58 * GetSystemMetrics(SM_CYSCREEN)) &&
    (p.y < .70 * GetSystemMetrics(SM_CYSCREEN)))
{
    if (mousedown)
    {
        mGameState = TCodeRex::LOAD;
        mGameLevel = L0;
    }
}
```

Code similar to this was repeated (without a loop) four times, because there were four buttons in the `MainMenu`. Of course, there were better (much better) ways to write this code. It is important to separate game stages from the `Graphics` class for one, and buttons can manage themselves if they are written correctly. However, the worst part of this old code base was how game stages were changed.

In that game, there was an `Update` function in the `Engine` class that contained a 507-line-long `switch` statement. This included a `switch` within a `switch` for situations where there needed to be a menu stage, but there were multiple menus to choose from. Here is some sample code from when a level needed to be loaded:

```
case TCodeRex::LOAD:
{
StopGameMusic();
StopMenuMusic();
switch (mGameLevel)
{
case TCodeRex::L0:
{
    grafx.LoadScreen(mLoading);
```

```
      mLoading = true;
      if (ObjectMgr->LoadLevel(".\\Levels\\Level_00.txt"))
      {
        mPlayer1->SetPhysics().setPosition(
        (Physics::real)ObjectMgr->PlayerX,
        (Physics::real)ObjectMgr->PlayerY, 0.0f);

        grafx.GetCamera().Move(
          ObjectMgr->PlayerX - 500,
          ObjectMgr->PlayerY - 500);

        ObjectMgr->AddToList(mPlayer1);
        mPlayer1->SetHealth(100);
        mBGTexture = grafx.GetTextureMgr().GetTile(49);
        mplaying = true;
        mGameState = TCodeRex::PLAY;
      }
        else
          mGameState = TCodeRex::MENU;
        break;
  }//end case TCODEREX::LOAD
```

If you feel like that is hard to look at, you are right. For some reason, the stage-switching code was responsible for setting the player's health and position, moving the camera, setting the background texture, and going back to the menu if something failed to load.

The reason we are showing this is so you can see an example of really bad code. This Engine class was tightly coupled with the graphics class, the physics class, the object manager class, and the player class. If any of these classes changed or were removed, the code in the Engine class needed to change. Another problem is that there are many dependencies here, which means a change to any of the classes above will cause the code to be recompiled as well.

One of the authors was in a similar situation a few years later while working on an iPhone game as contract programmer. The original design called for only two stages, the main menu and the gameplay. Since the plan was so simple, code similar to what we saw above was used. This soon became a problem, because all game designs change even if the project is only three months long.

After one month, the game was completed to specification, including a level editor so the designer could create as many levels as were needed. The goal was to spend the rest of the time adding effects and polish to the game. However, every week, the producer and designer would come and say they needed a new menu or transition screen.

In the end, the game design called for an options menu, a level select menu, a credits screen, a celebration screen every 10 levels, and a congratulations screen after completing the game. The simple two-stage code that was originally written ended up being a hacked-together mess because of the fast development timeline and the constant addition of new features. One horrible line of code was similar to this:

```
if(levelCounter == 81)
   ShowCongratsScreen();
```

This *worked* because there were 80 levels in the game and the `levelCounter` incremented after completing a level. After seeing game code like this, we hope you understand why it is important to plan for change to occur.

In `Chapter 3`, *Creating Flexibility with the Component Object Model*, we saw how to create components for our game object so we can easily handle changes to our object design. This is an important step in creating flexible code; however, when we create an object in our stage, we still must use new to hardcode the concrete types that make up our object:

```
M5Object* pObj                  = new M5Object(AT_Player);
GfxComponent* pGfxComp          = new GfxComponent;
PlayerInputComponent* pInput    = new PlayerInputComponent;
ClampComponent* pClamp          = new ClampComponent;
pObj->AddComponent(pGfxComp);
pObj->AddComponent(pInput);
pObj->AddComponent(pClamp );
//Set position, rotation, scale here
//...
M5ObjectManager::AddObject(pObj);
```

This means that our derived `M5Stage` class is tightly coupled to the components of this object type, and really all object types that need to be created in this level. If the objects need different components, or any of the components are changed or removed, then our `Stage` class must be changed.

One way to *solve* this (as we saw in `Chapter 3`, *Creating Flexibility with the Component Object Model*) is to put this code into our `M5ObjectManager` class. This way, our stages don't need to be constantly updated as our types are modified:

```
M5Object* M5ObjectManager::CreateObject(M5ArcheTypes type)
{
  switch(type)
  {
  case AT_Player:
    // Create player object
    M5Object* pPlayer               = new M5Object(AT_Player);
```

```
// Create the components we'd like to use
GfxComponent* pGfx              = new GfxComponent;
PlayerInputComponent* pInput    = new PlayerInputComponent;
ClampComponent* pClamp          = new ClampComponent;

// Attach them to our player
pObj->AddComponent(pGfx);
pObj->AddComponent(pInput);
pObj->AddComponent(pClamp);

   //Add this object to the M5ObjectManager
   AddObject(pPlayer);
   return pPlayer;
 break;
case AT_Bullet:
 //...More Code here
```

This solves the problem of needing to change our stages whenever an object is changed. However, we will still have to change our `switch` statement and the object manager if our objects or components change. Actually, except for this function, the Object Manager doesn't really care about any derived component types. It only needs to be dependent on the `M5Component` abstract class. If we can fix this function, we can completely decouple our derived component types from this class.

The solution to our problem is the same solution used to solve the stage management problem I faced years ago, *the Dependency Inversion Principle*.

The Dependency Inversion Principle

The concept of avoiding `concreate` classes isn't new. Robert C. Martin defined this idea in *The C++ Report* in May 1996 in an article titled *The Dependency Inversion Principle*. It is the D in his SOLID design principles. The principle has two parts:

- High-level modules should not depend on low-level modules. Both should depend on abstractions.
- Abstractions should not depend on details. Details should depend on abstractions.

While this may seem like a mouthful, the concept is actually very easy. Imagine we have a `StageManager` class that is responsible for initializing, updating, and shutting down all of the stages in our game. In this case, our `StageManager` is our high-level modules, and the stages are the low-level modules. The `StageManager` will control the creation and behavior of our low-level module, the stages. This principle says that our `StageManager` code shouldn't depend on derived stage classes, but should instead depend on an abstract stage class. To see why, let's look at an example of not following this principle.

Here our `StageManager` has a function called `Update`, which looks like this:

```
void StageManager::Update()
{
  Level1 level1;
  level1.StartGame();
  while(nothingChanged)
    level1.PlayGame()
  level1.EndGame();
}
```

Of course, this is just the first level of our game, so we will need to include code to update the main menu, and the second level of our game. Since these classes are unrelated, we will need a `switch` statement to make a choice between stages:

```
void StageManager::Update()
{
  switch(currentStage)
  {
  case LEVEL1:
  {
    SpaceShooterLevel1 level1;
    level1.StartLevel();
    while(currentStage == nextStage)
      level1.PlayLevel()
    level1.EndLevel();
    break;
  }
  case LEVEL2:
  {
    SpaceShooterLevel2 level2;
    level2.StartGame();
    while(currentStage == nextStage)
      level2.PlayLevel()
    level2.EndLevel();
    break;
  }
  case MAIN_MENU:
  {
```

```
        SpaceShooterMainMenu mainMenu;
        mainMenu.OpenMenu();
        while(currentStage == nextStage)
          mainMenu.Show()
        mainMenu.CloseMenu();
        break;
    }
}//end switch
}//end Update
```

You can see that as we continue to add more and more levels, this code will get large very fast and it will quickly become impossible, or just really difficult to maintain. This is because we will need to go into this function and remember to update the `switch` statement every time a new stage is added to the game.

The first part of this section, tells us that that our `StageManager` class shouldn't depend on levels or menus, but should instead depend on a common abstraction. That means that we should create an abstract base class for all of our stages. The second part says that the abstraction shouldn't care whether the stage is a level or a menu. In fact, it shouldn't even care that we are making a stage for a space shooter game, a platformer, or a racing game. A major benefit of using this principle, besides having more flexible code, is that our `StageManager` class will no longer depend on anything in this specific game, so we can reuse it for our next project:

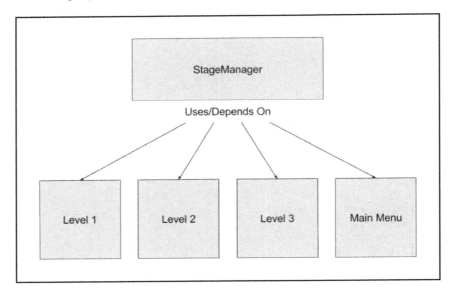

StageManager depends on specific classes

```
//Stage.h
class Stage
{
public:
  virtual ~Stage(void) {}//Empty virtual destructor
  virtual void Init(void)     = 0;
  virtual void Update(void)   = 0;
  virtual void Shutdown(void) = 0;
};

//StageManager.cpp
void StageManager::Update()
{
  //We will talk about how to get the current stage soon
  Stage* pStage = GetCurrentStage();

  //Once we have the correct Stage we can run our code
  pStage->Init();

  while(currentStage == nextStage)
    pStage->Update();

  pStage->Shutdown();
}


//Example of a derived class
//MainMenu.h
class MainMenu : public Stage
{
public:
  virtual ~MainMenu(void);
  virtual void Init(void);
  virtual void Update(void);
  virtual void Shutdown(void);
private:
  //Specific MainMenu data and functions here...
};
```

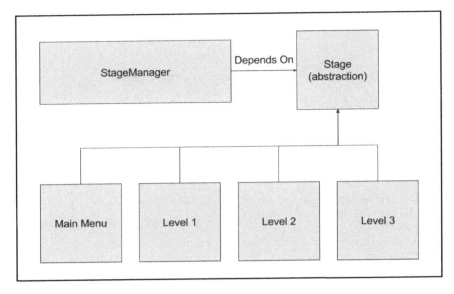

StageManager only depends on abstraction

Now the `Update` function of `StageManager` is much simpler. Since we are only dependent on the abstract class, our code no longer needs to change based on derived implementations. We have also simplified the interface of all stages. The functions of each stage no longer change based on the details of the class (menu, level, and so on); instead, they all share a common interface. As you can see, knowing about the Dependency Inversion Principle will not only make you a big hit at parties, it will also allow you to decouple your code base and reuse higher-level modules.

We still have the problem of selecting the correct derived class. We don't want to put a `switch` statement in the `Update` function of `StageManager`. If we do that, we will have dependency problems like before. Instead, we need a way to select the correct derived class while depending only on the base class.

The Factory method pattern

The Factory method pattern is exactly the design pattern we need to solve our problem. The purpose of this pattern is to have a way of creating the derived class that we want without needed to specify the `concreate` class in our high-level module. This is done by defining an interface for creating objects, but letting subclasses decide which class to instantiate.

In our case, we will create a `StageFactory` interface with a method called `Build` that will return a `Stage*`. We can then create subclasses such as `Level2Factory` to instantiate our derived classes. Our `StageManager` class now only needs to know about the `Stage` and `StageFactory` abstractions:

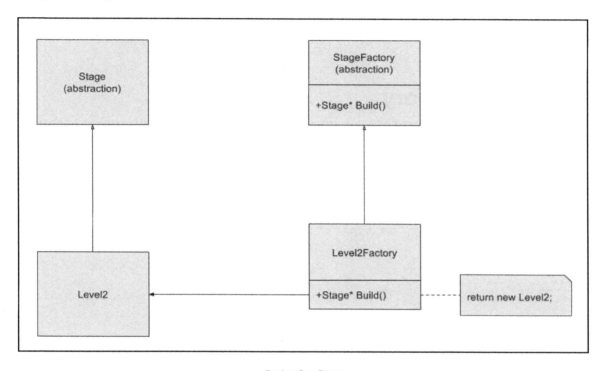

Creating a Stage Factory

```
//StageManager.cpp
void StageManager::Update()
{
Stage* pStage = m_stageFactory->Build();

pStage->Init();

  while(currentStage == nextStage)
    pStage->Update();

pStage->Shutdown();
m_StageFactory->Destroy(pStage);//stage must be destroyed
}
```

Notice that we have moved the call to new from our `StageManager::Update` function into derived `StageFactory` methods. We have successfully decoupled our `StageManager` from our derived `Stage` classes. However, the call to `Build` represents the creation of only one derived `Stage` class. We still need a way to choose which derived `Stage` we want to use and which derived `StageFactory` we need to instantiate. We need a way to choose between different types of factories. Before we look at the solution that was used in the Mach5 Engine, let's look at an alternative Factory method, the Static Factory.

The Static Factory

The simplest way to implement a factory method the way we want is with either a global function or a static class function. We could define a function called `MakeStage` outside of `StateMananger` that is responsible for instantiating the correct derived type based on a parameter. In this case, we will use an `enum` called `StageType` to help us choose our correct type:

```cpp
//MakeStage.cpp
Stage* MakeStage(StageType type)
{
  switch(type)
  {
    case ST_Level1:
      return new Level1;
    case ST_LEVEL2:
      return new Level2;
    case ST_MainMenu:
      return new MainMenu;
    default:
      //Throw exception or assert
  }
}
```

If we use this style of factory, our `StageManager::Update` function will look like this:

```
void StageManager::Update()
{
  Stage* pStage = MakeStage(currentStage);

  pStage->Init();

  while(currentStage == nextStage)
    pStage->Update();

pStage->Shutdown();
DestroyStage(pStage);//Clean up the stage when done
}
```

This version of the factory method works exactly as we want. We can now choose which derived `Stage` class is instantiated. We still have a switch statement that we must maintain, but at least our higher-level module is no longer dependent on derived classes. In the default case, where our `switch` statement can't match the correct type, we are left with the choice of using an assert to crash the program, throwing an exception and letting the client resolve the issue, or perhaps returning null, which still gives responsibility to the client.

The Static Factory successfully decouples our `StageManager` class from specific derived `Stage` classes, while allowing us to choose which stage will be instantiated at runtime. This is great, but as I said, this isn't how the Mach5 Engine implements `Stage` or component factories. Instead, Mach5 uses a more dynamic solution, so we will call it the Dynamic Factory.

The Dynamic Factory

While the Static Factory is simple enough for our purpose, the Mach5 Engine uses a different approach. This approach combines the polymorphic solution of the classic Factory method with the selection capability of the Static Factory. This new approach uses a searchable collection of derived `StageFactory` classes.

Remember that problem with the classic Factory method is that the method represents only one class to instantiate. This allows our code to be flexible because we don't depend on a derived `Stage` class or a call to the `new` operator. However, we still needed a way to get specific derived `StageFactory` instances.

In the Mach5 Engine, the names are changed a little. There is only one `StageFactory` class, which contains a collection of `M5StageBuilder` pointers (these are classic Factories), which implement a `Build` method. The design looks like this:

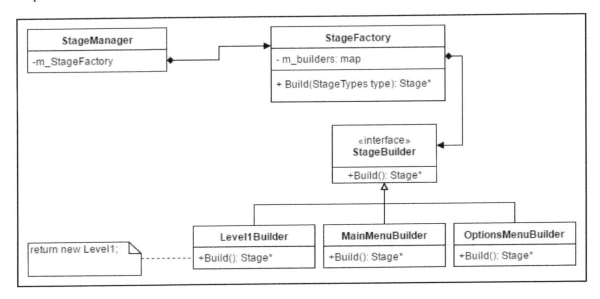

Design of Dynamic Factory

The first class we want to see is the base `M5Stage` class:

```
class M5Stage
{
public:
  virtual ~M5Stage(void) {} //Empty virtual destructor
  virtual void Load(void)      = 0;
  virtual void Init(void)      = 0;
  virtual void Update(float dt) = 0;
  virtual void Shutdown(void)  = 0;
  virtual void Unload(void)    = 0;
};
```

The base `M5Stage` class is a pretty simple abstract base class with a virtual destructor. The specific virtual functions in `M5Stage` aren't important for the details of the factory. We are simply showing the class here, because the `M5StageManager` and `M5StageFactory` will be using this abstraction.

C++ classes intended for polymorphic use, including abstract base classes, should always implement a virtual destructor, otherwise the correct derived class destructor cannot be called.

Creating our Stage Builders

Next let's look at our base builder class. Notice that this is the same type of interface that would be used in the classic Factory method pattern. This abstraction declares a method that returns another abstraction, in this case `M5Stage`.

Just like before, we need to have an empty virtual destructor so when we use this class in a polymorphic way, the correct destructor will be called. Also like before, the other methods are marked as purely `virtual`, which disallows direct instantiation of this class. That means we cannot create an `M5StageBuilder` directly. We must derive from it, and implement the pure virtual methods:

```
class M5StageBuilder
{
public:
  virtual ~M5StageBuilder() {} //Empty virtual destructor
  virtual M5Stage* Build(void) = 0;
};
```

Even though the name is different, this is how the classic Factory method would be implemented. The Mach5 Engine calls this a *Builder* instead of a *Factory* but it is only a change in the name and not the functionality. The name of the `Build` method isn't important. Some programs will call the method `Create` or `Make`. Mach5 calls it `Build` but any of these names are fine.

No matter what the name is, a user creating a game with the Mach5 Engine would want to derive their own specific stage builders for the stages in their game. For this book, we have stages for a space shooter game called `AstroShot`. In order to make builders for these stages, we need to derive from `M5StageBuilder` and implement the `Build` method. For example, if we had `M5Stage` derived classes called `SplashStage` and `MainMenuStage`, we would create builders like this:

```
//SplashStageBuilder.h
class SplashStageBuilder: public M5StageBuilder
{
public:
  virtual M5Stage* Build(void);
};
```

```
//SplashStageBuilder.cpp
M5Stage* SplashStageBuilder::Build(void)
{
return new SplashStage;
}

//MainMenuStageBuilder.h
class MainMenuStageBuilder: public M5StageBuilder
{
public:
   virtual M5Stage* Build(void);
};

// MainMenuStageBuilder.cpp
M5Stage* MainMenuStageBuilder::Build(void)
{
return new MainMenuStage;
}
```

Note here that the use of the keyword `virtual` in the derived classes is completely optional. In the pre C++ 11 days, programmers would mark the function `virtual` as a form of documentation to other programmers. These days, you can add the override specifier to a virtual function so the compiler can issue an error if the function isn't a true override.

To some, this might seem a little tedious. In fact, the biggest complaint I hear from people first learning about object-oriented programming is that they feel like they waste a lot time creating many files with small classes in them. To them, it feels like a lot of work for very little pay-off.

I agree that programming this way can require lots of files and lots of little classes. However, I disagree with it being a waste of time. I think these arguments are a result of shortsighted thinking. They are only thinking of the time it takes to write the original code, but they aren't thinking about the time it will save when making changes to the design or the time it will take to test and debug.

It doesn't take much time to create new files. With an integrated development environment such as Visual Studio, it takes less than 10 seconds to create a source and header file. Writing small classes such as the builders above doesn't take much time either. In total, writing these two classes takes less than five minutes. Of course, this is more than directly writing new into a high-level module, but remember that the goal is to write code that can adapt to change in our game design.

These shortsighted arguments are similar to the complaints of new programmers learning to write functions. We have already discussed the benefits of writing functions and those same benefits apply here. We shouldn't think only of the time it takes to write the initial code. We need to factor in how long it will take to test and debug the code, how likely it is to introduce new bugs into old code, how long it will take to modify if our design changes a month or year from now, and if the design does change, how likely is it that modifying our code will introduce bugs.

It is important to understand that by using design patterns we are writing more code upfront, so that we can cut down on the time it takes to test, debug, integrate, maintain, and change our code in the future. It is important to understand that writing the original code is easy and cheap, while changing it later is much harder and more expensive. In this case, cheap and expensive could be referring to hours worked or money spent paying programmers.

The template builder

Those worried about writing a lot of little classes are in luck. Most, if not all, of our builders will be the same except for the specific derived class they instantiate. That means we can use the power of C++ templates to create builders for us. Our templated builder will look like this:

```
//M5StageBuilder.h
template <typename T>
class M5StageTBuilder : public M5StageBuilder
{
public:
  virtual M5Stage* Build(void);
};

template <typename T>
M5Stage* M5StageTBuilder<T>::Build(void)
{
  return new T();
}
```

This code works great for most of our stages. The only time it doesn't work is when we need to do something more specific, such as call a non-default constructor, or a function specific to the derived stage.

Notice that the implementation of the `Build` function is also included in the `.h` file. This is because `template` functions are not the same as regular functions. They work as recipes so the compiler knows how to generate the function for the specific type. Each time we need to use this function, the compiler will need to know about the recipe. This allows the compiler to instantiate the function as opposed to requiring the user to explicitly instantiate the `Builder` classes they need before using them. So when we want to use this class, it will look something like this:

```
//SomeFile.cpp
#include "M5StageBuilder.h"
#include "MainMenuStage.h"

void SomeFunction(void)
{
  //Creating the class needs the type
  M5Builder* pBuilder = new M5StageTBuilder< SplashStage >();

  //But using the Build function doesn't need the type
  M5Stage* pStage = pBuilder->Build();
}
```

Creating the Dynamic Factory class

So far, we have only created our builders, which are equivalent to the classic Factory method pattern. However, we haven't seen the Factory part of the Dynamic Factory. Let's look at how the Mach5 Engine implements the `StageFactory` class:

```
class M5StageFactory
{
public:
~M5StageFactory(void);
void      AddBuilder(M5StageTypes name, M5StageBuilder* builder);
void      RemoveBuilder(M5StageTypes type);
void      ClearBuilders(void);
M5Stage* Build(M5StageTypes name);
private:
  typedef std::unordered_map<M5StageTypes,
    M5StageBuilder*> BuilderMap;
  typedef BuilderMap::iterator MapItor;

  BuilderMap m_builderMap;
};
```

As you can see, `M5StageFactory` isn't a very complicated class. Once you understand the design behind the patterns, implementing them is usually not very difficult. As for this class, it is only five methods and one member. The private section looks a little complicated because Mach5 prefers using a `typedef` for templated containers. Since the container is used in all of the private functions, let's look at the member before exploring the five methods.

Let's first look the `typedef`s:

```
typedef std::unordered_map<M5StageTypes, M5StageBuilder*> BuilderMap;
```

Since we want a container of `M5StageBuilders`, we have a few choices. We could use an STL vector or list, but those containers are not ideal for searching because of the potential lack of efficiency if we have many builders. However, this is exactly what the STL map and `unordered_map` are perfect for. They allow us to save key/value pairs and later use the key to efficiently find the value, even if we had thousands of builders. We will use the `M5StageTypes`enum as our key, and use a derived `M5StageBuilder*` as our value.

An STL map is implemented as a tree, while `unordered_map` is implemented as a hash table. In general, this means that the map will use less memory, but will be a little slower to search. `unordered_map` will use more memory but search much faster. In our games, we aren't likely to create thousands of stages, so the difference in speed isn't going to matter that much, especially since we won't be searching very often either. We choose the hash table because, on a PC, I am less concerned about memory and more concerned about speed. If you are interested in learning more, check out `http://www.cplusplus.com/reference/` for lots of information about the standard library.

We should also prefer to have as readable code as possible. Using a `typedef` will help others understand our code, because we only need to write the long `std::unordered_map< M5StageTypes, M5StageBuilder*>` code one time. After that, we can use the shorted name, in this case `BuilderMap`. This also gives us the ability to easily change containers if we later decide to use a map instead:

```
typedef BuilderMap::iterator MapItor;
```

The next `typedef` gives us a shorted name for our `BuilderMap` iterators.

> This is unnecessary with the C++ 11 auto keyword, but doesn't make our code less readable so we have chosen to use the `typedef`.

Finally, the actual member:

```
BuilderMap m_builderMap;
```

This will be our container that maps `M5StageTypes` to `M5StageBuilder*`. We should make it private because we want all builders to be added and removed with the class methods so the data can be validated.

Now for the class methods. Let's start with the most important method of the factory:

```
M5Stage* M5StageFactory::Build(M5StageTypes type)
{
   ArcheTypeItor itor = m_builderMap.find(type);
if (itor == m_builderMap.end())
   return nullptr;
else
   return itor->second->Build();
}
```

The `Build` method is where the *magic* happens, at least for the user. They pass in a stage type and we build the correct stage for them. Of course, we use the `find` method first to make sure the type has been added. If it can't be found, we use a debug assert to let the user know that this type wasn't added. In general, the `find` method is safer to use than the `operator[]` that exists in the map and unordered map. Using the `operator[]` will create and return a null value if the key doesn't exist. If that happened while trying to build, we would get a null pointer exception, which would crash the program without giving the user an explanation of why.

We have the choice of adding some default stage to the map, and building that if the correct type can't be found. However, there is a chance that the programmer won't notice that a mistake has been made. Instead, we have chosen to return a null pointer. The requires the user to check whether the builder is valid before using it, but also means that the code will crash if they don't fix the problem:

```
bool M5StageFactory::AddBuilder(M5StageTypes name,
   M5StageBuilder* pBuilder)
{
std::pair<MapItor, bool> itor = m_builderMap.insert(
```

```
        std::make_pair(name, pBuilder));

    return itor.second;
}
```

The `AddBuilder` method allows our user to associate an `M5StageTypes` value with a derived `M5StageBuilder`. In this case, our code doesn't know or care whether `pBuilder` is pointing to a templated class or not. All that matters is that it derives from `M5StageBuilder`.

Just as before, we should write our code to help the user find and fix bugs if they occur. We do that by testing the return value of the insert method. The `insert` method returns a pair in which the second element will tell us whether the insert was successful or not. Since a map and an `unordered_map` do not allow duplicates, we can test to make sure the user isn't associating an `M5StageTypes` value with two different builders. If the user tries to use an `enum` value twice, the second builder will not be inserted and false will be returned.

 The STL versions of map and `unordered_map` do not allow duplicate items. If you wish to have duplicates, you can replace the container with `multimap` or `unordered_multimap`, which do allow duplicates. It wouldn't be useful to use the multi versions in this class, but they are good tools to know about.

```
void M5StageFactory::RemoveBuilder(M5StageTypes name)
{
    BuilderMap::iterator itor = m_builderMap.find(name);

if (itor == m_builderMap.end())
    return;

    //First delete the builder
    delete itor->second;
    itor->second = 0;//See the note below

    //then erase the element
    m_builderMap.erase(itor);
}
```

By now, the pattern should feel routine. First we write code to make sure there are no errors, then we write the actual function code. In this function, we first check to make sure the user is removing a previously added builder. After we make sure the user didn't make a mistake, we then delete the builder and erase the iterator from the container.

TIP

Since we are immediately erasing the iterator after deleting the builder, it is unnecessary to set the pointer to 0. However, I always set the pointer to 0. This helps find bugs. For example, if I forgot to erase the iterator and tried to use this builder again, the program would crash, resulting from using the null pointer. If I didn't set the pointer to 0 but still tried to use it, I would instead get undefined behavior.

```
void M5StageFactory::ClearBuilders(void)
{
  MapItor itor = m_builderMap.begin();
  MapItor end  = m_builderMap.end();

  //Make sure to delete all builder pointers first
  while (itor != end)
  {
    delete itor->second;
    itor->second = 0;
    ++itor;
  }

  //Then clear the hash table
  m_builderMap.clear();
}
```

Just as with the `RemoveAllComponents` from the `M5Object`, the purpose of `ClearBuilders` is to help the destructor of the class. Since this code needs to be written anyway (it would go in the destructor), we think it is better to factor it into a separate function that the user can call if they need:

```
M5StageFactory::~M5StageFactory(void)
{
  ClearBuilders();
}
```

Finally, we have our factory destructor. This just ensures that we don't have any memory leaks by calling the `ClearBuilders` function.

Using the Dynamic Factory

Now that we have a completed `Factory` class, let's look at how we would use it. Since the goal of this class was to decouple our `M5StageManager` from our specific derived `M5Stage` classes, it makes sense that it will be used in the `M5StageManager` class:

```
class M5StageManager
{
public:
  //Lots of other stuff here...
  static void AddStage(M5StageTypes type, M5StageBuilder*
      builder);
static void RemoveStage(M5StageTypes type);
static void ClearStages(void);

private:
  //Lots of other stuff here
  static M5StageFactory s_stageFactory;
};
```

Since the factory will be private in the `M5StageManager`, we will add interface functions so the user can control the factory without knowing the implementation. This allows us to change the details, without affecting the user.

Inside the `M5StageManager::Update` function, we will use the factory to get access to the current stage. Notice that this class is completely decoupled from any specific `M5Stage` derived classes. This give the user freedom to change the game design, including stage types, stage count, and stage names, without needing to modify the `M5StageManager` class.

In fact, that is the purpose of creating the Mach5 Engine the way we are. It can be used and reused in many game projects without changing the engine code. Here is a simplified version (pausing/restarting code has been omitted) of the `M5StageManager::Update` showing code relevant to the stages and factory:

```
void M5StageManager::Update(void)
{
  float frameTime = 0.0f;
  /*Get the Current stage*/
  M5Stage* pCurrentStage = s_stageFactory.Build(s_currStage);

  /*Call the initialize function*/
  pStage->Init();

  /*Keep going until the stage has changed or we are quitting. */
  while ((s_currStage == s_nextStage) &&
      !s_isQuitting                    &&
```

```
        !s_isRestarting)
    {
        /*Our main game loop*/
        s_timer.StartFrame();/*Save the start time of the frame*/
        M5Input::Reset(frameTime);
        M5App::ProcessMessages();

        pStage->Update(frameTime);

        M5ObjectManager::Update(frameTime);
        M5Gfx::Update();
        frameTime = s_timer.EndFrame();/*Get the total frame time*/
    }

    /*Make sure to Shut down the stage*/
    pStage->Shutdown();

    ChangeStage();
}
```

As you can see, the M5StageManager is completely decoupled from any derived M5Stage classes. This allows the user to change, add, or remove any stages during development without needing to modify the M5StageManager class. This also allows the M5StageManager and M5StageFactory classes to be reused in another game, shortening the development time of that project.

Now that we have seen the dynamic factory and how to use it, an important question should come to your mind: what are the benefits of the Dynamic Factory? Both the Static and Dynamic Factories allow us to decouple our code. Since they both offer that benefit and the Static Factory is much easier to implement, why should we bother spending time on the Dynamic Factory? Asking questions like these is always a good idea. In this case, I think there are two benefits to using the Dynamic Factory over the Static Factory.

The first benefit of the Dynamic Factory is that it is dynamic, meaning that we can load builders from a file at runtime or remove a stage if we will never use it again (SplashStage). Being dynamic allows us to swap out a builder at runtime. For example, depending on the difficulty the player selects, we can swap out a difficulty component on enemies. The code to these difficulty component builders could be put into the menu, and the rest of our game no longer needs to care about the difficulty, the levels just create enemies the same way, no matter what.

The second and more important benefit of creating the Dynamic Factory comes in the next step. Since we have successfully created a StageFactory, we should do the same thing for components and game objects. In the next section, we will take a look at creating these factories.

Creating a component and Object Factory

Now that we have built a stage factory, building a component factory should be easy. Let's take a look at what a component and object factory would look like:

```cpp
//Component Factory
class M5ComponentFactory
{
public:
  ~M5ComponentFactory(void);
  void AddBuilder(M5ComponentTypes type,
                  M5ComponentBuilder* builder);
  void RemoveBuilder(M5ComponentTypes type);
  M5Component* Build(M5ComponentTypes type);
  void ClearBuilders(void);
private:
  typedef std::unordered_map<M5ComponentTypes,
                             M5ComponentBuilder*> BuilderMap;
  typedef BuilderMap::iterator MapItor;
  BuilderMap m_builderMap;
};

//Object Factory
class M5ObjectFactory
{
public:
  ~ M5ObjectFactory (void);
  void AddBuilder(M5ArcheTypes type,
     M5ObjectBuilder* builder);
  void RemoveBuilder(M5ArcheTypes type);
  M5Object* Build(M5ArcheTypes type);
  void ClearBuilders(void);
private:
  typedef std::unordered_map< M5ArcheTypes,
     M5ObjectBuilder *> BuilderMap;
  typedef BuilderMap::iterator MapItor;
  BuilderMap m_builderMap;
};
```

Looking at those classes, you will notice that they are almost identical to the M5StageFactory class. The only things that are different are the types involved. Instead of M5StageTypes, we use M5ComponentTypes or M5ArcheTypes. Instead of M5StageBuilder, we use M5ComponentBuilder or M5ObjectBuilder. Finally, instead of the Build method returning an M5Stage*, we return either an M5Component* or M5Object*.

If we were to implement these classes, the code would be identical as well. You might think that the `M5ObjectFactory` would be a little different since the `M5Object` isn't part of an inheritance hierarchy, but it actually doesn't matter. Even though the derived class builders are all doing different work, they are always just returning a single pointer type. The builders might be different, but the return type isn't.

The Templated Factory

Since we need to create different versions of the same algorithms using different type, we should again make use of C++ templates. This will allow us to write the code one time, and reuse it for any factory type we need.

First we need to factor out the types that are different. If you look at all three classes, you will see that three types are different. The enumeration type, the builder type, and the return type for the `Build` method is different in all three classes. If we make those template parameters, we can reuse the same code instead of recreating the same class three times. Here is how we should refactor our code:

```
//M5Factory.h
template<typename EnumType,
         typename BuilderType,
         typename ReturnType>
class M5Factory
{
public:
  ~M5Factory(void);
  void AddBuilder(EnumType type, BuilderType* pBuilder);
  void RemoveBuilder(EnumType type);
  ReturnType* Build(EnumType type);
  void ClearBuilders(void);
private:
  typedef std::unordered_map<EnumType, BuilderType*> BuilderMap;
  typedef typename BuilderMap::iterator MapItor;
  BuilderMap m_builderMap;
};
```

Notice that our class is now a template class with three template parameters, `EnumType`, `BuilderType`, and `ReturnType`. Instead of any specific types such as `M5StageTypes`, we have used our template parameters. One change that confuses many people is this line:

```
typedef typename BuilderMap::iterator MapItor;
```

In the original, non-templated `M5StageFactory` class, the compiler was able to look at the code `BuilderMap::iterator` and know for certain that iterator was a type inside `BuilderMap`. Now that we have a template class, the compiler can't be sure whether `BuilderMap::iterator` is a variable or a type, so we need to help the compiler by using the `typename` keyword to say that this is a type.

Since our factory is now a templated class, we should again put all functions implementations into the header file. In addition, each implementation must be marked as a template function. Here is an example of one of the `Build` methods:

```
//M5Factory.h
template<typename EnumType,
         typename BuilderType,
         typename ReturnType>
ReturnType* M5Factory<EnumType,
                      BuilderType,
                      ReturnType>::Build(EnumType type)
{
MapItor itor = m_builderMap.find(type);
M5DEBUG_ASSERT(itor != m_builderMap.end(),
  "Trying to use a Builder that doesn't exist");
  return itor->second->Build();
}
```

Except for the change in the function signature, the `Build` function is exactly the same. This is true of `AddBuilder`, `RemoveBuilder`, and all functions of the class. As I said, by making the Dynamic Factory a template class, we can reuse the same code for our stage factory, our component factory, and our object factory. Since that is the case, we won't spend time on making the template factory. However, we still need to see how to use this new class. Let's look at our `M5StageFactory` class:

```
class M5StageManager
{
public:
  //Same as before
private:
//static M5StageFactory s_stageFactory; //Our Old Code
static M5Factory<M5StageTypes,
               M5StageBuilder,
               M5Stage> s_stageFactory;//Our new code

};
```

That is the only change we need to make to our `M5StageFactory`. Everything else will work the exact same way. The nice thing is that once we have our template factory completed, using a component factory is easy. Here is how we can use our component factory and object factory inside our `M5ObjectManager` class:

```
class M5ObjectManager
{
public:
  //See M5ObjectManager.h for details
private:
  static M5Factory<M5ComponentTypes,
                  M5ComponentBuilder,
                  M5Component> s_componentFactory;
static M5Factory<M5ArcheTypes,
                M5ObjectBuilder,
                M5Object> s_ObjectFactory;
};
```

Reusing the code is simple once we have created the template version. We should have created that first, but most programmers have a hard time thinking about how to reuse a class until after the initial code has been written. I think it is easier and more natural to create the stage factory first, then refactor the code into a template class.

There is one more important thing to consider when using our factory: how to add our builders. For now, let's only consider the `M5Factory` inside the `M5StageManager` since we have seen that code already. Somewhere in our code, we must still instantiate our derived builders so we can add them to the `M5StageManager`. For example, we would need a function like this:

```
#include "M5StageManager.h"
#include "M5StageTypes.h"
#include "M5StageBuilder.h"
#include "GamePlayStage.h" //Example Stage
#include "SplashStage.h"   //Example Stage


void RegisterStages(void)
{
M5StageManager::AddStage(ST_GamePlayStage,
   new M5StageTBuilder< GamePlayStage >() );
M5StageManager::AddStage(ST_SplashStage,
   new M5StageTBuilder< SplashStage >() );
}
```

As you can see, this function is dependent on all stages in our game and is likely to change as we change our design. Unfortunately, this is as far as we can decouple our code. At some point, we need to instantiate derived classes. Even though this is necessary, later we will look at how to minimize the work involved in maintaining this code. In the case of the Mach5 Engine, this code is auto generated with a Windows batch file before the code is compiled. By auto generating our file, we reduce the chance of forgetting to add a stage, and also minimize the work when our code changes.

Architecting versus over-architecting

Over-architecting is the concept of spending time planning as well as writing code that includes completely unneeded and ultimately unused features. Since every project has a deadline, over-architecting means wasting time that could be better spent writing code that will be used.

In our effort to learn design patterns, we want to know not only how to use them, but also about when not to use them. When you are working on a project, you must always find the balance between writing flexible code and getting the project finished on time. It always takes more time to write flexible, reusable code, so you have to consider whether it is worth the extra time to write that code.

It would be great to spend time creating the ultimate graphics engine, or creating a content creation tool that can rival Unreal or Unity. However, if you strive to write perfect, flexible, 100% reusable code, you may never complete your game. You may end up writing a great particle system and have your designers only use 10% of the capabilities. This is why many companies choose to use a premade engine in the first place. Those companies don't want to spend time or money on creating a tool. They want to spend time making a game that is fun.

The opposite of this situation is just as bad. We don't want to write code that breaks whenever a change is introduced, or is impossible to use again. We can all imagine how ugly the code would be if an entire game was written in the standard `main` function. We might laugh at the thought of someone doing that, while at the same time hardcoding behavior with large if/else chains instead of using Finite State Machines.

Finding the balance between these two extremes is difficult. I already mentioned that besides writing the initial code, there are additional factors to consider. These include the time it takes to test and debug the code as well as time to modify code if and when change occurs.

Determining whether writing flexible code is worth the time also includes determining how likely that code is to change. This is why we are using Singleton classes for our core engines. These are unlikely to change during the project. Of course, if we need to support multiple graphics APIs, multiple platforms, or even a multithreaded environment, we might make a different decision. This is also why using the Component Object Model and Finite State Machines are very useful, since our game objects and their behavior are likely to change constantly.

In this case, we need to choose between using the Static Factory or the Dynamic Factory. The Static Factory is very simple to write and use. Since it is so simple, testing and debugging should be easy. It is likely to change, but those changes should be easy as well. However, when using the Static Factory, we must write, test, debug, and maintain code for at least three separate types in our game: the stages, components, and objects. These will change often during the development cycle. Each time a change occurs, you would need to go back and modify these functions.

The templated Dynamic Factory is a little more difficult to implement, especially if you aren't very familiar with using templates. However, the major benefit of using the templated Dynamic Factory is that we only need to write the code once, and we can use it for stages, components, and objects. In addition, we have the ability to add, remove, or change items in our factories at runtime. As I mentioned, this could mean changing archetype builders based on difficulty to create harder versions of the same archetype without needing new enumeration values. Finally, we have the option of using this code again in another project, which is unlikely if we stick with the Static Factory.

In the end, the `M5Factory.h` file that contains the templated Dynamic factory is only around 125 lines of code, with maybe 30% of that being comments and white space. It may be a little more difficult, but I don't think it is so difficult that someone should prefer the Static Factory.

Summary

In this chapter, we focused a lot on decoupling code. Since our game design is very likely to change, we want to make sure that our high-level modules don't depend on derived stages or components. That is why we should follow the Dependency Inversion Principle, which says the following:

- High-level modules should not depend on low-level modules. Both should depend on abstractions.
- Abstractions should not depend on details. Details should depend on abstractions.

In simpler terms, this means that all our code should be built around the interfaces. We used the example of our `M5StageManager` not being dependent on derived `M5Stage` classes. Since we want to avoid class dependencies like this, we learned that we should also avoid *hard coding*, including using calls to the `new` operator. In order to avoid direct calls to the `new` operator, we learned about three ways to make Factories.

The first method was the classic Gang of Four Factory method, which says we should create a hierarchy of classes, each capable of instantiating a single class. This method helped us get to our final solution, but wasn't quite good enough, because we want to be able to select which derived class to instantiate via a string or an enum.

The second method we learned was the Static Factory Method, which uses a simple global or static function and a switch statement to allow us to select our desired derived class. This works great for our needs, but we decided to go one step further and create an even more flexible, reusable factory.

Finally, we learned about the Dynamic Factory, specifically the templated version of the Dynamic Factory, which combines both the classic Factory method and the Static Factory. The best part is that since we are using the power of C++ templates, we can reuse the code for stages and components, as well as objects.

Throughout this chapter, but especially in the last section, we discussed the balance between spending time writing flexible code versus over-architecting. Of course, one strong reason to study design patterns is to learn how to write great reusable code, but we always want to make sure it fits the project and fits within the project deadline.

The goal of this book is to help you understand when and where we should apply these patterns throughout a game. We already know how to create flexible game objects using components and Finite State Machines. Now that we know about the Dynamic factory, we have decoupled our stage and component creation from our core engine, making everything more reusable.

However, the ultimate goal is to make things so flexible that they can be changed from a text file or tool without the need to recompile anything. That is what we will learn how to do next.

6

Creating Objects with the Prototype Pattern

We saw in the last chapter how using a Dynamic Factory can help us decouple our high-level modules, such as the `M5StageManager` or `M5ObjectManager` from the implementation details of our derived `M5Stage` or `M5Component` classes. We did this by pushing those dependencies into derived builder classes that would be used by a Dynamic Factory. This allowed us the freedom to change our derived stage and component classes without needing to modify our higher level modules. C++ template classes made using the Dynamic Factory very easy, since we were not required to create a derived class builder for every stage and component.

However, we are required to create a builder for each `M5Object` type we want, since they will contain a set of components that are unique to each object. Unfortunately, these builders may require frequent changes as we playtest, balance, and modify our game design. Each time these builders change, the game will be need to be recompiled.

The goal would be to have our game object types be completely defined in a file. This would give the game designer the ability to test, tweak, and balance the game without needing to touch C++ code or ever recompile. Of course, all of this could be done in a level editor tool, which could also be given to players, allowing them to create additional game content.

In this chapter, we will explore the Prototype pattern and how it can help us define objects completely within a text file. We will do this by first looking at a simple example of the pattern, then looking at how the Mach5 Engine, and the `M5ObjectManager` specifically, makes use of this pattern to read game object definitions from a file. Along the way, we will look at some language features of C++ that will help us write better, safer code.

Your objectives

Here is an outline of the topics we will cover and your tasks for this chapter:

- Learn the trouble with using a factory for game objects
- Implement the Prototype pattern
- Learn how the Mach5 engine uses the Prototype pattern
- Implement components within the Mach5 Engine
- Learn how to define objects completely in a file

The trouble with using a factory for game objects

In Chapter 5, *Decoupling Code via the Factory Method Pattern* we learned how to use a Dynamic Factory to decouple our stages, components, and objects from higher level modules. We did this by placing the dependencies of each derived class into a separate builder class instead of a high-level module. Let's look at an example of creating a derived type stage builder:

```
//SplashStageBuilder.h------------------
#include "M5StageBuilder.h"

class SplashStageBuilder: public M5StageBuilder
{
public:
  virtual M5Stage* Build(void);
};

//SplashStageBuilder.cpp--------------------
#include "SplashStageBuilder.h"
#include "SplashStage.h"

M5Stage* SplashStageBuilder::Build(void)
{
  return new SplashStage();
}
```

The reason we did this is so that changes to the `SplashStage` class only affect this file as opposed to the `M5StageManager`, for example. This means any changes to derived stage or stage builder classes cannot break other code, because the other code will only be using an `M5Stage` pointer. Changes to this class could still break other code, particularly if this stage was removed from the game altogether. However, by minimizing dependencies, we reduce the chances that other code will need to be changed in the future.

In the Mach5 Engine, the `M5Stage` derived classes only need a default constructor. This is by design to keep the builder classes as simple as possible. Each stage class will read its own required data from a file. The logic for which file to read is written into the constructor. The same simple default constructor design is used in the `M5Component` derived classes as well. What this means is that instead of needing to create a builder class for each stage or component, we can instead use the power of C++ templates:

```
//M5StageBuilder.h
class M5StageBuilder
{
public:
  virtual ~M5StageBuilder(void) {} //empty virtual destructor
  virtual M5Stage* Build(void) = 0;
};

template <typename T>
class M5StageTBuilder: public M5StageBuilder
{
public:
  virtual M5Stage* Build(void);
};

template <typename T>
M5Stage* M5StageTBuilder<T>::Build(void)
{
  return new T();
}
```

By using C++ templates, we can reduce the number of small classes that need to be manually created while still gaining the decoupling benefits of the factory. Of course, it is always possible that a few stages or components will need more complex constructors or builder classes. In that case, we can easily create the required classes when the need arises. Unfortunately, we don't get the option of using templates with our object types.

Using builders with objects

Our game objects are mostly just collections of components. Each object type will have different components and component data based on the decisions of the designer. As the development progresses, those collections are likely to change. Remember, even though each individual component has a builder in the factory, the object will need to somehow instantiate the separate components. Let's look at shortened examples of using builders for the `Player` and `Raider` objects:

```cpp
//PlayerBuilder.h--------------------
#include "M5ObjectBuilder.h"

class PlayerBuilder: public M5ObjectBuilder
{
public:
virtual M5Object* Build(void);
};

//PlayerBuilder.cpp--------------------
#include "PlayerBuilder.h"
#include "M5Object.h"
#include "M5ObjectManager.h"

M5Object* PlayerBuilder::Build(void)
{
M5Object* pObj = new M5Object;
//Build and set Gfx component for player
GfxComponent* pGfx =
    M5ObjectManager::CreateComponent(CT_GfxComponent);
pGfx->SetTexture("playerShip.tga");
pGfx->SetDrawSpace(DS_WORLD);

//Build and set input component for player
PlayerInputComponent* pPI =
   M5ObjectManager::CreateComponent(CT_PlayerInputComponent);
pPI->SetSpeed(100);
pPI->SetRotationSpeed(10);

pObj->AddComponent(pGfx);
pObj->AddComponent(pPI);

//...add more components here

return pObj;
}

//RaiderBuilder.h--------------------
```

```
#include "M5ObjectBuilder.h"

class RaiderBuilder: public M5ObjectBuilder
{
public:
virtual M5Object* Build(void);
};

// RaiderBuilder.cpp--------------------
#include "RaiderBuilder.h"
#include "M5Object.h"
#include "M5ObjectManager.h"

M5Object* RaiderBuilder::Build(void)
{
  M5Object* pObj = new M5Object;
  //Build and set Gfx component for Raider
  GfxComponent* pGfx =
     M5ObjectManager::CreateComponent(CT_GfxComponent);
  pGfx->SetTexture("enemyBlack3.tga");
  pGfx->SetDrawSpace(DS_WORLD);

  //Build and set behavior for Raider
  ChasePlayerComponent* pCP =
     M5ObjectManager::CreateComponent(CT_ChasePlayerComponent);
  pPI->SetSpeed(40);

  pObj->AddComponent(pGfx);
  pObj->AddComponent(pCP);

return pObj;
}
```

In these two simple examples, we can see why each object builder needs to be different. Each specific object type will have a unique set of components. These examples only use two components each, but we haven't considered our physics colliders, any weapon components, or additional behaviors. Even in these short examples, both object types use a GfxComponent but the differences in data, such as texture, mean that we need different code. Since there is only one object class, as opposed to a hierarchy of derived classes, there is no way to let the object manage the creation of the necessary components.

To deal with this, we will either need a builder class for each object type or one object builder with a `switch` statement and a case for each object type. The problem with both solutions is that the list of components and the data for each component is likely to change often. Now, instead of being worried about high-level modules and dependencies, we have two new problems to be worried about.

The first problem is constant, and possibly long, compile times. We already know that as development continues, the game design will change. This could mean not only changing components, but also changing values inside those components. At some point, especially toward the end of development, the game may be complete, but not quite balanced. During this phase, game objects and the code responsible for them will be constantly tweaked. Changes in health, damage, speed, and other attributes could be changed frequently causing the code to be recompiled.

There are a lot of factors that can affect how long it takes to compile a project. In the best-case scenario, we would only change one file, and recompiling could be very fast. However, even a short build time such as 10 seconds can get annoying if the only thing that changed is a speed value from 10 to 11. Something as simple as balancing a single unit can take all day, and then still need additional tweaks as other units get balanced. Our goal here is to make modifying the object and seeing the results of the modification as fast as possible.

The second problem that comes up is related to who is responsible for making these balance changes. One scenario is that the programmer is responsible because all balance changes are code changes. This is a bad situation because, as we already mentioned, balancing can take a long time, and now both the designer and the programmer are involved. The designer may not be able to properly explain the desired result to the programmer, so they must sit together tweaking and compiling, repeatedly. It would be better if the designer was free to balance, and the programmer was free to fix bugs or optimize code where needed.

The other scenario is that the designer is responsible for making these balance changes to the code. The problem here is that the designer may not be as familiar with the engine, or with the programming language. It is very possible that the designer doesn't have programming experience at all, so they would not be familiar with IDEs or version control systems. The chance of introducing bugs or breaking the project could be very high.

Solution - reading from files

Our solution to both problems is to move all hard-coded values into text or binary files that will be read by the engine at runtime. Since we are using a component-based system in our game, this means being able to define which components belong to an object in the file as well. The benefit of this approach is that these files could be created with a level editor or some other content creation tool by a designer. For now, we won't focus on how these files get created, but instead on how they are read into our engine and how we can use them in place of an object builder class.

Now that we have decided to define our objects in files, we need to think about when they will be read by our engine. There are a few different solutions to our problem. The first solution is to simply have our builder read a file every time we need a new Raider, Bullet, or Asteroid. This is a common first thought, but is a very bad idea. Reading files from the hard disk is very slow compared to accessing data already in RAM. Depending on the factors, it can be anywhere from 10,000 to 50,000 times slower or more. This is like a normal 5 minute drive to the store taking 173 days, 14 hours, and 40 minutes. If you started your drive on January 1st, you would arrive at the store on June 21st.

This doesn't mean that we should never read files from the hard disk. It just means that we need to be more strategic about it. Using this solution would mean we could be reading the exact same file many times during the same frame. This would be like taking that half-year trip to the store to buy eggs, going home, then immediately going back to the store to buy milk. Instead of reading the same file many times we should read it once and store the data into RAM. Since it is so slow, we should avoid reading and writing files during gameplay and instead load as much from our files during load time as we can.

In large scale games, such as *Rockstar's Grand Theft Auto 3*, there is too much data to keep in RAM all at once. A game like this will be constantly reading data from files that aren't currently in memory, and releasing resources that are no longer in use. This is done by reading files on separate threads so the main gameplay isn't paused or slowed down. There is a lot of work involved in this file streaming process, including making sure that key gameplay elements are in memory when the player needs them so gameplay isn't affected. However, even games that stream data like this don't waste time reading files repeatedly once they are in memory.

We won't be worrying about threads for now. So, a more common solution for us would be to read the file once during a load screen to create the object types we need, then simply to copy these objects whenever we need a new instance of them. This will allow us to focus on the pattern, as well as solve key issues related to this problem, without worrying about the difficulties involved in multithreaded architecture.

Even without using threads, we still have a problem. How do we copy the object that contains components without knowing the types? Typically, when creating new objects, we need the new keyword, which means we also need a constructor to call. Of course, we have an enum for the type, which means we could use a switch statement and call the correct copy constructor. However, we already know that switch statements can be difficult to maintain and should be avoided.

The component factory will create a new component of the correct type, but we would still need to write a copy function that can copy the data once it has been created. It would be nice if we had a function that would construct and copy the data, based on the type of object it is. We need a constructor that works like a virtual function.

The Prototype pattern explained

The Prototype pattern gives us a way to copy a class without knowing the actual type of that class. This is often referred to as a virtual constructor because we can use it to create and copy a derived class while only using a base class pointer or reference. This pattern is most powerful when used with object hierarchies, but it doesn't only need to be used with virtual functions. Another purpose of the Prototype pattern is simply to create a prototypical (or archetypical) instance of an object and to use that to copy from.

Imagine that we are creating a level editor. In the middle of the tool we would have the map of the level. Here we can place tiles, power-ups, enemies, and players. Along the side of the map, we would have all the objects and tiles used in our game that can be placed on the map. This can be seen in the following screenshot:

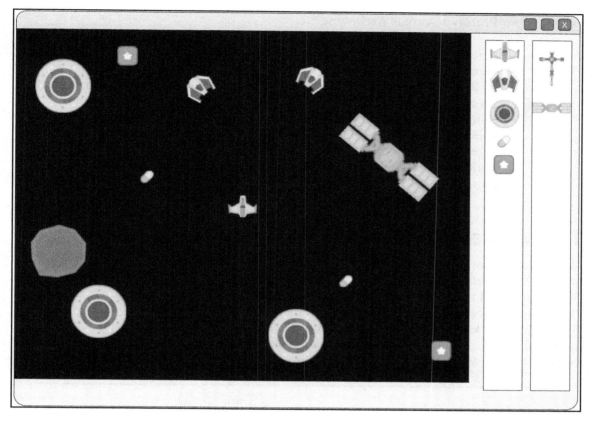

Figure 6 1 - Example of a Simple Level Editor

Since we are striving for clean code, we have a clear separation between the part of the code that handles drawing, the part of the code that handles clicking and manipulating the objects on the side, and the part of the code that defines our specific object type. However, when we click and drag an object from the side, we would make a new instance of the object that was clicked and would draw it at the mouse location, and eventually on the map where the user places it. Based on the Dependency Inversion Principle, we know we don't want our high-level modules depending on our low-level objects. Instead, they should both depend on abstractions.

Prototype versus Archetype

Before we learn more about this pattern we should talk a little about word choice. In the Mach5 Engine, the files we will be reading and creating, as well as the enumerations we will be using, are called archetypes instead of prototypes. An Archetype is a perfect, unchanging, ideal example of a thing. A prototype is typically an early, usually unrefined version of something that later versions can depart from. While both words could be correct, the authors use the word Archetype to refer to the object definitions in the files, even though the pattern is called the Prototype pattern.

The virtual constructor

The Prototype pattern is simple. It involves giving an object for which you might want to copy a `Clone` method, and letting the object know about the details of how to perform the clone. The actual name of the method isn't important. `Clone` is just one common example. This is most powerful when used with object hierarchies in which you want to copy an object, but don't know the type of derived object you might be holding. Simply add a `Clone` method to the interface of a hierarchy and have the derived classes each implement the method. Let's look at a simple example to start off:

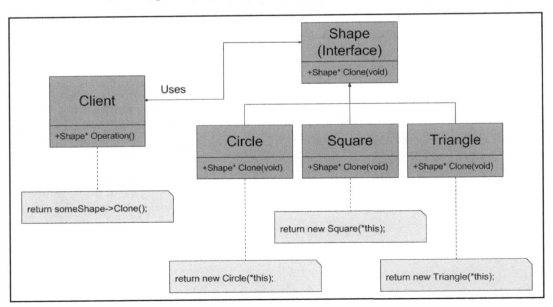

In the following code, we have our interface object, Shape. We will just be talking about simple shapes in this example. Since this class will be used as an interface, we must mark the destructor as virtual so the correct destructor will get called when derived classes are deleted. Next, we have two pure virtual methods. The Draw method could be any action that we need virtual behavior with. In this simple case, we will just be using printed statements instead of drawing shapes on the screen. The Clone method will be our virtual constructor. This method will know how to copy itself and return a new instance:

```
class Shape
{
public:
  virtual ~Shape(void) {}//empty base class constructor
  virtual void Draw(void) const    = 0;
  virtual Shape* Clone(void) const = 0;
};
```

Now, let's look at the derived class examples:

```
class Circle : public Shape
{
public:
  virtual void Draw(void) const
  {
    std::cout << "I'm a Circle" << std::endl;
  }
  virtual Shape* Clone(void) const
  {
    return new Circle(*this);
  }
};

class Square : public Shape
{
public:
  virtual void Draw(void) const
  {
    std::cout << "I'm a Square" << std::endl;
  }
  virtual Shape* Clone(void) const
  {
    return new Square(*this);
  }
};

class Triangle : public Shape
{
public:
```

```
   virtual void Draw(void) const
   {
      std::cout << "I'm a Triangle" << std::endl;
   }
   virtual Shape* Clone(void) const
   {
      return new Triangle(*this);
   }
};
```

Of course, our derived classes know how to draw themselves. To keep things simple, the `Draw` methods are just printing to the console. The important part here is that each `Draw` method has a different behavior; in this case, a hardcoded string to print. The `Clone` methods are where the real magic happens--each one returns a new instance of itself. Specifically, they are calling their own copy constructors. This will allow the client to hold a pointer to any `Shape`, and get a copy of the correct derived type without knowing or caring which constructor to call. Let's look at an example of this using code:

```
int main(void)
{
   //seed the RNG
   std::srand(static_cast<unsigned>(time(0)));
   //Create my shapes
   const int MAX = 3;
   Shape* shapes[MAX] = { new Circle(),
                          new Square(),
                          new Triangle() };

      for (int i = 0; i < MAX * 2; ++i)
   {
      Shape* pCopy = shapes[std::rand() % MAX]->Clone();
      copy->Draw();
      delete pCopy;
   }

   //make sure to delete my original shapes
   for (int i = 0; i < MAX; ++i)
      delete shapes[i];

   return 0;
}
```

The first few lines are simply initializing the random number generator and the array of shapes. In the array, you can see that we create a new instance of a `Circle`, `Square`, and `Triangle`. These will be our prototype `Shapes` to clone.

The next section is a loop to show the `Clone` method at work. We use a random index into the array and clone an object. Since it is random, we can't know which `Shape` will be cloned. This is simulating a random click by the user. Once we clone the `Shape`, we are free to call `Draw` or any other interface method we need. At the end of the loop, we delete the cloned `Shape` but, of course, that doesn't delete our prototype `Shape` from the array because it was a copy of the object. After the loop, we go through our prototype array and delete each of those shapes as well.

The following is the output for the preceding code:

```
I'm a Triangle
I'm a Square
I'm a Square
I'm a Circle
I'm a Circle
I'm a Square
```

The problem with constructors

Now that we have seen a little about virtual constructors and the Prototype pattern, let's look at exactly what problem we are trying to solve.

To understand the problem of construction, we first need to understand the difference between a class and an object of that class. Classes are what the programmer creates. They are the code template or recipe that the program uses to create objects. In C++, we cannot create classes at runtime. We don't have a way to introduce new code while the program is running.

This is because C++ is a statically typed language. This means that the language tries to prevent operations if they can't be performed on that type at compile time. For example, we can't divide a float by a `void*` because the C++ compiler checks a compile time if the operation makes sense, and will issue an error if it doesn't.

This static typing in C++ is why we are forced to declare a type for every variable. It is also why we are required to specify the constructor in a case like this:

```
Base* p = new Derived;
```

In this case, the compiler must know the class that we are trying to create. Unfortunately, in C++, classes do not have first class status. That means we can't pass a class as an argument to a function or use a class as a return value. We can't copy a class, save it in a variable, or create one at runtime. Some languages do have these features. Here is an example of what you could do if classes had first class status in C++:

```
//This isn't real C++ code
Shape* CreateShape(class theShape)
{
  Shape* pShape = new theShape;
  return pShape;
}
```

While this might be useful, we would be trading some type safety for flexibility. The static type checking that the C++ compiler performs has the chance to catch problems before they become bugs at runtime. This is a good thing. We should enjoy the type checking C++ provides. We should also recognize when it has an impact on our code flexibility.

Even though C++ is a statically typed language, we have ways of getting around this problem. One such way was with the factories that we created in the last chapter. We were forced to write the factories ourselves, but we still can choose which class gets created at runtime, while getting the benefits of static typing for all other classes and types. Factories are just one way we can avoid the rigidity of classes not having first class status. The virtual constructor is another way.

The benefits of a virtual constructor

Using a virtual constructor can be very powerful. The biggest benefit is that we can now treat classes as if they had first class status. We can make copies of an object without knowing the exact type of the object. We can use the Prototype pattern in our level editor example, but we could also use it in our game. Anytime we need to make a copy without truly knowing the type, we can use this pattern. As we said before, C++ is a statically typed language, meaning the compiler will make sure we are using the correct types at compile time. This static type checking helps us write safer code.

By using Dynamic Factories and virtual constructors, we are bypassing this type checking a little. The compiler is still doing the type checking on the pointers we are working with, but we are choosing our derived class at runtime. This has the chance to lead to bugs that are difficult to find if we somehow mix up the types we are cloning. That doesn't mean we shouldn't use the patterns; it is just good to understand that we are giving up a little safety for flexibility.

We don't need to know the type

As we said, the biggest benefit of using the Prototype pattern is that we can make copies without knowing the type. This means we can make a copy of a function parameter or function return type without caring about the derived class involved. This also means that we can share a pointer with another class or method and we don't need to care if the type is modified.

In the following example, we have a `SpawnShape` class with the ability to spawn a specific type of shape. By using the Prototype pattern, the class doesn't need to care what type it is spawning. The constructor takes a pointer to some shape and then it just needs to call the `Clone` method. If the base class pointer is pointing to a `Circle`, then a circle will be created. However, if we have a pointer to a `Triangle`, then a triangle will be created. Here is an example that shows the Prototype pattern in action:

```
class ShapeSpawner
{
public:
ShapeSpawner (Shape* pShape, float maxTime):
  m_pToSpawn(pShape),
  m_spawnTime(0.f),
  m_maxSpawnTime(maxTime)
{

  }
void Update(float dt)
{
  m_spawnTime += dt;
  if(m_spawnTime > m_maxSpawnTime)
  {
    //The class doesn't care what type it is cloning
    Shape* pClone = m_pToSpawn->Clone();

    //...Register the clone somehow

    //Reset timer
    m_spawnTime = 0;
  }
}
private:
  Shape* m_pToSpawn;
  float  m_spawnTime;
  float  m_maxSpawnTime;
};
```

Our `SpawnShape` class doesn't care if it is spawning a `Circle`, `Square`, or `Triangle`, or any new shape we might create later. It can make copies without knowing the real type of the shape. If we add a public `SetShape` method, we could even change the type that spawns at runtime. Compare this with a more rigid example that can only spawn `Circles`:

```cpp
class CircleSpawner
{
public:
CircleSpawner (Circle* pCircle, float maxTime):
  m_pToSpawn(pCircle),
  m_spawnTime(0.f),
  m_maxSpawnTime(maxTime)
{
}
  void Update(float dt)
{
  m_spawnTime += dt;
  if(m_spawnTime > m_maxSpawnTime)
  {
    //Use copy constructor
    Circle* pClone = new Circle(*m_pToSpawn);

    //...Register the clone somehow

    //Reset timer
    m_spawnTime = 0;
  }
}
private:
  Circle* m_pToSpawn;
  float    m_spawnTime;
  float    m_maxSpawnTime;
};
```

In the second example (not using the Prototype pattern) we are forced to use the copy constructor of the derived class, in this case the `Circle`. If we want to spawn a `Square` or a `Triangle`, we would need to create a `SquareSpawner` or `TriangleSpawner`. That is a lot of repeated code. It could get worse as we add even more shapes. By using the Prototype pattern, we can reduce the number of classes we need.

No need to subclass

The reduction in classes is another big benefit of using a virtual constructor. In the case above, we only needed a single `SpawnShape` instead of duplicating our spawn class or making derived versions. Consider our factory builder classes that we saw before. We were forced to create an abstract base class and create derived classes for every new `M5Component` and `M5Stage` that we used. C++ templates helped us autogenerate that code, but the code still exists.

By using a virtual constructor, we don't need derived builder classes for every `M5Stage`, `M5Component`, `Shape`, or other inheritance hierarchy. We can let the objects copy themselves. Does that mean we should remove our factories and always use the Prototype pattern? It depends.

Remember that with the Prototype pattern, we must first instantiate an object before it can be cloned. This is fine with shapes or components because these types are very small. However, the `M5Stage` derived classes may be very big and they also may cause side effects. This means that the constructor of a stage may add objects to the `M5ObjectManager` or may load textures or another large resource.

Since using C++ templates made creating our builders so easy, we can keep using them for stages and components. However, we want to avoid making builders for the `M5Object` because those builders are very likely to change during development. By using virtual constructors and creating prototypes (or archetypes) that can clone themselves, the rest of our code will not be affected by changes to our types.

It's easy to make exact copies

Here, the concept of a prototype doesn't need to be used with virtual functions. We may have a group of objects, for example, easy, hard, and insane enemies that we want to copy. These objects may be the exact same class type, but they could have very different values for health, speed, and damage. In this case, we have our prototypical example that we want to copy from. Of course, in this case we could also just use a copy constructor, but it is possible, as in the case of the Mach5 Engine, that the copy constructor doesn't exist.

Either way, since we don't need to create derived builder classes, we can add prototypes at runtime. Take the above example of the easy, hard, and insane enemy types. We could have just a single file that defines the health of an easy enemy with a value of 50, for example. Then at runtime we could create a hard enemy prototype with a health of 100 and an insane enemy with a health of 200. We could always just double the values of health and damage for each hard and insane enemy, or the file could contain the scale factor for the hard and insane versions.

Another example where we might want to modify the data would be if we had an enemy base that spawned enemies after a set time (like our `ShapeSpawner` from above). In this example, the base might increase the health and damage of the object over time. So, the base might initially create enemies with health of 50, but after each spawn, the health is increased by 5. So, the second enemy has a health of 55. The third enemy has a health of 60. Since each base has a specific instance, each base would be spawning enemies with different health values.

The object could also be modified via an in-game level editor. Imagine the benefit of play testing a level only to realize that enemies are killed too easily. With the Prototype pattern and an in-game level editor, we could pause the game, edit attributes of an object type, and continue playing. This method wouldn't require programmers, or recompile times. It doesn't even require a game restart. Of course, this same effect could also be done with a separate level editor or by just modifying the Archetype files and reloading the files at runtime. In these situations, we can see that creating copies of a specific instance is very easy and very useful.

Examples of the clone method in Mach5

So far, we have seen simple examples of how the Prototype pattern is implemented. If you thought that the examples were easy, you are in luck--it doesn't get much harder than that. We also discussed a few ways in which an object instance and a virtual constructor can be useful in a game. Now let's look at how the Mach 5 Engine uses the Prototype pattern in the `M5Component` and `M5Object` classes. Since the `M5Object` class uses the `M5Component` `Clone` method, let's look at the components first.

In Chapter 3, *Improving on the Decorator Pattern with the Component Object Model*, we examined almost all the methods and member variables in the M5Component class. However, the method we didn't talk about was the Clone method:

```
//! M5Component.h
class M5Component
{
public:
//! virtual constructor for M5Component, must override
virtual M5Component* Clone(void) const = 0;

//The rest of the class is the same as before
};
```

As you can see, the M5Component class implements a pure virtual Clone method just like we saw above in the Shape class. Since the M5Component class is used only as an abstract base class, we don't want to provide any default behaviors for cloning. Cloning only makes sense for derived classes. This part of the component was shown again so we can understand what the interface for overloading this method should be.

The Gfx and collider components

Now that we have seen the interface, let's look at two very important components. These are important because they allow game objects to interact with two of the other core pieces of our engine, graphics and physics.

The first one we will look at is the GfxComponent class. This class allows the game object to have a visual representation in the game. It contains the two minimum pieces of information to draw an object in the game:

```
//GfxComponent.h
enum DrawSpace
{
  DS_WORLD,
  DS_HUD
};

class GfxComponent : public M5Component
{
public:
  GfxComponent(void);
  ~GfxComponent(void);
  void Draw(void) const;
  virtual void Update(float dt);
```

```
     virtual GfxComponent* Clone(void) const;
     virtual void FromFile(M5IniFile& iniFile);
     void SetTextureID(int id);
     void SetDrawSpace(DrawSpace drawSpace);
  private:
     int        m_textureID;   //!< Texture id loaded from graphics.
     DrawSpace m_drawSpace;    //!The space to draw in
  };
```

The two pieces of information we need to draw an object are which texture to draw and which space to draw in. Of course, we need a texture to draw, but the draw space may be a bit more confusing. It is just an enum letting us know which type of graphics projection should be used with the object. For now, it is enough to know that the HUD draw space is always on top and isn't affected by camera movement or camera zoom. Of course, there could be more data, such as texture color and texture coordinates. These could be added in a derived class if we wanted. Here we are just showing the basics.

There are a few functions used to set these values, as well as a FromFile function that we talked about a little before. The Update function doesn't do anything for this component because there is nothing to update. The Draw function will be called by the graphics engine, making each M5Component responsible for drawing itself. However, the most important function for this chapter is the Clone:

```
GfxComponent* GfxComponent::Clone(void) const
{
   //Allocates new object and copies data
   GfxComponent* pNew = new GfxComponent;
   pNew->m_pObj = m_pObj;
   pNew->m_textureID = m_textureID;
   pNew->m_drawSpace = m_drawSpace;

   if (m_drawSpace == DrawSpace::DS_WORLD)
     M5Gfx::RegisterWorldComponent(pNew);
   else
     M5Gfx::RegisterHudComponent(pNew);

   return pNew;
}
```

In this function, we simply create a new `GfxComponent` and copy the relevant data from this object to the newly created one. What you don't see is that in the `GfxComponent` constructor, the component type is set by calling the `M5Component` component constructor which, of course, also gives this component a unique ID. The last thing we do is register this component with the graphics engine depending on the draw space. This class automatically unregisters itself when it is destroyed:

```
GfxComponent::GfxComponent(void) :
  M5Component(CT_GfxComponent),
  m_textureID(0),
  m_drawSpace(DrawSpace::DS_WORLD)
{
}
GfxComponent::~GfxComponent(void)
{
  M5Gfx::UnregisterComponent(this);
}
```

Now that we have seen the `GfxComponent`, let's look at the most basic of all physics colliders. The Mach5 Engine `ColliderComponent` is as simple as possible for a 2D game. For now, it is only concerned with circle versus circle collisions. It could easily be extended to test for rectangle collision as well:

```
//ColliderComponent.h
class ColliderComponent : public M5Component
{
public:
  ColliderComponent(void);
  ~ColliderComponent(void);
  virtual void Update(float dt);
  virtual void FromFile(M5IniFile& iniFile);
  virtual ColliderComponent* Clone(void) const;
  void TestCollision(const ColliderComponent* pOther);
private:
  float m_radius;
};
```

This class is a lot like the previous one because it is connected to one of the core pieces of the game engine. Just like all components, `FromFile` must be overloaded to read component data from an `.ini` file. `Update` must also be overloaded but, just like with the `GfxComponent`, this doesn't do anything in this simple version. If the class used oriented bounding boxes, the `Update` function could be used to update the corner points of the oriented box. The `TestCollision` function is also important. It is called by the **Physics Engine** to test if this object is colliding with another object. If it is, the two objects are added to a list of colliding pairs that can be resolved later. Again, the most important function for this chapter is the `Clone`:

```
ColliderComponent* ColliderComponent::Clone(void) const
{
   ColliderComponent* pNew = new ColliderComponent;
   pNew->m_radius = m_radius;
   pNew->m_pObj   = m_pObj;
   M5Phy::RegisterCollider(pNew);

   return pNew;
}
```

Just like the `GfxComponent`, this component first creates a new version of itself, then copies the important information into the new component. Before returning the new component, it first registers itself with the physics engine. Since it is registered, it must be unregistered when it is destroyed, so we do that in the destructor:

```
ColliderComponent::ColliderComponent(void) :
   M5Component(CT_ColliderComponent), m_radius(0)
{
}
ColliderComponent::~ColliderComponent(void)
{
   M5Phy::UnregisterCollider(this);
}
```

There are a few things to point out with both classes. First, notice that we don't clone the `m_type`, the `m_id`, or the `isDead` variables. This isn't necessary. The type is set by the constructor in the `M5Component` base class when we call the constructor. The id is also set in the base class, but it is important to point out that the purpose of the `m_id` is to be unique. It wouldn't serve the correct purpose if we also copied the id. Instead, we are copying the rest of the important data but we recognize that this is a separate component, not just an exact copy. For the same reason, we also don't copy the `isDead` variable. We are creating a new component that is like the old one, but still a unique component. If we copied the `isDead`, this component would be deleted in this frame or the next.

Next, both classes register themselves with engines in the clone method instead of the constructor. This is because of how they are intended to be used. Our object manager will hold a collection of these pre-created prototype components at the start of the game so they are ready to be cloned. We don't want these initial components to pollute the graphics or physics engine.

However, we are assuming that an object is being cloned and it also needs to live in the game world, so we register at that time. This seems like the most standard reason for cloning. It is better for the user to only worry about cloning, than to worry about cloning, registering, and then unregistering. If the user wishes to do something non-standard, they are free to unregister after cloning.

Cloning an object

We have seen a few examples of how M5Component derived classes use the Prototype pattern. We will look at a few more important ones a little later, but for now let's look at how the M5Object class uses these Clone methods, and how the M5Object itself is cloned. Recall that the M5Object also had a Clone method. Even though this class isn't part of a hierarchy, it can still use the concept of the Prototype pattern to create cloneable instances. Here is the Clone method of the M5Object:

```
//M5Object.h
class M5Object//Everything is the same as before
{
public:
  M5Object*    Clone(void) const;
};
//M5Object.cpp
M5Object* M5Object::Clone(void) const
{
  //create new object
  M5Object* pClone = new M5Object(m_type);
  //copy the internal data
  pClone->pos         = pos;
  pClone->vel         = vel;
  pClone->scale       = scale;
  pClone->rotation    = rotation;
  pClone->rotationVel = rotationVel;

  //clone all components
  size_t size = m_components.size();
  for (size_t i = 0; i < size; ++i)
  {
    M5Component* pComp = m_components[i]->Clone();
```

```
        pClone->AddComponent(pComp);
    }
    return pClone;
}
```

The important thing when we clone is that we copy all the relevant data from the old object. This includes not only things like the position and velocity but also all the components. So, we start off the function by both creating a new instance of the object we will be creating and passing the correct type to the constructor. This will set the m_type and m_id variables. Remember, even though we are cloning, we want to make sure that each object has a unique ID. Next, we copy the data. Just as with components, we don't need to copy the isDead value.

Finally, we have a loop to clone all components in the current object. This shows the power of the Prototype pattern. We don't need to know the types of each component--all we need to do is loop, call Clone to make our copy, then add that copy to the newly created object. Remember that the AddComponent method will change the m_pObj in each component. This will ensure that all components point to their correct owners.

In the end, the Prototype pattern is easy. Each component's Clone method is simple, and using them to clone an object is simple. Even using these cloned objects in the M5ObjectManager is easy. We will look at that in the next few pages, but first let's talk about a few details that some readers may have noticed. The first is that we didn't use a copy constructor in any of the Mach5 Clone methods, even though we did in the Shape example. The next is that the return types of the GfxComponent and CollideComponent are different from the return type in the M5Component interface.

Choosing a copy constructor

As we said, and as you saw in the code examples above, we didn't use copy constructors in any of the component Clone methods. We also didn't use them in the Clone method of M5Object. By default, classes have copy constructors and assignment operators generated by the compiler. In the Shape example above, we used the compiler generated copy constructor in our Clone methods.

However, in the Mach5 Engine there is an important choice to consider. What should the copy constructor do about the `m_id` variable value? Remember that this ID is supposed to be unique for every object and every component. However, if we use the compiler generated copy constructor, each variable, including `m_id`, will be copied by value. This would mean that any time we use the copy constructor, we would have two objects with the exact same ID.

Sometimes this is what we want, such as if we wanted to have a vector of objects instead of pointers to objects, for example. When using standard vectors (and other containers), the copy constructor gets called when adding to the container. If we were to add an object, we probably would want it to copy the ID. It is also possible that we would want to shift the position of the object around the container. Most likely, we would want it to keep the same ID.

However, this is not the behavior we want in our `Clone` methods. We want each clone to be a separate entity with a different unique ID. Of course, we could write our own copy constructor and give a different ID to each newly created object or component, just as we do in the default constructors. Unfortunately, if we did that using standard containers we would be generating new IDs for every time they internally called the copy constructor. In this case, the IDs wouldn't match up to the correct objects or components.

In the Mach5 Engine we use containers of pointers instead of containers of objects or components, so the authors decided to remove the copy constructors (and assignment operators) all together. This will remove all confusion about the process. If you want a copy, you call the `Clone` method, because you can't call the copy constructor. It is fine to make a different decision. In a different engine that uses containers of objects instead of pointers, a different decision would probably be made.

In the Mach5 Engine, we remove these methods from the object by making them private so that they can't be called. In C++ 11, you can mark them as deleted so the compiler won't generate them for you. The assignment operators will already be removed because these classes contain `const` data that can't be reassigned:

```
//In M5Object.h
M5Object(const M5Object& rhs) = delete;

//In M5Component.h
M5Component(const M5Component& rhs) = delete;
```

Covariant return types

Astute readers will also have noticed that the return types of each `Clone` method in the Mach5 Engine are actually different. The base `M5Component` class returns an `M5Component*`, however the derived classes return pointers to their own class types. This is a feature of C++ (as well as some other languages) known as covariant return types. Let's look at this feature using the `Shape` class from above:

```cpp
class Shape
{
public:
  virtual ~Shape(void) {}//empty base class constructor
  virtual void Draw(void) const    = 0;
  virtual Shape* Clone(void) const = 0;
};

class Circle : public Shape
{
public:
  virtual void Draw(void) const;
  virtual Shape* Clone(void) const;
};

int main(void)
{
  Circle* pCircle = new Circle();

   //The line won't compile
  Circle* pClone = pCircle->Clone();

  delete pClone;
  delete pCircle;
  return 0;
}
```

If the `Clone` method of the `Circle` class returns a `Shape*`, the compiler won't allow us to directly assign the result to a `Circle*`. We would need to do either a `static_cast` or `dynamic_cast`, meaning we would have to write code like this:

```
Circle* pCircle = new Circle();
Shape* pClone  = pCircle->Clone();

Circle* pCircle2 = dynamic_cast<Circle*>(pClone);
if (pCircle2)
{
   //do something specific to circle
}
```

In both cases, the `Clone` method will return a circle. However, there is no way for the compiler to know this, so we are forced to do the cast. The standard rule for using virtual functions is that the function signature must be the same, including the return type. With covariant return types, the compiler will allow us to replace the base class of a return type with a more specific type in the inheritance hierarchy:

```
class Circle : public Shape
{
public:
  virtual void Draw(void) const;
   //Example of using a covariant return type
  virtual Circle* Clone(void) const;
};

int main(void)
{
  Circle* pCircle = new Circle();
  //No need to cast
  Circle* pClone = pCircle->Clone();

  //... Do something Circle specific with pClone

  delete pClone;
  delete pCircle;
  return 0;
}
```

By using covariant return types, we can eliminate the need for unnecessary casting in cases where we clone an object that needs to access properties of its true type. It is worth noting that this feature only works with pointers or references. That means if the `Clone` method of `Shape` was returning a shape, instead of `Shape*`, we wouldn't have the option of doing this.

Loading archetypes from a file

Now that we have seen the Prototype pattern in detail and discussed how it is used with the components of the Mach5 Engine, let's look at how we can use it to load object data from a file. To do that, we will need to first look at the object files, then look at specific methods in the `M5ObjectManager` used to load and create these objects.

Archetype files

The first thing we need to do is look at how we define our object archetype within a file. The Mach5 Engine uses `.ini` files for archetypes, levels, and anything related to initialization of the engine. A more standard file format would be XML or JSON if you wanted to keep them as human readable and modifiable. If you didn't want them to be modified by users, the files could always be saved as binary.

We have chosen `.ini` files because they are easy to read by both humans and a computer program. They only have a few simple rules, so they are easy to explain in just a few sentences. They only contain named sections which are defined by square brackets `[ ]`, and key value pairs in the form of `key = value`. The only exception is the global section, which doesn't have a name and therefore no square brackets. Let's look at a basic example of an Archetype file. This is an example of `Player.ini`:

```
posX        = 0
posY        = 0
velX        = 0
velY        = 0
scaleX      = 10
scaleY      = 10
rot         = 0
rotVel      = 0
components = GfxComponent PlayerInputComponent ColliderComponent

[GfxComponent]
texture       = playerShip.tga
drawSpace     = world
```

```
[PlayerInputComponent]
forwardSpeed  = 100
speedDamp     = .99
bulletSpeed   = 7000
rotationSpeed = 10

[ColliderComponent]
radius        = 5
```

As you can see, the global section of the `Player.ini` file contains values for everything variable that is defined in `M5Object`. Except for the components key, everything is read in the `FromFile` method of the `M5Object`. In this case, most of our starting values are zero. This is because things like the starting position for the player object will depend on the level, so this data will be modified after creation.

The more important part is the components. The components key contains a list of components that the object will use. These strings will be used by the `M5ObjectManager` to create a component and then read the specific component data defined in each section. This allows us to reuse components, such as the `ColliderComponent`, because each object that uses them can have different component data. In this case, the player object will have a radius of `5`, but a bullet might have a radius of `1`.

The object manager

The `M5ObjectManager` is a singleton class that is responsible for, among other things, loading archetypes and creating objects. There are a lot of members and methods in this class so looking at everything would take too long. In this section, we will only go over the methods specifically related to loading and creating an object from an Archetype file. Remember that since the class is a singleton, we have global access. For that reason, every member and method is static:

```
class M5ObjectManager
{
public:
  static M5Object* CreateObject(M5ArcheTypes type);
  static void AddArcheType(M5ArcheTypes type,
                           const char* fileName);
  static void RemoveArcheType(M5ArcheTypes type);

  //Plus other methods

private:
  typedef M5Factory<M5ComponentTypes,
                    M5ComponentBuilder,
```

```
                              M5Component>  ComponentFactory;
        typedef std::unordered_map<M5ArcheTypes,
                                    M5Object*>  ArcheTypeMap
  static ComponentFactory  s_componentFactory;
  static ArcheTypesMap      s_archetypes;

  //Plus other members
  };
```

Here we have the most important members and methods to show how objects are loaded from a file. What we haven't shown here are methods related to destroying or searching for specific objects. If you are interested in those functions, feel free to review the full source code that comes with this book.

In the public section, the AddArcheType method will be used to read an archetype file, create the object, and store it for later. The RemoveArcheType method is used to delete the object when it is no longer needed. Finally, the CreateObject method will be used to clone one of the previously loaded archetypes. In the private section, we have a few types defined for creating easier names. You can see we are using the templated Dynamic Factory that we created in Chapter 5, *Decoupling Code via the Factory Method Pattern*. We also have a map of the loaded Archetype objects.

Let's take a closer look at these methods:

```
void M5ObjectManager::AddArcheType(M5ArcheTypes type,
    const char* fileName)
{
  MapItor found = s_archetypes.find(type);
  M5DEBUG_ASSERT(found == s_archeypes.end(),
      "Trying to add a prototype that already exists");

  M5IniFile file;
  file.ReadFile(fileName);
  M5Object* pObj = new M5Object(type);
  pObj->FromFile(file);

  std::string components;//A string of all my components
  file.GetValue("components", components);

//parse the component string and create each component
  std::stringstream ss(components);
  std::string name;

//Loop through the stream and get each component name
  while (ss >> name)
  {
```

```
        M5Component* pComp = s_componentFactory.Build(
                         StringToComponent(name));
        pComp->FromFile(file);
        pObj->AddComponent(pComp);
    }
  //Add the prototype to the prototype map
    s_archeypes.insert(std::make_pair(type, pObj));
  }
```

This might seem like a difficult function, but this is where the magic happens. Let's start at the beginning. This function takes two parameters, an enumeration ID specifying the type to create, and a file name to associate with that enum ID. Next, we need to check if this M5Archetypes ID has been loaded before. If it has, there must be an error. After checking for the enum error, we read the .ini file. If the file does not exist, the ReadFile method will assert.

If there haven't been any errors, we create a brand new M5Object, and pass the M5ArcheTypes ID to the constructor. This simply sets the type of the object, but doesn't do anything else. To set the data for the object, we call the FromFile method to read the global section from the .ini file. This will set the position, scale, rotation, and everything else in the object except the actual component, which needs to be handled differently.

The trouble with the components is that the file contains the component names as strings but, for the sake of performance during the game, we want to avoid doing string comparisons. This means we need to somehow convert these strings to an enum value. This is the purpose of the StringToComponent function. This function is an if/else chain that will return the correct enum based on the parameter. Functions like this can be a problem to maintain. We will discuss in a later chapter about how to use Windows batch files to automate this process.

After we read the object data from the file, we read the component list from the file. This is a list of component names separated by a space. There are lots of ways we could extract each individual component name, but one of the easiest ways is to use an STL stringstream object. This allows us to extract separate strings from the stream, just like std::cin.

After creating our stringstream object, we loop through the stream and extract the name. We then use s_componentFactory to build the correct component, after it has been converted to a M5ComponentTypes enum. After the correct component is built, we pass the .ini file to the component's FromFile method to let the derived component read its own data. Then we make sure to add the component to the object. Finally, after all components have been read, we add the type and object pointer to our s_archetypes map.

This may seem like a complicated way of loading objects. However, this function doesn't need to know about any derived component types, or which components go with a specific object type. If our archetype .ini files change, we don't need to recompile this code. We are free to add, remove, or change objects in our game and our high-level module, the M5ObjectManager, doesn't need to change:

```cpp
void M5ObjectManager::RemoveArcheType(M5ArcheTypes type)
{
  MapItor found = s_archetypes.find(type);
  M5DEBUG_ASSERT(found != s_archetypes.end(),
     "Trying to Remove a prototype that doesn't exist");

  delete found->second;
  found->second = 0;
  s_archetypes.erase(found);
}
```

The RemoveArcheType method is much simpler than the AddArcheType. All we need to do here is make sure the type to delete exists in the map, which we do by first finding and using a debug assert if it isn't there. Then we delete the prototype object and erase the iterator within the map.

The RemoveArcheType method doesn't need to be called since all archetype objects will be deleted when the game exits. However, this could be used if the user wanted to minimize which archetypes existed throughout the game. By default, the Mach5 Engine automatically loads all archetype .ini files before the game begins:

```cpp
M5Object* M5ObjectManager::CreateObject(M5ArcheTypes type)
{
  MapItor found = s_archetypes.find(type);
  M5DEBUG_ASSERT(found != s_archetypes.end(),
     "Trying to create and Archetype that doesn't exist");

  M5Object* pClone = found->second->Clone();
  s_objects.push_back(pClone);//A std::vector<M5Object*>
  return pClone;
}
```

Finally, we have the method that allows the user to create Archetype objects. Here, the user supplies the `M5ArcheTypes` type that they want to create. First, the method does the standard error checking that we are familiar with. Then, after finding the correct iterator, we make use of the Prototype pattern's `Clone` method to copy all data and components from the Archetype object. After creating the object, we automatically add it to the list of active game objects and return the pointer to the user so they can modify things such as position and velocity if needed.

Summary

In this chapter, we focused a lot on creating flexible code. Since we are using the Component Object Model with our game objects, we want to make sure that, as our objects change, they handle that change well. This means we don't want to modify lots of other files as we playtest and balance our objects.

We said at the beginning of this chapter that the goal for our game objects is to completely define them in a file. Since we are using components in our objects, we want to define the components that are used by the objects within the file as well. By defining objects in a file, our programmers are free to work on other code and the designers can work on balance and play testing without fear of breaking the game or introducing bugs.

After looking at a simple example of the Prototype pattern, we looked at how it is used in the Mach5 Engine. We saw both the `M5Component` class and the `M5Object` use a `Clone` method to make copying objects easy. These of course, were used by the `M5ObjectManager` to allow the user to create objects based on the `M5ArcheTypes` enum.

Now that creating objects can be done through a file, we should focus on a problem that is more difficult to see. Since we are using lots of object pointers that will have lots of component pointers, we should talk about a few problems related to memory. This is what we will cover in the next chapter.

7

Improving Performance with Object Pools

In programming languages, one of the most time-consuming things for the computer to do is deal with memory allocation. It's fairly inefficient and, depending on the resources being used, could slow down your game drastically.

A common element found in shooter games, or any game with explosions or bullets, is to create and destroy many objects in quick succession. Take, for example, the *Touhou Project* series of games, where there are many bullets being fired by both the player and enemies. When done in the simplest manner, calling `new` when you want to create a bullet and `delete` when you want to remove it will cause our game to lag or freeze over time.

To prevent this from happening, we can make use of the Object Pool pattern.

Chapter overview

In this chapter, we will create an object pool that will allow players to spawn a large number of bullets on the screen for the game.

Your objectives

This chapter will be split into a number of topics. It will contain a simple step-by-step process from beginning to end. Here is the outline of our tasks:

- Why we should care about memory
- The Object Pool pattern explained
- Using memory pools--overloading `new` and `delete`
- Design decisions

Why you should care about memory

As a programmer, you're probably already used to using `new` and `delete` (or `malloc` and `free` if you're writing C), and you may be wondering why you would want to handle memory by yourself when it's already built into the language and is easy to use. Well, the first thing is that like most aspects of using a high-level programming language, you do not know what is going on behind the scenes. If you write your own logic to handle memory, you can create your own statistics and additional debugging support, such as automatically initializing data. You can also check for things such as memory leaks.

However, for game developers the most important aspect to look into is that of performance. Allocating memory for a single object or thousands of them at once is approximately the same time as the computer needs to look through your computer's memory for an opening that isn't being used, and then give you the address to the beginning of that contiguous piece of memory. If you keep requesting small pieces of memory over and over again this can lead to memory fragmentation, which is to say that there isn't enough free continuous space when you want to get a larger object.

We may start off with some memory like this, with the gray sections being free memory and black being memory set aside because we called `new` for that amount of data. Each time we call for new, the computer needs to look for the first address that is open which has enough space to fit the object type we provide:

Later on, we remove some of the memory and that opens up some space, but the computer will need to look at each address and spend more time searching:

Finally, we get to a spot where we have very little open data and it requires a lot of work to find a place to insert new data, due to the memory becoming fragmented.

This is especially important if you are developing titles for a console or for a mobile device, as the size of memory you have to work with is much smaller than what you're used to working with on a PC. If you used computers five or more years ago you may remember the idea of defragging your computer, in which your computer would shift pieces of memory over in order to create larger blocks that could be used later. But this was a very time-consuming process.

Mach5 doesn't easily give us the ability to support having game objects being created in this way but, if you are interested in doing this, we do have a way that can use the concepts of an object pool in order to not waste resources; we will discuss that later on in the chapter.

 An excellent article on writing memory managers for game programming can be found at `http://www.gamasutra.com/view/feature/2971/play_by_play_effectiv e_memory_.php`.

The Object Pool pattern explained

Previously, we talked about the Singleton design pattern and how it's used to create a single instance of something inside of our project, often something static. We know there is only one and it's only created once, and that we can share it with the rest of our project without issues. However, the Singleton pattern only works when the instance is initialized.

The object pool is similar but, instead of one object, we want to have a group (or pool) of objects (or instances) that we can refer to within the rest of the project. Whenever the project wants to access these objects, we have another object called an **object pool**, which acts as a liaison between the project and the objects themselves.

Also called a resource pool or an N-ton elsewhere in computer science (but most frequently in game development referred to as an object pool) you can think of the object pool as having a similar role to a manager. When our program wants an object to work with, the manager knows which objects are currently being used and will give you one that isn't, or expand to create a new one. This promotes reusing previously created objects instead of creating and deleting them on the fly. This provides a number of advantages when the cost of initializing a class instance is an expensive operation, or when the rate of instantiation is high and the amount of time the objects are being used is low.

Let's consider our space shooter game as an example. Any time we press the spacebar, we have been creating a new object of the laser we want to shoot out. Also, any time we shoot something, we have to destroy them. This will slow down the performance of our game. This is not a huge issue now with such a simple game, but in AAA games we use this idea a lot, for example, in any of the games in the Naughty Dog's *Uncharted* series or most FPS titles. The enemies in these games are very complex, and having them in the game is very expensive. Instead of having a bunch of enemy objects in the game what will often be done instead is, after using enemies and having them die, they just turn invisible and when you need a new enemy, the dead object gets moved to a new position and gets turned on again.

The very basic elements of an object pool will look something like this:

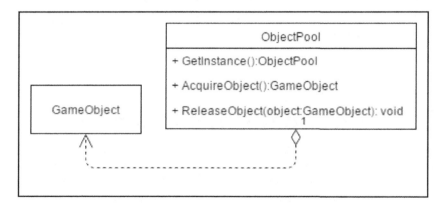

In our object pool's case, we have some type of variable that we want to hold the copies of. In this case, I've named it `GameObject`, but you'll also hear it referred to as a `Reusable` or `Resource` class instead. We use the `AcquireObject` function to get an object from our object pool, and we use the `ReleaseObject` function when we are finished working with it. The `GetInstance` function works in a similar manner to how it did with the Singleton class we talked about earlier, by giving us access to the `ObjectPool` referred to by it.

In the Mach5 Engine, there isn't an included object pool by default, so we will actually need to extend the engine to support it. That means we'll need to actually build one from scratch.

There are multiple ways to implement the Object Pool pattern or to get a similar behavior. We'll go over some of the commonly seen versions and the cons before moving to our final version.

Implementing a basic object pool

Let's first start off by creating an object pool for a simple class that we can create multiples of:

```
class GameObject
{
private:
  // Character's health
  int currentHealth;
  int maxHealth;

  // Character's name
  std::string name;

public:
  GameObject();
  void Initialize(std::string _name = "Unnamed",
    int _maxHealth = -1);
  std::string GetInfo();

};
```

So, this sample `GameObject` class contains a name of the object to identify it by and some example properties to make the class seem more game-object-like. Obviously, you can easily add more properties and the same principles apply. In this case, we have a function called `Initialize`, which provides both a `set` and `reset` of values for the class. Finally, I added in a `GetInfo` function to print out information about the class so we can verify that things are working correctly.

The implementation for the class will look something like this:

```
/****************************************************************/
/*!
Constructor that initializes the class' data
*/
/****************************************************************/
GameObject::GameObject()
{
    Initialize();
}

/****************************************************************/
/*!
Initializes or resets the values of the class
*/
/****************************************************************/
void GameObject::Initialize(std::string _name, int _maxHealth)
{
    name = _name;
    maxHealth = _maxHealth;
    currentHealth = maxHealth;
}

/****************************************************************/
/*!
Prints out information about the class
*/
/****************************************************************/
std::string GameObject::GetInfo()
{
    return name + ": " + std::to_string(currentHealth) + "/" +
        std::to_string(maxHealth);
}
```

Now that we have our game objects created, we need the pool to be created:

```
class GameObject;

class ObjectPool
{
private:
    std::list<GameObject*> pool;
    static ObjectPool* instance;

    // Private constructor so users are unable to create without
    // GetInstance
    ObjectPool() {}
```

```
public:

    static ObjectPool* GetInstance();
    GameObject* AcquireObject();
    void ReleaseObject(GameObject* object);
    void ClearPool();

};
```

To start off with there are two variables: `pool`, which will contain all of the available objects within our object pool, and `instance`, which is a way for us to access it. Note that our object pool uses the Singleton design pattern, in that there can only be one per type of object you'd like to have copies of. In this instance, we have the same issues that we talked about earlier, namely that you have to actually delete the pool and remove all of the elements that were created, which is why we added in a `ClearPool` function which does exactly that. The implementation for the class will look something like this:

```
ObjectPool* ObjectPool::GetInstance()
{
    if (instance == nullptr)
    {
        instance = new ObjectPool();
    }
    return instance;
}
```

In this preceding function, we first check if `instance` is set. If it's not, we dynamically allocate memory for it and set the `instance` variable to it. Either way, we'll have an instance afterwards, and that is what we return:

```
/**************************************************************************/
/*!
Returns the first available object if it exists. If not, it will create a
new
one for us
*/
/**************************************************************************/

GameObject* ObjectPool::AcquireObject()
{
    // Check if we have any objects available
    if (!pool.empty())
    {
        // Get reference to an avaliable object
        GameObject* object = pool.back();

        // Since we are going to use it, it's no longer available,
```

```
      // so we need to remove the last element from our list
      pool.pop_back();

      // Finally, return the reference
      return object;
    }
    else
    {
      // If none are available, create a new one
      return new GameObject()
    }
}

/***********************************************************************/
/*!
Marks an object as being available again

\param
The object to be made available again
*/
/***********************************************************************/
void ObjectPool::ReleaseObject(GameObject* object)
{
  // Reset the object
  object->Initialize();

  // Add it to our avaliable list
  pool.push_back(object);
}


/***********************************************************************/
/*!
Takes care of removing all of the objects from the pool whenever we're
finished
working with it.
*/
/***********************************************************************/
void ObjectPool::ClearPool()
{
  while (!pool.empty())
  {
    GameObject * object = pool.back();
    pool.pop_back();
    delete object;
  }
}
```

The `ClearPool` function will continuously remove objects from the pool until it is empty. We first get a reference to the object, by retrieving the last element using the `back` function.

We then remove the element from the pool before deleting the object itself safely:

```
ObjectPool* ObjectPool::instance = 0;
```

Finally, C++ requires that we initialize the `instance` variable, so we add that last.

Once we have this foundational code in, we can start to use the classes. An example usage could be the following:

```
ObjectPool* pool = ObjectPool::GetInstance();
GameObject * slime = pool->AcquireObject();

std::cout << "Initial: " << slime->GetInfo() << std::endl;

slime->Initialize("Slime", 10);

std::cout << "After Assignment: " << slime->GetInfo() <<
std::endl;

pool->ReleaseObject(slime);

slime = pool->AcquireObject();

std::cout << "Reused: " << slime->GetInfo() << std::endl;

pool->ClearPool();
delete pool;
```

If we save this script and run it in a blank project, you'll see the following:

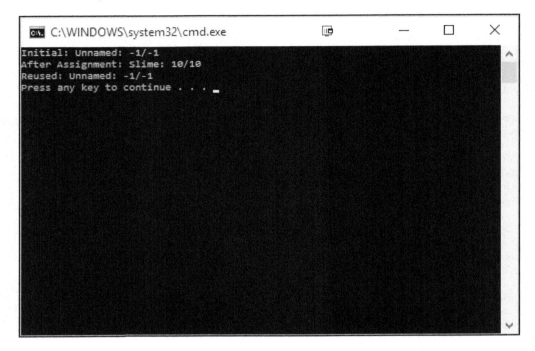

In this case, we first get our `ObjectPool` that makes use of the `GetInstance` function, and then obtain an object from the object pool using the `AcquireObject` function (which calls `new` to create the object). From there we print out its values and, due to the constructor, it is set to our predefined default values. We then assign the values and use it. Afterward, we release it from the list in which we placed it on the pool, to be reused when we are ready. We then get the object again and show that it's already reset to be reused in exactly the same way as before!

Operator overloading in C++

We now have a good foundation to build on, but we can actually make our object pool much nicer to use. One of the cooler features in C++ is the fact that you can override the default behaviors of operators, typically referred to as **operator overloading**. This is done with functions being created with specific names that contain the operator keyword, followed by what operator you want to define. Just like regular functions, they have return types as well as parameters that get passed to them.

For more information on operator overloading and how it works in C++, check out
`http://www.cprogramming.com/tutorial/operator_overloading.html`.

In addition to common operators, such as +, −, and /, we also have the ability to overload the `new` and `delete` operators as well, allowing us to use our own custom object pool instead!

To do this, we will need to add the following to the end of the `GameObject` class, and add the following bold lines to the class definition:

```
class GameObject
{
private:
  // Character's health
  int currentHealth;
  int maxHealth;

  // Character's name
  std::string name;

public:
  GameObject();
  void Initialize(std::string _name = "Unnamed",
    int _maxHealth = -1);
  std::string GetInfo();

  void* operator new(size_t);
  void operator delete(void* obj);

};
```

Here, we added two new functions to the `GameObject` class--one for us to create our own version of `new` and another for our version of `delete`. Then, we need to add the implementations:

```
void* GameObject::operator new(size_t)
{
  return ObjectPool::GetInstance()->AcquireObject();
}

void GameObject::operator delete(void* obj)
{
  ObjectPool::GetInstance()->ReleaseObject(static_cast<GameObject*>(obj));
}
```

In our case, we are just using the `ObjectPool` class' functions to acquire and release our objects when needed, instead of just allocating memory all of the time. Then, we can modify the original implementation code as follows:

```
ObjectPool* pool = ObjectPool::GetInstance();
GameObject * slime = new GameObject();

std::cout << "Initial: " << slime->GetInfo() << std::endl;

slime->Initialize("Slime", 10);

std::cout << "After Assignment: "
    << slime->GetInfo() << std::endl;

delete slime;
slime = new GameObject();

std::cout << "Reused: " << slime->GetInfo() << std::endl;

pool->ClearPool();
delete pool;

return 0;
```

Now, don't run the code just yet. If you remember, we call the `new` and `delete` operators inside of our `ObjectPool` class, so running the code now will cause a stack overflow error, because when `AquireObject` calls `new`, it will call the `GameObject` class' version of `new`, which in turn calls the `AquireObject` function, and so on and so forth. To fix this, we'll need to use the C version of allocating memory, the `malloc` and `free` functions, in order to get memory from the system:

```
/**************************************************************/
/*!
Returns the first available object if it exists. If not, it will create a
new
one for us
*/
/**************************************************************/

GameObject* ObjectPool::AcquireObject()
{
  // Check if we have any objects available
  if (!pool.empty())
  {
    // Get reference to an avaliable object
    GameObject* object = pool.back();
```

```
        // Since we are going to use it, it's no longer available, so
        // we need to remove the last element from our list
        pool.pop_back();

        // Finally, return the reference
        return object;
    }
    else
    {
        // If none are avaliable, create a new one
        return static_cast<GameObject*>(malloc(sizeof(GameObject)));
    }
}


/******************************************************************/
/*!
Takes care of removing all of the objects from the pool whenever we're
finished
working with it.
*/
/******************************************************************/
void ObjectPool::ClearPool()
{
    while (!pool.empty())
    {
        GameObject * object = pool.back();
        pool.pop_back();
        free(object);
    }
}
```

Now we should be able to run and see if everything is working the way we intended! This version works fairly well as long as you want your users to still call new and delete; however, it gives you a performance boost over time.

Building the object pool for Mach5

Now that we've seen an object pool in action, let's next learn how we can integrate the Object Pool pattern into the Mach5 game engine. Since we are creating a shooter game, one of the things that we spawn a lot during gameplay are the laser bullets from our ship, which makes it perfect for using object pool functionality. And unlike the previous examples, we'll see a version of the object pool that will not need to use pointers to access the pool, and we'll not have to worry about the pool being created. To do this, we'll need to make some adjustments to the starter project. First, we are going to need to change how our bullets are destroyed.

If you go into the `Bullet.ini` file located at `Mach5-master\EngineTest\EngineTest\ArcheTypes`, you'll see the following:

```
posX = 0
posY = 0
velX = 0
velY = 0
scaleX = 2.5
scaleY = 2.5
rot = 0
rotVel = 0
components = GfxComponent ColliderComponent OutsideViewKillComponent

[GfxComponent]
texture = bullet.tga
drawSpace = world
texScaleX = 1
texScaleY = 1
texTransX = 0
texTransY = 0

[ColliderComponent]
radius = 1.25
```

Go in and remove `OutsideViewKillComponent` and replace it with `BulletComponent`. We are replacing `OutsideViewKillComponent` because when it leaves the screen, it will set the object's `isDead` property to `true`, which will call `delete` on it and remove it from the world. We are actually going to take care of this ourselves, so let's replace this with our own behavior, which we will write inside of the `BulletComponent` script that we will write later on in this chapter.

Next, we will want to create a new place for our `ObjectPool` so, with that in mind, go to the **Solution Explorer** tab and then right-click on the **Core/Singletons** folder and select **New Filter**. Once you create one, name it `ObjectPool`. From there, right-click on the newly created folder and select **New Item...**. Then, from the menu select the **Header File (.h)** option and give it a name of `M5ObjectPool.h`.

In the `.h` file, we'll put in the following code:

```
/****************************************************************/
/*!
\file    M5ObjectPool.h
\author  John P. Doran
\par     email: john\@johnpdoran.com
\par     Mach5 Game Engine
\date    2016/11/19

Globally accessible static class for object caching to avoid creating new
objects
if we already have one not being used.

*/
/****************************************************************/
#ifndef M5OBJECT_POOL_H
#define M5OBJECT_POOL_H

#include <vector>
#include <queue>

#include "EngineTest\Source\Core\M5Object.h"

template <M5ArcheTypes T>
class M5ObjectPool
{
public:
  // Gives to us the first available object, creating a new one if none is
available
  static M5Object * AcquireObject();

  // Returns the object to the pool making it available for reuse
  static void ReleaseObject(M5Object* object);

  // Removes all of the objects in the pool and removes references
  // as needed
  static void ClearPool();

private:
  // All of the objects in the object pool
```

```
    static std::vector<M5Object*>  pool;

    // All of the objects that are currently available
    static std::deque<M5Object*> available;
};

#endif //M5OBJECT_POOL_H
```

You'll notice that the class is very similar to what we've done in the past but, instead of using the `GameObject` class, we are going to use the Mach5 engine's `M5Object` class. We've also templatized the class to make it so that this will work with any kind of object archetype that exists (including our bullet, which is represented by `AT_Bullet`). I've also added a new variable called `available`, which is a **deque** (pronounced **deck**), which stands for a double-ended queue. This variable will contain all of the objects that both exist and are unused, so we can easily tell if we have any objects that we can use or if we need to create a new one.

 If you want to learn more about the deque class, check out `http://www.cplusplus.com/reference/deque/deque/`.

We'll also want to create an `M5ObjectPool.cpp` file as well. In the `.cpp`, we'll write the following code:

```
/***************************************************************************/
/*!
\file    M5ObjectPool.cpp
\author  John P. Doran
\par     email: john\@johnpdoran.com
\par     Mach5 Game Engine
\date    2016/11/19

Globally accessible static class for object caching to avoid creating new
objects
if we already have one not being used.

*/
/***************************************************************************/
#include "M5ObjectPool.h"
#include "Source\Core\M5ObjectManager.h"

template class M5ObjectPool<AT_Bullet>;// explicit instantiation

/***************************************************************************/
/*!
```

```
Returns the first available object if it exists. If not, it will create a
new
one for us
*/
/***************************************************************************/

template <M5ArcheTypes T>
M5Object * M5ObjectPool<T>::AcquireObject()
{
  // Check if we have any available
  if (!available.empty())
  {
    // Get reference to an available object
    M5Object * object = available.back();

    // Since we are going to use it, it's no longer available,
    // so we need to remove the last element from our list
    available.pop_back();

    // Finally, return the reference
    return object;
  }
  else
  {
    M5Object * object = M5ObjectManager::CreateObject(T);

    pool.push_back(object);

    return object;
  }
}
```

In this instance, we are first going to check if we have any objects inside of the available list. If none exist we will spawn a new object, making use of the M5ObjectManager class' CreateObject function. We then add it to the pool as it is an object in our object pool, but we do not make it available as it's going to be used upon being acquired:

```
/***************************************************************************/
/*!
Marks an object as being available again

\param
The object to be made available again
*/
/***************************************************************************/
template <M5ArcheTypes T>
void M5ObjectPool<T>::ReleaseObject(M5Object * object)
{
```

```
    // If it's valid, move this object into our available list
    if ((object->GetType() == T) &&
      (std::find(pool.begin(), pool.end(), object) != pool.end())))
    {
      //Make sure we haven't already been added already
      if(std::find(available.begin(), available.end(), object) ==
available.end())
      {
        available.push_back(object);
      }
    }

}
```

In this case, the `ReleaseObject` function marks an object as being available for reuse. But, we want to do some error checking to make sure that the function is being used properly and isn't being provided with an invalid object.

First, the code makes sure that the object is the same type as the object pool's and that it is actually located inside the pool somewhere. This ensures that we will only be adding objects that are valid into our available deque. If we know the object is valid, we then look through the objects we already have in the deque and make sure that the object hasn't already been added before. If it hasn't, we then add it into the available deque:

```
/*************************************************************************/
/*!
Takes care of removing all of the objects from the pool whenever we're
finished working with it.
*/
/*************************************************************************/
template<M5ArcheTypes T>
void M5ObjectPool<T>::ClearPool()
{
    //  Go through each of our objects and destroy them
    for (int i = pool.size() - 1; i >= 0; --i)
    {
      M5ObjectManager::DestroyObject(pool[i]);
      pool.pop_back();
    }

    // Now clear out the available queue
    available.clear();
}
```

In the `ClearPool` function, we just go through every object in the pool and destroy that game object. Then, we clear out the available list:

```
template<M5ArcheTypes T>
std::vector<M5Object*>  M5ObjectPool<T>::pool;

template<M5ArcheTypes T>
std::deque<M5Object*>  M5ObjectPool<T>::available;
```

Finally, we need to declare the pool and available objects so they can be created in the future.

Now that we have this base functionality, we need to return these objects back to our available pool. To do this, we'll need to add the `BulletComponent` component we mentioned previously. Since this component is exclusive to our game, let's move over to the `SpaceShooter/Components` filter and create a new filter called `BulletComp`. From there, create two new files, `BulletComponent.h` and `BulletComponent.cpp`, making sure the location is set to the `Mach5-master\EngineTest\EngineTest\Source\` folder.

In the `.h` file, put in the following:

```
#ifndef BULLET_COMPONENT_H
#define BULLET_COMPONENT_H

#include "Core\M5Component.h"

//!< Removes The parent Game Object if it is outside the view port
class BulletComponent : public M5Component
{
public:
  BulletComponent();
  virtual void Update(float dt);
  virtual M5Component* Clone(void);
};

#endif // !BULLET_COMPONENT_H
```

Next, inside of the `.cpp` file, use the following:

```
#include "BulletComponent.h"
#include "Core\M5Gfx.h"
#include "Core\M5Math.h"
#include "Core\M5Object.h"
#include "EngineTest\M5ObjectPool.h"

BulletComponent::BulletComponent():
M5Component(CT_BulletComponent)
{
}

void BulletComponent::Update(float /*dt*/)
{
  M5Vec2 pos = m_pObj->pos;
  M5Vec2 scale = m_pObj->scale;
  scale *= .5f;
  M5Vec2 botLeft;
  M5Vec2 topRight;
  M5Gfx::GetWorldBotLeft(botLeft);
  M5Gfx::GetWorldTopRight(topRight);

  if (pos.x + scale.x > topRight.x || pos.x -
      scale.x < botLeft.x ||
    pos.y + scale.y > topRight.y || pos.y - scale.y < botLeft.y)
  {
    M5ObjectPool<AT_Bullet>::ReleaseObject(m_pObj);
  }

}

M5Component * BulletComponent::Clone(void)
{
  BulletComponent * pNew = new BulletComponent;
  pNew->m_pObj = m_pObj;
  return pNew;
}
```

Save your files. This will make it so that if the object has a bullet component, it'll be returned to the list; but we have to first make our objects. Go into the `PlayerInputComponent.cpp` file and update the section of code for creating bullets in the `Update` function, as follows:

```
//then check for bullets
if (M5Input::IsTriggered(M5_SPACE) || M5Input::IsTriggered(M5_GAMEPAD_A))
{
```

```
M5Object* bullet1 = M5ObjectPool<AT_Bullet>::AcquireObject();
M5Object* bullet2 = M5ObjectPool<AT_Bullet>::AcquireObject();
bullet2->rotation = bullet1->rotation = m_pObj->rotation;

M5Vec2 bulletDir(std::cos(bullet1->rotation),
std::sin(bullet1->rotation));
M5Vec2 perp(bulletDir.y, -bulletDir.x);
bullet1->pos = m_pObj->pos + perp * .5f * m_pObj->scale.y;
bullet2->pos = m_pObj->pos - perp * .5f * m_pObj->scale.y;

M5Vec2::Scale(bulletDir, bulletDir, m_bulletSpeed * dt);

bullet1->vel = m_pObj->vel + bulletDir;
bullet2->vel = m_pObj->vel + bulletDir;

}
```

Notice that we've replaced the creation of `bullet1` and `bullet2` to use our `ObjectPool` class' `AcquireObject` function, instead of our `ObjectManager` class' version.

Now it will be difficult for us to see if we are using objects that have just been created or if they are things we are reusing. Let's go back into `BulletComponent` and modify a property before we give it back to the object pool:

```
void BulletComponent::Update(float /*dt*/)
{
  M5Vec2 pos = m_pObj->pos;
  M5Vec2 scale = m_pObj->scale;
  scale *= .5f;
  M5Vec2 botLeft;
  M5Vec2 topRight;
  M5Gfx::GetWorldBotLeft(botLeft);
  M5Gfx::GetWorldTopRight(topRight);

  if (pos.x + scale.x > topRight.x || pos.x - scale.x < botLeft.x ||
    pos.y + scale.y > topRight.y || pos.y - scale.y < botLeft.y)
  {

    m_pObj->scale = M5Vec2(1.5f, 1.5f);
    M5ObjectPool<AT_Bullet>::ReleaseObject(m_pObj);
  }

}
```

Now we can go ahead and save our scripts and run our game!

You'll notice that, at the beginning of play, the objects have a scale of 2.5, 2.5. However, once some objects go off the screen, you'll see something similar to the following screenshot:

When we shoot the new bullets, they have been scaled down! With this, we know that our pool is working correctly, and that we are reusing the objects we've made before!

Issues with object pools

Now, as great as object pools are, we should take some time to talk about times when you would not want to use object pools, and the alternatives out there.

First of all, you need to remember that when you are using a memory manager, you are telling the computer that you are smarter than them and that you know how the data should be handled. This is more power than other languages tend to give you, and using Uncle Ben's famous line, *"with great power comes great responsibility"* as we mentioned previously in this book in Chapter 2, *One Instance to Rule Them All - Singletons*. When using an object pool, you typically want to use it when objects only have a limited lifetime and a lot of them will be created, but not all at the same time. If at one point in time you'll have 10,000 on the screen, but the rest of the game you'll have 30 max, that 9,970 other objects' worth of memory will just be standing there waiting for you in the unlikely event that you want to use it again.

An alternative method of handling a lot of objects at once is through a circular linked list, in which the last element connects to the first. This will guarantee that you'll never create more things than you have allocated memory for. If you happen to go all the way around you'll just be replacing the oldest one and, if you have so many things on the screen at once, users will not notice the oldest one being removed. This can be useful for things such as particle systems which we will be talking about in Chapter 10, *Sharing Objects with the Flyweight Pattern*. If you're spawning many particles, people probably will not notice the game replacing the oldest particles with new ones.

For more information on circular linked lists, check out https://www.tutorialspoint.com/data_structures_algorithms/circular_linked_list_algorithm.htm.

We were also using a type of object pool that allocated one element at a time. Alternatively, you could allocate memory for a large number of them at a time to ensure that you'll always have that memory reserved. While it's not needed in this case, it's definitely something to use for large classes.

While the code samples listed are in C#, Michal Warkocz lists some very good examples of why an object pool may be a bad choice to use here: `https://blog.goyello.com/2015/03/24/how-to-fool-garbage-collector/`.

Summary

In this chapter, we have used object pools to reduce system resources and user frustration by storing and reusing objects instead of creating and removing them. After spending this time polishing your work, you'll probably want to spend time modifying the UI of your game, which is what we will be talking about in the next chapter!

8

Controlling the UI via the Command Pattern

In the last chapter, we dived deeply into the bits and bytes of computer memory so we could make our components more efficient and easier to debug. Understanding these details can be the difference between a game running at 60 frames per second or 30 frames per second. Knowing how to control memory usage is an important aspect of becoming a great programmer. It is also one of the hardest things about programming. In this chapter, we will take a break from low-level programming and look at something high level.

The user interface, or UI, is just as important as memory management or stage switching. You could even argue that it is more important because the player doesn't care about the low-level details. They just want a game that is fun. However, it doesn't matter how fun the gameplay is; if the UI is difficult to navigate or control, the fun level drops fast.

Can you remember a time when you played a game with terrible controls? Did you keep playing the game? It is interesting because, for something so important, it often has the chance of being left until the end of a project. Even in this book, we had to wait until the eighth chapter to cover it. However, great games make the design of the UI and the user experience a top priority.

There are a lot of great books on how to design user interfaces and craft the user experience. This isn't one of those books. Instead, we will look at how the code behind the UI can be implemented in a flexible way that works with the rest of our engine. The first step to making a great UI is designing the code that will make buttons and other input easy to create and change.

We will start by looking at a very simple but powerful pattern that allows us to decouple our function calls from the objects that want to call them. While we are discussing the pattern, we will look at some of the syntactically ugly and confusing ways C++ allows us to treat functions as if they were objects. We will also see how the Mach5 Engine uses this pattern to create clickable UI buttons.

Chapter overview

This chapter is all about separating the user interface and input from the actions they perform. We will learn about the Command pattern and how it can help us decouple our code. We will do this by first understanding the problem then looking at how this could be solved in a C style fashion. Then after looking at the Command pattern in depth, we will see how it is implemented in the Mach5 Engine.

Your objectives

The following lists the things to be accomplished in this chapter:

- Learn the naive approach to handling input and why it should be avoided
- Implement the Command pattern using function pointers and the class method pointer
- Learn how the Mach5 Engine uses the Command pattern
- Implement UI buttons within the Mach5 Engine

How can we control actions through buttons?

In Chapter 3, *Improving on the Decorator Pattern with the Component Object Model*, we implemented game objects. Now that we have them, it seems trivial to create buttons on the screen. In fact, in genres such as real-time strategy, there is no difference between clickable buttons and game objects. The player can click on any unit or building and give them orders.

At first thought, our buttons could just be game objects. They both have a position, scale, and texture, and that texture will be drawn to the screen. Depending on the game, you might draw your buttons using orthographic projection while the objects will be drawn using perspective projection. However, the differences go deeper than that.

At its core, a button has an action that needs to be performed when it is clicked or selected. This behavior is usually simple; it doesn't require creating an entire state machine class. It does however, require a little thought so we don't end up hardcoding button functionality all over our high-level modules or repeating similar code in many different places.

In Chapter 5, *Decoupling Code via the Factory Method Pattern*, we saw an extremely naive way to handle a button click on a menu screen. Recall that this code was written by one of the authors early in their programming career:

```
if ((p.x > .15 * GetSystemMetrics(SM_CXSCREEN)) &&
    (p.x < .42 * GetSystemMetrics(SM_CXSCREEN)) &&
    (p.y > .58 * GetSystemMetrics(SM_CYSCREEN)) &&
    (p.y < .70 * GetSystemMetrics(SM_CYSCREEN)))
{
  if (mousedown)
  {
    mGameState = TCodeRex::LOAD;
    mGameLevel = L0;
  }
}
```

There are a lot of problems with this code:

- First, the rectangular click region is hardcoded to the aspect ratio in full screen mode. If we were to switch from widescreen 16:9 aspect ratio to standard 4:3 aspect ratio or even if we changed from full screen to windowed mode, this code wouldn't work correctly.
- Second, the click region is based on the screen and not the button itself. If the button position or size were to change, this code wouldn't work correctly.
- Third, this menu screen is coupled to the Windows GetSystemMetrics function instead of an encapsulated platform code class like the M5App class. This means if we want to run on a different operating system or platform, this menu and possibly all menus need to be modified.
- Finally, the state (stage in Mach5) switching action is hardcoded to the menu. If we decide to perform a different action, we need to modify the menu. If this action can be performed by both a button click and keyboard input, we need to update and maintain both sections of code.

As you can see, this isn't an ideal way to handle buttons in a game. This is basically the worst way you can implement buttons. This code is very likely to break if anything changes. It would be nice if the author could say this code was only written as a demonstration of what not to do. Unfortunately, a book like the one you are reading didn't exist at the time, so he had to learn the hard way.

Callback functions

A better way to deal with these button actions is with callback functions. Callback functions in C/C++ are implemented using pointers to functions. They allow you to pass functions around as if they were variables. This means functions can be passed to other functions, returned from functions, or even stored in a variable and called later. This allows us to decouple a specific function from the module that will call it. It is a C style way to change which function will be called at runtime.

Just as pointers to `int` can only point at `int`, and pointers to `float` can only point at `float`, a pointer to a function can only point at a function with the same signature. An example would be the function:

```
int Square(int x)
```

This function takes a single `int` as a parameter and returns an `int`. This return value and parameter list are the function's signature. So, a pointer to this function would be:

```
int (*)(int);
```

We haven't given the function pointer a name, so it should look like this:

```
int (*pFunc)(int);
```

 Note that the parentheses around the variable name `pFunc` are required, otherwise the compiler will think this is a prototype of a function that returns a pointer to an `int`.

We can now create a pointer to a specific function and call that function through the variable:

```
int (*pFunc)(int);
pFunc = Square;
std::cout << "2 Squared is "<< pFunc(2) << std::endl;
```

The output for the preceding code is as follows:

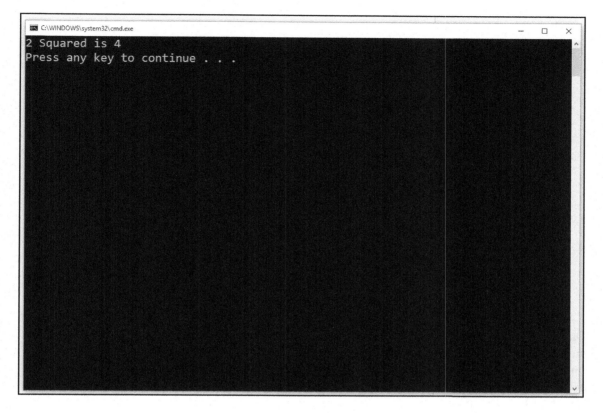

Figure 8 1 - Function pointer output

Notice that we didn't need to take the address of the Square function (although that syntax is allowed); this is because in C and C++ the name of the function is already a pointer to that function. That is why we can call pFunc without needing to dereference it. Unfortunately, everything about function pointers is weird until you get used to them. You must work at remembering the syntax since it doesn't work the same as pointers to variables.

By looking at a larger example, we can get familiar with this syntax. Let's write a program with three different ways to fill an array with values and a way to print the array:

```
//Fills array with random values from 0 to maxVal - 1
void RandomFill(int* array, int size, int maxVal)
{
    for (int i = 0; i < size; ++i)
        array[i] = std::rand() % maxVal;
```

```
}

//Fills array with value
void ValueFill(int* array, int size, int value)
{
  for (int i = 0; i < size; ++i)
    array[i] = value;
}

//Fills array with ordered values from 0 - maxVal - 1 repeatedly
void ModFill(int* array, int size, int maxVal)
{
  for (int i = 0; i < size; ++i)
    array[i] = i % maxVal;
}


//Helper to print array
void PrintArray(const int* array, int size)
{
  for (int i = 0; i < size; ++i)
    std::cout << array[i] << " ";
  std::cout << std::endl;
}
```

Our goal with this program is to write a function that can fill an array with any fill function, including one that hasn't been written yet. Since we have a common function signature, we can create a function called FillAndPrint that will take a pointer to any function with a matching signature as a parameter. This will allow FillAndPrint to be decoupled from a specific fill function and allow it to be used with functions that do not exist yet. The prototype for FillAndPrint will look like this:

```
void FillAndPrint(void (*fillFunc)(int*, int, int), int* array, int size,
int param);
```

This is incredibly ugly and difficult to read. So, let's use a typedef to clean up the code a little. Remember that a typedef allows us to give a different, hopefully more readable, name to our type:

```
//Defines a function pointer type named FillFUnc
typedef void(*FillFunc)(int*, int, int);

void FillAndPrint(FillFunc pFunc, int* array, int size, int param)
{
  pFunc(array, size, param);
  PrintArray(array, size);
}
```

In main, the user of this code can pick which fill function they want to use or even write a completely new one (if the signature is the same), without changing `FillAndPrint`:

```
int main(void)
{
  const int SIZE = 20;
  int array[SIZE];
  //See the Random number generator
  std::srand(static_cast<unsigned>(time(0)));
  FillAndPrint(ValueFill, array, 20, 3);
  FillAndPrint(RandomFill, array, 10, 5);

  return 0;
}
```

Here is what this code would output to the command line:

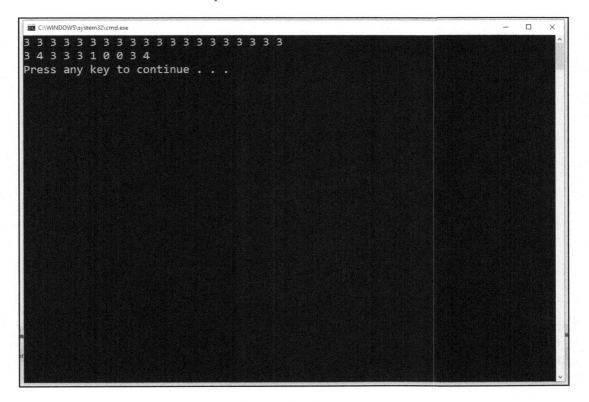

Figure 8 2 - Using FillAndPrint in different ways

We could even allow the user to pick the fill at runtime if we included a `helper` function to select and return the correct fill function:

```cpp
FillFunc PickFill(int index)
{
  switch (index)
  {
  case 0:
    return RandomFill;
  case 1:
    return ValueFill;
  default:
    //We could report an error if the value is outside of the
    //range, but instead we just use a default
    return ModFill;
  }
}


//Our Second main example
int main(void)
{
  const int SIZE = 20;
  int array[SIZE];
  int fillChoice;
  int param;

  //This doesn't properly explain to the user,
  //but it is just an example
  std::cout << "Enter a Fill Mode and parameter to use"
            << std::endl;
  std::cin  >> fillChoice;
  std::cin  >> param;
  //See the Random number generator
  std::srand(static_cast<unsigned>(time(0)));
  FillAndPrint(PickFill(fillChoice), array, 20, param);

  return 0;
}
```

This is a very simple example, but you can already see how using function pointers allows us to write flexible code. `FillAndPrint` is completely decoupled from any specific function call. Unfortunately, you can also see two flaws with this system. The functions must have the exact same signature, and the parameters of the function must be passed to the user of the function pointer.

These two problems make function pointers interesting and powerful, but not the best solution for in-game buttons that need to support a wide variety of actions with varying parameter lists. Additionally, we might want to support actions that use C++ member functions. So far, all the examples that we have seen were C style global functions. We will solve these problems in a moment, but first we should look at how we will trigger our button click.

Repeated code in the component

We have the problem of wanting to decouple a specific function call from the place that calls it. It would be nice to be able to create a button component that could save a function pointer or something like it, and call it when the component is clicked.

One solution could be to create a new component for every action we want to execute. For example, we might want to create a component that will change the stage to the main menu. We could create a component class that knows how to perform that exact action:

```cpp
//MainMenuComponent.h
class MainMenuComponent : public M5Component
{
public:
  MainMenuComponent(void);
  ~MainMenuComponent(void);
  virtual void Update(float dt);
  virtual void FromFile(M5IniFile&);
  virtual MainMenuComponent* Clone(void) const;
private:
};

//MainMenuComponent.cpp
void MainMenuComponent::Update(float /*dt*/)
{
  M5Vec2 mouseClick;
  M5Input::GetMouse(mouseClick);


  if(M5Input::IsTriggered(M5_MOUSE_LEFT) &&
    M5Intersect::PointRect(clickPoint,
      m_pObj->pos, m_pObj->scale.x, m_pObj->scale.y))
  {
    M5StageManager::SetNextStage(ST_MainMenu);
  }
}
```

The preceding case is a very simple example because it is only calling a static function with the parameter hardcoded, but the function pointer as well as the function parameters could easily be passed in to the constructor of this component. In fact, we could pass any object to the constructor and hardcode a specific method call in the update function. For example, we could pass an M5Object to a component such as the one above. The button click might change the texture of the object. For example:

```cpp
// SwapTextureComponent.cpp
void SwapTextureComponent::Update(float /*dt*/)
{
  M5Vec2 mouseClick;
  M5Input::GetMouse(mouseClick);

  if(M5Input::IsTriggered(M5_MOUSE_LEFT) &&
     M5Intersect::PointRect(clickPoint,
     m_pObj->pos, m_pObj->scale.x, m_pObj->scale.y))
{
  //Get the Graphics Component
  M5GfxComponent* pGfx = 0;
    m_savedObj->GetComponent(CT_GfxComponent, pGfx);

    //Do something to swap the texture...
  }
}
```

Unfortunately, there is a big problem with code like this; the action is completely coupled to the button click. This is bad for two reasons. First, we can't use this action for a keyboard or controller press unless we add additional keys to our UI button click component. Second, what happens when we have a list of actions that we want to perform? For example, synchronizing the movement of multiple UI objects, or scripting an in-game cut scene. Since the actions require the mouse to be pressed on the object, our action is very limited.

The other reason this approach is bad is because we must repeat the exact same mouse click test code in every button component that we create. What we would like to do is decouple the action from the button click component. We would need to create a separate UI button component and an action class. By doing that, we would factor out the part of the code that repeats, and we would gain the ability to use the actions on their own.

The Command pattern explained

The Command pattern is exactly the pattern that solves our problem. The purpose of the Command pattern is to decouple the requester of an action from the object that performs the action. That is exactly the problem we have. Our requester is the button, and it needs to be decoupled from whatever specific function call will be made. The Command pattern takes our concept of a function pointer and wraps it into a class with a simple interface for performing the function call. However, this pattern allows us more flexibility. We will easily be able to encapsulate function pointers with multiple parameters, as well as with C++ object and member functions. Let's start off easy with just two simple functions that have the same parameter count and return type:

```
int Square(int x)
{
   return x * x;
}

int Cube(int x)
{
   return x*x*x;
}
```

The Command pattern encapsulates a request into an object, and it gives a common interface to perform that request. In our example, we will call our interface method `Execute()`, but it could be called anything. Let's look at the `Command` abstract class:

```
//Base Command Class
class Command
{
public:
   virtual ~Command(void) {}
   virtual void Execute(void) = 0;
};
```

As you can see, the Command pattern interface is very simple--it is just a single method. As usual, we mark the method as pure virtual so the base class can't be instantiated. Additionally, we create an empty virtual destructor so the correct derived class destructor will be called when needed. As I said, the name of the method isn't important. I have seen examples such as `Do`, `DoAction`, `Perform`, and so on. Here we call it `Execute` because that was the name in the original book written by the Gang of Four.

Right from the start, we gain a benefit over function pointers by using this pattern. For every derived class we are writing the `Execute` method, which means we can directly hardcode any function and any parameters in that `Execute` function. Recall that when using function pointers, we needed to pass in parameters at the time of the call:

```
//Derived command classes
class Square5Command: public Command
{
public:
  virtual void Execute(void)
  {
    std::cout << "5 squared is " << Square(5) << std::endl;
  }
};
```

In this example, we are just hardcoding the function call and the function parameter in place. This may not seem very useful now for such a simple function, but it could be used in-game. As we will see later, the Mach5 Engine has a command to quit the game. The command directly calls `StageManager::Quit()`.

In most cases, we probably don't want to hardcode the function and parameters. This is where the power of this pattern shows. In this next example, we can use the fact that both functions have the same signature. That means we can create a function pointer, and pass the function, and parameters to the command. The benefit here is that because the command is an object, it has a constructor. So, we can construct an object with an action and the parameters that will be used by that action:

```
//The function signature of both Square and Cube
typedef int (*OneArgFunc)(int);

//Command that can use any function of type OneArgFunc
class OneArgCommand: public Command
{
public:
  OneArgCommand(OneArgFunc action, int* pValue):
    m_action(action), m_pValue(pValue)
  {
  }
  virtual void Execute(void)
  {
    *m_pValue = m_action(*m_pValue);
  }
private:
  OneArgFunc m_action;
  int*       m_pValue;
};
```

There are a few interesting things going on here. The first is that this command can call any function that returns an `int` and takes one `int` as a parameter. That means it can work for Square and Cube, but also any other functions that we come up with later. The next interesting thing is that we can set the action and parameter in the constructor; this allows us to save parameters within the class and use them later. We could not do this by using function pointers alone. Finally, you may have noticed that we are passing in a pointer to an `int`, instead of just an `int`. This demonstrates how we can save the return value of a function call, and also allows us to think about these commands in a more flexible way.

Commands are not just for quitting the game or changing the stage. We could have a command that changes the position of a game object when executed, or perhaps swaps the position of the player and an enemy based on some user input or a button click. By using commands, we can control everything about the game via the UI. That sounds a lot like a level editor.

Now that we have seen two types of commands, let's look at how the client would use them. We will start out with a simple main function. We will be constructing the command in the same function that calls it, but these could be set via a function call instead. The important thing is that at the point where the client calls Execute, they don't need to know which function is being called, or what parameters (if any) are needed:

```cpp
int main(void)
{
  const int SIZE = 3;
  int value = 2;
   //This commands could be loaded via another function
  Command* commands[SIZE] = {
    new Square5Command,
    new OneArgCommand(Square, &value),
    new OneArgCommand(Cube, &value),
  };

  //The Client Code
  commands[0]->Execute();//Square5
  std::cout << "value is " << value << std::endl;
  commands[1]->Execute();//OneArg Square
  std::cout << "value is " << value << std::endl;
  commands[2]->Execute();//OneArg Cube
  std::cout << "value is " << value << std::endl;

  for (int i = 0; i < SIZE; ++i)
    delete commands[i];

  return 0;
}
```

The output for the preceding code is as follows:

```
5 squared is 25
value is 2
value is 4
value is 64
```

As we can see, the client could call different functions using the same interface, and does not need to care about function parameters. For such a simple pattern, the Command pattern is amazing. And it gets even better.

Two parameters and beyond

We saw that one limitation of using function pointers was that the signatures must be the same. They must have the same return type, as well as the same parameter types and count. We can already see that this isn't true with the Command pattern. The client doesn't need to know or care about the specific signature at call time since every command shares the common Execute interface. As an example, let's look at a function with more than one parameter and create a command for that type. Here is the function:

```
int Add(int x, int y)
{
  return x + y;
}
```

As we mentioned before, the complexity of the function isn't important. For now, let's focus on functions that take more than one parameter, as in the case of this Add function. To make our code easier to read, let's create a typedef for this signature too:

```
typedef int (*TwoArgsFunc)(int, int);
```

Finally, let's create a Command for all functions that match this signature:

```
class TwoArgCommand: public Command
{
public:
  TwoArgCommand(TwoArgsFunc action, int x, int y) :
    m_action(action), m_first(x), m_second(y)
  {
  }

  virtual void Execute(void)
  {
    std::cout << "The Result is "
              << m_action(m_first, m_second)
```

```
                        << std::endl;
    }
private:
  TwoArgsFunc m_action;
  int         m_first;
  int         m_second;
};
```

The `main` function is now updated to the following. Here we are only showing the parts of the code that changed:

```
Command* commands[SIZE] = {
    new Square5Command,
    new OneArgCommand(Square, &value),
    new OneArgCommand(Cube, &value),
    new TwoArgCommand(Add, 5, 6)
};

//The Client Code
  commands[0]->Execute();//Square5
  std::cout << "value is " << value << std::endl;
  commands[1]->Execute();//OneArg Square
  std::cout << "value is " << value << std::endl;
  commands[2]->Execute();//OneArg Cube
  std::cout << "value is " << value << std::endl;
  commands[3]->Execute();//TwoArg
```

The output for the preceding code is as follows:

```
5 squared is 25
value is 2
value is 4
value is 64
The Result is 11
```

As you can see, we can easily create a new command for every function pointer signature we need. When the client calls the method, they don't need to know how many parameters are used. Unfortunately, even though our commands can take multiple arguments, those arguments are stuck using only the `int`. If we wanted them to use the float, we would need to make new commands or use the create a template command.

In a real-world scenario, you could get away with creating the commands as you need them, and only creating them for the types you need. Another option, and one that is more common, is to have commands call C++ class methods, since the method has the option to use class variables instead of passed in parameters.

Pointers to member functions

So far, we have seen how we can use the Command pattern with function pointers and allow the client to call our functions without caring about the parameter types or counts. This is incredibly useful. But what about using commands with C++ objects? While we can get commands to work with objects, we need to think about the problem a little first.

The most basic way to call member functions is to simply hardcode them in the Execute method. For example, we could pass in an object to a command constructor and always call a very specific function. In the example, `m_gameObject` is a pointer to an object that was passed to the constructor. However, `Draw` is the hardcoded method that we always call. This is the same as hardcoding the function in `Square5Command`:

```
//Example of hard-coding a class method
virtual void Execute(void)
{
  m_gameObject->Draw();
}
```

Since `m_gameObject` is a variable, the object that will call `Draw` can change, but we are still always calling `Draw`. In this case, we don't have the option to call something else. This is still useful, but we would like the ability to call any method on a class type. So, how do we get this ability? We need to learn about pointers to member functions.

Using pointers to member functions isn't that different from pointers to non-member functions. However, the syntax is a little stranger than you might expect. Recall that when calling a non-static class method, the first parameter is always implicit to the pointer:

```
class SomeClass
{
public:
  //Example of what the compiler adds to every
  //Non-static class method. THIS IS NOT REAL CODE
void SomeFunc(SomeClass* const this);
private:
  int m_x;
};
```

The `this` pointer is what allows the class method to know which instance of the class it needs to modify. The compiler automatically passes it in as the first parameter to all non-static member functions, and the address of the `this` pointer is used as an offset for all member variables:

```
SomeClass someClass;
//when we type this
someClass.SomeFunc();

//The compiler does something like this
SomeClass::SomeFunc(&someClass);
```

Even though it is implicitly passed in and is not part of the parameter list, we still have access to the `this` pointer in our code:

```
void SomeClass::SomeFunc(/* SomeClass* const this */)
{
//We can still use the this pointer even though it isn't
//in the parameter list
this->m_x += 2;

//But we don't have to use it.
m_x += 2;
}
```

It is important to understand this because normal functions and member functions are not the same. Class members are part of the class scope and they have an implicit parameter. So, we can't save pointers to them like normal functions. The signature of a class method includes the class type, meaning we must use the scope resolution operator:

```
SomeClass someClass;
//This doesn't work because they are not the same type
void (*BadFunc)(void) = &SomeClass::SomeFunc;

//We must include the class type
void (SomeClass::*GoodFunc)(void) = &SomeClass::SomeFunc;
```

Just having the correct pointer type is not enough. The class member access operators, known as the dot operator (.) and arrow operator (->), are not designed to work with arbitrary function pointers. They are designed to work with known data types or known function names as declared in the class. Since our function pointer isn't known until runtime, these operators won't work. We need different operators that will know how to work with member function pointers. These operators are the pointer to member operators, (.*) and (->*).

Unfortunately, these operators have lower precedence than the function call operator. So, we need to add an extra set of parentheses around our object and our member function pointer:

```
SomeClass someClass;
void (SomeClass::*GoodFunc)(void) = &SomeClass::SomeFunc;

//this doesn't work. GoodFunc isn't part of the class
someClass.GoodFunc();
//Extra parenthesis is required for .* and ->*
(someClass.*GoodFunc)();
```

There is a lot more to pointers to members. This section here was just a short introduction. If you want more information, please go to https://isocpp.org/wiki/faq/pointers-to-members.

Pointer to member command

Now that we know how to use pointers to member functions, we can create commands that can take an object and a specific member function to call. Just like before, we will use a simple example. The example class isn't designed to do anything interesting, it is just used to demonstrate the concepts:

```
class SomeObject
{
public:
  SomeObject(int x):m_x(x){}

  void Display(void)
  {
    std::cout << "x is " << m_x << std::endl;
  }
  void Change(void)
  {
    m_x += m_x;
  }
private:
  int m_x;
};
```

Here is a simple class called `SomeObject`. It has a constructor that takes an `int` parameter and uses it to set the private member variable `m_x`. It also has two functions: one that will print the value to the screen and one that changes the value. For now, we are keeping things simple by giving both member functions the same signature and not taking any arguments. This allows us to create a `typedef` for this type of method. Remember that the class type is part of the function signature:

```
typedef void (SomeObject::*SomeObjectMember)(void);
```

This creates a type called `SomeObjectMember` that can easily be used as a function parameter, function return type, or even saved as a member to another class (of course, that is exactly what we will do next). Even if you feel very comfortable with the syntax of function pointers and pointer to member functions, it is still good practice to make these `typedef`s. They make the code more readable for everyone, as you will see in the next code example:

```
class SomeObjectCommand: public Command
{
public:
  SomeObjectCommand(SomeObject* pObj, SomeObjectMember member) :
    m_pObj(pObj), m_member(member)
  {
  }
  virtual void Execute(void)
  {
    (m_pObj->*m_member)();
  }
private:
  SomeObject*      m_pObj;
  SomeObjectMember m_member;
};
```

Since the syntax of calling a member function pointer can be tricky to get right, it can be useful to use a `#define` macro. While most of the time, macros should be avoided, this is one of the few times they can help by making your code more readable:

```
#define CALL_MEMBER_FUNC(pObj, member) ((pObj)->*(member))
```

This changes our `Execute` function to this:

```
virtual void Execute(void)
{
  CALL_MEMBER_FUNC(m_pObj, m_member)();
}
```

All we have done is hide the ugliness away in a macro, but at least people will have a better understanding of what it is doing. It is important to note that this macro only works with object pointers because it uses the arrow star operator ($->*$).

Now, in main we can create commands to object members:

```cpp
int main(void)
{
  const int SIZE = 6;
  int value = 2;
  SomeObject object(10);
  Command* commands[SIZE] = {
    new Square5Command,
    new OneArgCommand(Square, &value),
    new OneArgCommand(Cube, &value),
    new TwoArgCommand(Add, 5, 6),
    new SomeObjectCommand(&object, &SomeObject::Display),
    new SomeObjectCommand(&object, &SomeObject::Change)
  };

  //The Client Code
  commands[0]->Execute();//Square5
  std::cout << "value is " << value << std::endl;
  commands[1]->Execute();//OneArg Square
  std::cout << "value is " << value << std::endl;
  commands[2]->Execute();//OneArg Cube
  std::cout << "value is " << value << std::endl;
  commands[3]->Execute();//TwoArg


  //Member function pointers
  commands[4]->Execute();//Display
  commands[5]->Execute();//Change
  commands[4]->Execute();//Display

  for (int i = 0; i < SIZE; ++i)
    delete commands[i];

  return 0;
}
```

The following is the class diagram of command hierarchy:

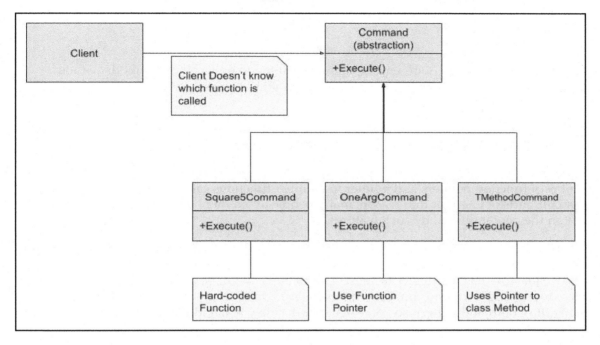

Figure 8.3 - The command hierarchy

Even though this is just a simple demo, we can see the client code is the same whether they are calling a function pointer or a pointer to a member function, and regardless of parameter count. Unfortunately, we still need to create a `typedef` for every function and class type we need. However, C++ templates can help us here too. We can create a template command class that can call class methods of a specific signature (in our case, `void (Class::*)(void)`) that will work for all classes:

```
template<typename Type, typename Method>
class TMethodCommand: public Command
{
public:
  TMethodCommand(Type* pObj, Method method) :
     m_pObj(pObj), m_method(method)
  {
  }

  virtual void Execute(void)
  {
    (m_pObj->*m_method)();
```

```
    }
  private:
    Type*  m_pObj;
    Method m_method;
  };
```

As you can see in the `Execute` method, this is limited to only calling methods without arguments, but it could easily be modified to suit your game's needs.

The benefits of the command pattern

If looking at all that crazy code makes your eyes glaze over, you are not alone. The complex syntax of function pointers and pointer to member functions calls are some of the most difficult parts of C++. For that reason, many people avoid them. However, they also miss out on the power offered by such features.

On the other hand, just because something is powerful, it doesn't mean it is always the right tool for the job. Simple is often better and, because of the many levels of indirection, code like we just saw has the chance to cause a lot of bugs. It will be up to you to decide if using these tools is right for your project. That being said, let's discuss some of the benefits of using the Command pattern so you can better decide when and where to use it.

Treating a function call like an object

The biggest benefit of using the Command pattern is that we are encapsulating the function or method call and the parameters. This means that everything needed for the call can be passed to another function, returned from a function, or stored as a variable for later use. This is an extra level of indirection over only using function or method pointers, but it means the client doesn't need to worry about the details. They only need to decide when to execute the command.

This might not seem very useful since we need to know all the function arguments before we pass it to the client. However, this situation can happen more often than you might think. The fact that the client doesn't need to know the details of the function call means that systems such as the UI can be incredibly flexible, and possibly even read from a file.

In the above example, it is obvious that at the time of the call, the client doesn't know which command exists at a given array index. This is by design. What might not be so obvious, is that the array could have been populated using the return value from a function instead of hardcoded calls to a new operator (which we learned in Chapter 5, *Decoupling Code via the Factory Method Pattern*, leads to inflexible code). This flexibility means that the function to be executed can be changed at runtime.

A perfect example of this is a context sensitive *action button* in a game. Since there is a limited number of buttons on a gamepad, it is often useful to have the action of button change depending on what the player is doing. This could mean one button is responsible for talking to an NPC, picking up an item, opening a door, or triggering a *quick time event* depending on the player's location and what they are doing.

Without the Command pattern, the logic involved in organizing, maintaining, and executing all the possible actions in a game would be incredibly complex. With the Command pattern, it is giving every actionable item a command, and making it available when the player is near.

Physically decoupling the client and the function call

One aspect of good design is low coupling. We have talked about this a lot before, and it applies here as well. First, since the client is only dependent on the base Command class, it is easier to test. This is because both the client and the specific function calls or actions can be tested independently to ensure that they work. Furthermore, since these unit tests are testing smaller amounts of code, we can be more confident that all possible cases are tested. This also means that the client or the commands have a better chance to be reused because of the low coupling within this project.

Second, the client is less likely to break when changes to the code base occur. Since the client doesn't know which functions or methods are called, any changes to parameter counts or method names are local only to the commands that implement the changed methods. If more commands need to be added, those commands will automatically work with the existing client because they will use the Command class interface.

Finally, compile times can be reduced because the client needs to include fewer header files. Including fewer header files can lower the compile time since every time the header changes, every source file that includes it must be recompiled. Even the smallest change to a comment in a header file means that all the function calls from that header need to be rechecked for correct syntax at compile time and relinked at link time. Since our client doesn't know the details of the functions calls, there are no header files to include.

Temporal decoupling

This type of decoupling isn't talked about much because it only applies to a few situations and, most of the time, this isn't what we want. Usually, when we call a function we want it to execute immediately. We have a specific algorithm in our code and the timing and order of that code is very important. This isn't true of all code. One situation is multithreaded code, in which multiple paths of code are executing simultaneously. Other situations are UI or context sensitive buttons, where the action to be executed is set up in advance instead of hardcoded in place. Let's look at some code as an example:

```
//Examples of setting up function calls
//Immediate execution
Add(5, 6);
//Delayed execution
Command* p1 = new TwoArgCommand(Add, 5, 6);

//Immediate execution
someObject.Display();
//Delayed execution
Command* p2 = new SomeObjectCommand(&object,&SomeObject::Display);
```

In all four of the above situations, the functions and parameters are given. However, the command versions can be passed to other methods, called and/or recalled based on the need of the client.

Undo and redo

Another major benefit of having the call details packaged together in a class is the ability to undo an operation. Every modern desktop application, as well as the best web applications being made these days, features the ability to undo the last action or actions. This should be a standard that you strive to follow when implementing a level editor for your game.

Implementing a single level of undo in an application can seem like a large task. The naive approach might be to save the entire state of the application, possibly to a file, and reload that state when we need to undo. Depending on the application, there might be a lot of data to save. This method doesn't scale well in applications that can have dozens or hundreds of levels of undo. As the user does more actions, you would need to make sure to delete the oldest state before saving the current one.

This simple approach is even more difficult when you also need to implement redo. Obviously, the text editors and tools that we use every day don't store hundreds of undo and redo files on the hard drive. There must be a better way.

Instead of saving the entire state of the program, you only need to save information about the action that happened, and what data was changed. Saving a function and the parameters to the function sounds a lot like the Command pattern. Let's look at a simple example of moving a game object from one place to another in a level editor. We could create a command like this:

```
class MoveCommand: public Command
{
public:
MoveCommand (Object* pObj, const Vec2D& moveTo) :
  m_pObj(pObj), m_method(method), m_oldPos(pObj->pos)
{
}
virtual void Execute(void)
{
  m_pObj->pos = m_moveTo;
}

//Add this method to the Command Interface
virtual void Undo(void)
{
  m_pObj->pos = m_oldPos;
}
private:
Object* m_pObj;
Vec2D   m_moveTo;
Vec2D   m_oldPos;//Save the old position so we can redo
};
```

By adding the Undo method to the command interface and making sure to save the old data that will be modified in the Execute method, performing undo and redo becomes incredibly simple. First, we need to implement a command for every action that can be performed in our editor. Then, when the user interacts with the editor, instead of directly calling a function, they always call a command and add it to the end of our array of commands. Undoing and redoing is just a matter of calling the Execute or Undo method of the current array index.

It might seem like a lot of work to create all those commands, and it is. However, that work is replacing the work of hardcoding function calls when a user presses keys or clicks the mouse. In the end, you will build a better system that people will want to use.

Easy UI with commands in Mach5

Now that we have seen what the Command pattern is, let's look at how it is used in the Mach5 Engine. You will be surprised that there isn't much code here. That is because using the Command pattern is easy once you understand the code behind it. In this section, we will look at both the component responsible for the mouse click and the commands that are used within the engine.

Let's have a look at the M5Command class:

```
class M5Command
{
public:
  virtual ~M5Command(void) {}//Empty Virtual Destructor
  virtual void Execute(void) = 0;
  virtual M5Command* Clone(void) const = 0;
};
```

Here is the M5Command class used in the Mach5 Engine. As you can see, it looks almost identical to the Command class we used in the example. The only difference is that since we plan on using this within a component, it needs to have a virtual constructor. That way we can make a copy of it without knowing the true type.

The code for the UIButtonComponent class is as follows:

```
class UIButtonComponent: public M5Component
{
public:
  UIButtonComponent(void);
  ~UIButtonComponent(void);
  virtual void Update(float dt);
```

```
    virtual UIButtonComponent* Clone(void) const;
    void SetOnClick(M5Command* pCommand);
private:
    M5Command* m_pOnClick;
};
```

As you can see, our UI button is a component. This means that any game object has the potential to be clicked. However, this class is specifically designed to work with objects that are in screen space, which is how the operating system gives us the mouse coordinates. The rest of the code here looks like you might expect. As part of the UIButtonComponent class, we have a private M5Command. Although this class is simple, it will be worth it for us to go through and see what each method does:

```
UI Button Component::UI Button Component(void) :
    M5Component(CT_UIButtonComponent), m_pOnClick(nullptr)
{
}
```

The constructor is simple (as are most component constructors) since they are designed to be created via a factory. We set the component type and make sure to set the command pointer to null so we set ourselves up for safer code later:

```
UIButtonComponent::~UIButtonComponent(void)
{
    delete m_pOnClick;
    m_pOnClick = 0;
}
```

The destructor is where that null pointer comes in handy. It is perfectly legal to delete a null pointer, so we know that this code will work, even if this component never receives a command:

```
void UIButtonComponent::Update(float)
{
    if (M5Input::IsTriggered(M5_MOUSE_LEFT))
    {
        M5Vec2 clickPoint;
        M5Input::GetMouse(clickPoint);
        if (M5Intersect::PointRect(clickPoint, m_pObj->pos,
            m_pObj->scale.x, m_pObj->scale.y))
        {
            M5DEBUG_ASSERT(m_pOnClick != 0,
                "The UIButton command is null"):
            m_pOnClick->Execute();
        }
    }
}
```

The `Update` function is where we perform the test to see if the mouse click intersects the rectangle created by the object. As we mentioned before, this class could work with all objects, but to simplify the code we decided we would only use this class for screen space items. The code that is important in this decision is the `GetMouse` function. This function always returns coordinates in screen space. It would be possible to check if the object was in screen space or world space and convert the coordinates using the `M5Gfx` method `ConvertScreenToWorld`.

That null pointer comes in handy here as well. Since we know that the command pointer is valid or null, we can do a debug assert to test our code before we execute it:

```
UIButtonComponent* UIButtonComponent::Clone(void) const
{
UIButtonComponent* pClone = new UIButtonComponent();
pClone->m_pObj = m_pObj;

if(pClone->m_pOnClick != nullptr)
  pClone->m_pOnClick = m_pOnClick->Clone();

return pClone;
}
```

The `Clone` method looks like you might expect after reading Chapter 6, *Creating Objects with the Prototype Pattern*. This is one situation where we always need to test for null before using the command. We can't clone a null command and it is completely valid to clone this component, whether the command has been set or not:

```
void UIButtonComponent::SetOnClick(M5Command* pCommand)
{
//Make sure to delete the old one
delete m_pOnClick;
m_pOnClick = pCommand;
}
```

The `SetOnClick` method allows us to set and reset the command that is associated with this component. Again, we don't need to test our command before deleting. We also don't need to test if the method parameter is non-null, because a null value is perfectly acceptable.

Even though we haven't done it for this class, this class could easily be expanded to include an `OnMouseOver` event that gets triggered when the mouse is inside the object rectangle but the mouse isn't clicked. A feature like this could have lots of uses for both UI and world objects. Implementing it would be as easy as swapping the two conditional statements in the `Update` function:

```cpp
void UIButtonComponent::Update(float)
{
  M5Vec2 clickPoint;
  M5Input::GetMouse(clickPoint);
  if (M5Intersect::PointRect(clickPoint, m_pObj->pos,
    m_pObj->scale.x, m_pObj->scale.y))
  {
    if (M5Input::IsTriggered(M5_MOUSE_LEFT))
    {
      //Do onClick Command
    }
    else
    {
      //Do onMouseOver Command
    }
  }
}
```

Using commands

Now that we have seen the base `M5Command` class and `UIButtonComponent` class, let's look at one of the derived commands to see how it is used in the game. The command that we will look at is a common one needed in games. This is the action that will allow us to change stages from one to the next:

```cpp
class ChangeStageCommand: public M5Command
{
public:
ChangeStageCommand(M5StageTypes nextStage);
ChangeStageCommand(void);
virtual void Execute(void);
void SetNextStage(M5StageTypes nextStage);
virtual ChangeStageCommand* Clone(void) const;
private:
  M5StageTypes m_stage;
};
```

When used with a `UIButtonComponent`, this will allow the user to click a button and change to a new stage. As you can see, there are two ways to change the stage in the constructor and in the `SetNextStage` method. This allows the user the ability to create a command and decide later what stage it will switch to. The `Execute` method is as simple as can be since the `StageManager` is a Singleton:

```
void ChangeStageCommand::Execute(void)
{
    M5StageManager::SetNextStage(m_stage);
}
```

The following is the output:

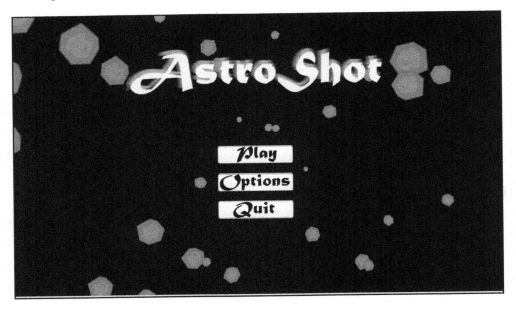

Figure 8-4 - An example of UIButtons in the Mach5 Engine

To be truly flexible, we would want all `UIButtons` loaded from a file. As with game objects, it would be best if menus and levels were not coupled to specific commands. At the very least, we would prefer to avoid hardcoding positions and sizes for each button. This proved to be easy with game objects. The Player or Raider game objects are so specific that when reading a level file, we only need to overwrite the position of each object. The size, texture name, and other attributes can be read from the more specific archetype file.

Buttons are more difficult since each one may use a different texture name, have a different size, and use a different command. We can't set this data in a button archetype file because all buttons will be different. Furthermore, game commands that need to control a specific game object are difficult to load from file since we have no information about the object except the type. This means that while we could create and load a command that controls the player, which we only have one of, we can't create and load a command that controls an arbitrary Raider, since we could have many per stage.

Having a high-quality level editor would solve both issues because the tool can manage data better. This could even include assigning object IDs that could be used by commands in the game. For this book, defining archetypes for every button worked well. While this may seem like a lot of work, the data in each archetype file would have otherwise been hardcoded into a .cpp file.

Summary

In this chapter, we focused on creating flexible, reusable buttons. Even though the UI may not be as fun to code or talk about as gameplay mechanics, to the player, it is just as important. That is why creating a good system to add and manage the UI in an intelligent way is so vital to making a great game.

We took an in-depth look at C++ function pointers and pointers to members. This is well known for being confusing and difficult. However, by mastering the techniques, we could create flexible commands that can call any C style function or C++ object method.

While this technique isn't always needed, in the case of UI, it allowed us to create an incredibly flexible system. Our UI objects and most commands can be set up and read from a file. If you were to create a level editor, you could easily use this system to create and read all UI buttons and commands from a file.

Now that we have a flexible system for creating the UI, let's move on to another problem everyone has when making games. In the next chapter, we will talk about a pattern that will allow us to better separate our engine code from our gameplay code.

9
Decoupling Gameplay via the Observer Pattern

Wow! The last two chapters were full of pointer craziness. Those two chapters combined, cover what are probably considered the hardest parts of C++. While all design patterns deal with pointers and using virtual functions at some level, it doesn't get much more difficult than what was covered in Chapter 7, *Improving Performance with Object Pools* and Chapter 8, *Controlling UI via the Command Pattern*.

In Chapter 7, *Improving Performance with Object Pools*, we went very low-level into the guts of C++ memory. This involved casting and strange pointer manipulation that most people tend to avoid. In Chapter 8, *Controlling UI via the Command Pattern*, we dealt with controlling the UI, which is more high-level. However, we learned how to control C++ objects and their methods in a way that allows us to create flexible code, but can also be very confusing.

If you feel comfortable with those chapters, then you are doing great. If you felt that those topics were a little difficult, you are not alone. Either way, you should be excited to know that this chapter covers a pattern that is easy to understand, easy to implement, and easily allows us to decouple our core systems from the gameplay specific code that is likely to change often.

In this chapter, we will cover a pattern called **Observer**, which is used to connect objects together in a decoupled way. As you will see, it is very simple to implement and can be applied in many places throughout our code base.

Chapter overview

This chapter is all about learning how to decouple code using the Observer pattern. This chapter is a little different than the others because it isn't about using the Observer pattern to solve one big pattern; it is about learning to apply it to the many little situations that lead to sloppy code throughout a game's development. The Observer pattern will show you that there is a better way.

First, we will explore the inevitable situation of gameplay code leaking into our engine code. Then, we will learn about the Observer pattern and how it can improve these situations. Along the way, we will look at some example code from the Mach5 Engine. However, since this pattern has so many uses, we will focus on how it can be incorporated into a game, as opposed to showing one large specific example.

Your objectives

- Learn two ways that gameplay code can cause trouble for your engine code
- Implement the simple Observer pattern example
- Learn the pros and cons of the Observer pattern

How gameplay creeps into every system

The first time someone makes a game, there is very likely no distinction between the game and the engine. This is usually because there is no engine. A common first game would include Ticktacktoe or Hangman. Games like these are simple enough that they can be completely written in main, or possibly using a few functions. They are also simple enough that they don't require complex systems like graphics or physics. There is no need for reusable engine code.

As you are learning to program more, you may decide to try making a 2D game using a graphics API, like DirectX or OpenGL. Code like this can be very difficult the first time it is used, so writing cleanly separated code isn't a top priority. Just as before, the game is made with just a few functions or classes. Drawing code is often mixed with collision code in one single file.

At some point, we all get to a place where the code is too complex and fragile. Hardcoding too many game object types or too many levels make us wish for a better way. Of course, that is the reason for this book. We are trying to find a better way to create games. Throughout this book there has been one major theme: things always change!

To cope with this change, we have tried to create a clear distinction between the parts of our game that will change and the parts of the game that are unlikely to change. In clear terms, we are trying to separate our engine code from our gameplay code. This clear separation of parts has lead us through eight chapters of patterns that solve very large and specific problems in games. Every game must deal with creating flexible game objects with complex behaviors. So, we learned about the Component Object Model and Finite Stage Machines. Every game must deal with creating an easy to modify UI. So, we learned about using the Command pattern to read actions from a file. These are common problems with common solutions.

However, as you write more code and you start to add more features to your game, you will always find that the clear separation between engine and gameplay starts to blur. One place that this becomes obvious is physics. The physics engine is responsible for moving objects as well as testing for and resolving collisions.

While this engine should be purely mathematical, the fact is that a game is made up of more than just physics objects. It is made of bullets, raiders, players, and more. When a bullet collides with a player, we must execute some very specific gameplay code, such as deleting the bullet, creating a small particle effect at the collision point, and subtracting player health. The question is, where should this code be executed? If the code is placed inside the physics engine, it is highly coupled with every game object type. If it is executed outside of the engine, we need to get the collision information to the correct location in a clean way.

The same problem of creeping gameplay code occurs with achievements. Achievements are always game specific but they end up getting mixed all throughout a code base. They can range from tracking behavior such as how many bullets the player fired, to tracking total time played or how long the game has been paused. However, they could always be related to engine specific behavior such as how many times the resolution has been changed, how many network connections have been made, how many times a UFO game object was created or destroyed, or how many collision events of a certain kind have occurred. This blurred line between engine and gameplay code, as well as general increased dependencies, makes code reuse very difficult.

Hardcoding requirements

We know that introducing gameplay code to our engines increases dependencies and limits code reuse. We also know that for a given action, the requirements are likely to change as gameplay features are added. Imagine the situation of adding controller support for split screen multiplayer in our space shooter. As more controllers are plugged in, additional players are created, the game difficulty is increased, and we split the screen to follow the new player. In this case, the original controller detection occurs in the Input Manager, but we need to notify a few other engines that something has changed. An example of this code might look like this:

```
//Not real code, just an example!
void InputManager:Update(void)
{
int controllerCount = GetControllerCount();
if(controllerCount > m_currentControllerCount)
{
  m_currentControllerCount = controllerCount;
  Object* pObj = ObjectManager::CreatePlayer(controllerCount);
  GameLogic::SetDifficulty(controllerCount);
  //player position is the camera location for the screen
  Graphics::SetScreenCount(controllerCount, pObj->pos);

  }
}
```

We might be reasonably certain that this code won't change. If we are, then hardcoding the requirements is fine. However, if we are not certain, it is good to assume that requirements always change. We might need to support online multiplayer and send a message to the Network Manager. We might allow the player to choose which type of space ship they want from a list of possible player ships, so we need to call a different Object Manager function or pause and switch to a new Ship Selection Stage via the Stage Manager.

In this case, we have a set of objects that need to be notified when an event occurs. We want the notification to happen automatically, but we don't want to change the Input Manager every time a new object needs to be notified. More generally, we have a broadcasting object that we don't want to change every time there is a new object that needs to listen. This would be like a Wi-Fi router needing to be updated every time a new device is in range.

The situation above describes interactions between different core engines. However, these interactions only happen this way because of the specific requirements of the game. Even though there is no gameplay code, the functionality of the specific game has crept into the input engine, and would need to be changed if we were making a different game. Of course, we could try to factor out some of this code into a game logic engine or just put similar code into a stage. Is there another way? We will consider that, but first, we will explore the problem from the other side.

Polling

Despite your best efforts, gameplay often turns into a mess. There are so many interacting parts that it is impossible to completely reduce coupling of gameplay code. While it makes sense that a graphics engine and a physics engine can be completely independent and decoupled, we shouldn't even try to do this with gameplay. Gameplay code is the game. The best we can do is to attempt to handle modifications to the game design gracefully.

The most obvious case of this is the state machines that we saw from Chapter 4, *Artificial Intelligence using the State Pattern*. The states often need access to the Object Manager and so scan the entire list of objects looking for an object. They may also need access to physics to see if they are colliding with this frame or the next. The gameplay code is the code that glues everything else together, so it can't really be completely decoupled.

Another example of this could be drawing HUD objects in screen space. If the window resolution changes, the objects need to be reoriented. A button in the center of the screen at 800 x 600 must still be in the center of the screen at 1280 x 1024. That means the position can't be hardcoded and must automatically adjust when the resolution changes. There are two ways of doing this. The first is the same as the example above; we could have the change resolution button call methods of other systems that care. The second would be for objects that care about resolution changes to ask the application for the resolution:

```
void RepositionComponent::Update(float /*dt*/)
{
  M5Vec2 windowSize = M5App::GetResolution();
  m_pObj->pos.x = windowSize.x * m_xScale;
  m_pObj->pos.y = windowSize.y * m_yScale;
}
```

Here is an example RepositionComponent. Every frame, it asks the M5App for the window resolution and sets the object to the specified scale of the window. An object that needed to be in the center of the screen would have x and y scale values of .5. If the resolution is 800 x 600, the position of the object will be x = 400, y = 300. If the resolution changes to 1280 x 1024, the position of the object will be x = 640, y = 512.

This works exactly as expected, but it does a lot of unnecessary work. The problem isn't that this code will make your game slow; you could have thousands of objects doing this before seeing slowdown. Still, this component is asking for the resolution 60 times a second, when a resolution change might only happen once per play session. More likely, the player will choose a resolution once, and the game settings will save it to a file and automatically load it every session after that.

The problem with this polling method is that the `RepositionComponent` has no way of knowing when the resolution changes. It would be nice if this code ran only when the data changed. Instead, it constantly asks for the exact same data, and calculates the exact same position every frame.

The example above is small. Problems like this may seem trivial. Individually, they won't even be a problem but, when added together, they can affect your game. This is true of all the examples so far in this chapter. They seem easy to solve one by one, but they can add up to lots of wasted CPU cycles as well as wasted developer time. It would be nice to have a pattern that is easy to implement that can solve little problems like these that pop up all over a game. Luckily, the Observer pattern will do exactly that.

The Observer pattern explained

The intent of the Observer pattern is to define a one-to-many relationship between objects. When the state of one object changes, all its dependents are notified. The typical names for the objects in this pattern are the **Subject** (the one), and the **Observers** (the many). The Subject will contain data that the Observers need to know about. Instead of the usual situation of classes requesting data from another (polling), our Subject will notify a list of Observers when the data has changed.

The terms Subject and Observers may seem a little confusing at first. However, this concept is very easy, and one that most of us are familiar with. When trying to understand the Observer pattern, think of a blog and subscribers. In this case, the blog is the Subject and the subscribers are the Observers.

A blog may be updated once a day, once a week, once a month, or even less. Readers of the blog have the option to check for updates as much as they want, however this can waste a lot of time if the readers check more frequently than the blog is updated. Instead, fans will often choose to subscribe to an e-mail list so they can be notified of updates as they come. The blog keeps a list of subscribers and sends an e-mail to everyone on the list when an update is posted.

The Subject and Observer

Let's look at a code example to understand this pattern better. There are a few different ways to implement this pattern, so we will discuss implementation strategies along the way:

```
class Observer
{
public:
  virtual ~Observer(void) {}
  virtual void Update(float currentHealth, float maxHealth) = 0;
};
```

We start off with our `Observer` interface. As always, we make our destructor virtual. The only method we need is an `Update` method however, as always, the name isn't important. This is the method that the Subject will use to notify the Observers that something has changed. One thing you might notice is that the update is very specific. In this case, it has two floats as arguments. This is a dependency that might change and cause our code to break. We will address improvements a little later.

You might also notice that there is no member data. It could be possible to give the base class a pointer to the Subject, and have this class be responsible for registering and unregistering (subscribing and unsubscribing) with the Subject. We decided to move that behavior into the derived classes so we could keep the base class as simple as possible:

```
class Subject
{
public:
  virtual ~Subject(void) {}
  virtual void RegisterObserver(Observer* pToAdd)      = 0;
  virtual void UnregisterObserver(Observer* pToRemove) = 0;
  virtual void Notify(void)                            = 0;
};
```

Our Subject is almost as simple as the Observer. The key methods we need are ways for the Observers to subscribe and unsubscribe to the Subject. Here, we called those methods `RegisterObserver` and `UnregisterObserver`. We have also added a `Notify` method which will be used to call `Update` on all registered Observers. There is no reason that this method needs to be public or even exist at all. As long as the derived class calls `Update` on the registered Observers, we are using the pattern correctly.

Again, you will notice that there are no data members in this class. We could easily add a vector of Observer pointers here in the base class. In fact, we could easily implement these methods because they will almost always be the same. However, we have chosen to keep this class simple and let the derived classes choose how to implement these methods.

The Player

To demonstrate how the Observer pattern can be used, we will look at a common situation in games. We will have a Player with some health that will need to be shared. The health of the Player can often be used for many things in a game. The value of health might be displayed as part of the HUD. It can also be displayed as a colored health bar in either the HUD or directly at the top or at the bottom of the Player. Additionally, the game may switch to a game over screen when the Player health is at or below zero.

These display elements, as well as the stage switching mechanisms, are dependent directly on the Player's health. Since it is very unlikely that these variables are all in the same scope, it would take some work if we tried to implement this via polling. In that case, each object would need to find the Player and ask for the health value. Since the health of the Player is unlikely to change every frame, most of this work is being wasted. Instead, we will make the Player derive from the Subject so it can notify all Observers when the health has changed:

```
class Player: public Subject
{
public:
  Player(float maxHealth);
  void AdjustHealth(float health);
  virtual void RegisterObserver(Observer* pToAdd);
  virtual void UnregisterObserver(Observer* pToRemove);
  virtual void Notify(void);
private:
  typedef std::vector<Observer*> ObserverVec;

  float       m_maxHealth;
  float       m_health;
  ObserverVec m_observers;
};
```

This `Player` class is very simple. Since this is only an example, we will only be focusing on the health. In the constructor, we can set the max health. The `AdjustHealth` method will be used to make the health change. Of course, we also implement each of the base class virtual methods. In the `private` section, we use an STL vector to keep track of our Observers. We also store our constructor value, as well as a variable for our current health:

```
Player::Player(float maxHealh):
  m_maxHealth(maxHealth),
  m_health(maxHealth)
{
}
```

The `Player` constructor sets data passed in by the user. Since the base `Subject` class has no data, there is nothing special to do here:

```
void Player::RegisterObserver(Observer* pToAdd)
{
  ObserverVec::iterator itor;
  itor = std::find(m_observers.begin(),
                    m_observers.end(),
                    pToAdd);

  assert(itor == m_observers.end());
  m_observers.push_back(pToAdd);
}
```

The `RegisterObserver` method takes a pointer to an Observer and adds it to the vector of the Observers. Depending on the behavior of the Observer, being added to the list twice could cause a lot of problems and could be a difficult bug to track down. In this example, we have chosen to assert if the same Observer is added twice. After that, we add it to our vector:

```
void Player::UnregisterObserver(Observer* pToRemove)
{
  ObserverVec::iterator itor;
  itor = std::find(m_observers.begin(),
                    m_observers.end(),
                    pToRemove);

  if (itor != m_observers.end())
  {
    std::swap(*itor, *(--m_observers.end()));
    m_observers.pop_back();
  }
}
```

Our `UnregisterObserver` class is a little more forgiving. If we don't find the Observer in the vector, we ignore it, instead of throwing an assert. This will make a little more sense later. You will see that our Observers will automatically remove or unregister in their own destructors. However, unregistering twice is unlikely to cause a problem. The line `std::swap(*itor, *(--m_observers.end()))` might look a little scary. Remember that the end method returns an iterator to one past the end of the vector. So, before we dereference, we decrement our iterator so it is pointing at the last element in the vector. Then we swap and pop, removing the correct element:

```
void Player::Notify(void)
{
  size_t size = m_observers.size();
```

```
     for (size_t i = 0; i < size; ++i)
       m_observers[i]->Update(m_health, m_maxHealth);
  }
```

As we said before, the `Notify` method doesn't need to exist. It would be fine if the class logic notifies the Observers internally, perhaps in `Setter` methods or when the data changes as in our `AdjustHealth` method. However, if there was more than one piece of data that the Observers cared about, the user could make many changes and send all the data to the Observers just once. Or, perhaps initializing the Observer data before the game has started.

This method is simple. It loops through the vector of the Observers and calls the `Update` method, sending the health data to those that care:

```
void Player::AdjustHealth(float adjustHealth)
{
  m_health += adjustHealth;
  Notify();
}
```

This method simulates the Player gaining or losing health. As you can see, after the health is modified, the class calls its own `Notify` method, letting all Observers know about the change.

The Observers

For this example, we have the three Observers that we mentioned before. Two are related to displaying the health of the Player in different ways; the other is used for quitting when the health of the Player is zero or less:

```
//Used to quit the game when the "game", when the player's health
//is less than or equal to 0
class StageLogic : public Observer
{
public:
  StageLogic (Subject* pSubject);
  bool IsQuitting(void) const;
  ~StageLogic(void);
  virtual void Update(float currentHealth, float maxHealth);
private:
  bool     m_isQuitting;
  Subject* m_pSubject;
};

//Used to Color the player health bar based on the how full it is
```

```
class PlayerHealthBar : public Observer
{
public:
  PlayerHealthBar(Subject* pSubject);
  ~PlayerHealthBar(void);
  void Display(void) const;
  virtual void Update(float currentHealth, float maxHealth);
private:
  float        m_percent;
  std::string m_color;
  Subject*    m_pSubject;
};

//Used to Display the health of the player as a value
class PlayerDisplay : public Observer
{
public:
  PlayerDisplay(Subject* pSubject);
  ~PlayerDisplay(void);
  void Display(void) const;
  virtual void Update(float currentHealth, float maxHealth);
private:
  float     m_health;
  Subject* m_pSubject;
};
```

As you can see, each derived `Observer` class overloads the `Update` method from base. You will also notice that each constructor takes a pointer to a Subject as the only parameter, and saves that pointer into a member variable. This isn't necessary, but it makes registering and unregistering more convenient because the objects take care of themselves. In this example, all three of the Observers' constructors and destructors do the exact same thing. Here is one:

```
PlayerDisplay::PlayerDisplay(Subject* pSubject) :
  m_health(0.0f),
  m_pSubject (pSubject)
{
  m_pSubject ->RegisterObserver(this);
}

PlayerDisplay::~PlayerDisplay(void)
{
  m_pSubject ->UnregisterObserver(this);
}
```

The choice of keeping a pointer to the Subject is up to you. It has some problems, which we will look at a little later; however, it allows the Observer to unregister in the destructor. This means that the user doesn't need to do it, which makes using the `Observers` classes very easy. If we don't keep this pointer, unregistering must be done manually and could be difficult depending on how you access the Subject and Observers.

The rest of the `Observer` methods are simple and don't interact with the Subject at all. Instead, the `Update` methods do some logic based on the values of `currentHealth` and `maxHealth`. For the two display elements, this means calculating some values; for the `StageLogic` class, this means setting `m_isQuitting` to true if the value of current health is zero or less. Let's look at an example `Update` from one of the Observers:

```cpp
void PlayerHealthBar::Update(float currentHealth, float maxHealth)
{
  m_percent = (currentHealth / maxHealth) * 100.f;

  if (m_percent >= 75.0f)
    m_color = "Green";
  else if (m_percent < 75.0f && m_percent > 35.0f)
    m_color = "Yellow";
  else
    m_color = "Red";

}
```

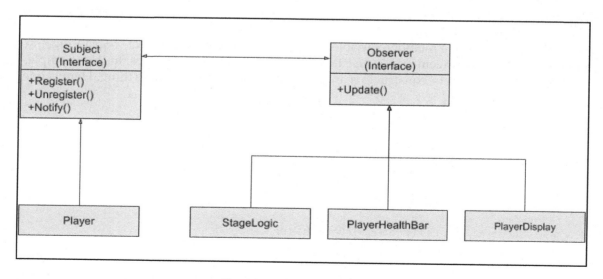

Figure 9 1 Interaction of Subjects and Observers

As you can see, the `Update` methods aren't very complicated. Nothing about the above method is using the Subject. The data could have come from anywhere. The part that is most interesting is how simple these objects are to use now. All three Observers are using the Player's health, but they don't need to call any `Player` methods. Even though these four objects interact, using them is incredibly simple. Let's look at how we can use these objects together:

```
int main(void)
{
  //Our value to decrement by
  const float DECREMENT      = -1.0f;
  const float STARTING_HEALTH =  5.0f;

  //creating our objects
  Player          player(STARTING_HEALTH);
  PlayerDisplay   display(&player);
  PlayerHealthBar bar(&player);
  StageLogic      stageLogic(&player);

  //Set the initial values to print
  player.Notify();

  //loop until player is dead
  while (!stageLogic.IsQuitting())
  {
    display.Display();
    bar.Display();
    player.AdjustHealth(DECREMENT);
  }

  return 0;
}
```

The `main` function starts out with a few `const` values to improve readability. After that, we create our objects. We first create our `Player`, which is our Subject. Then we create our Observers. Each Observer gets a pointer to the Subject. Remember, they are only dependent on the Subject interface, not to the derived `Player` class. Once all the Observers are created, the `Player` does an initial `Notify` call so the Observers start out with the correct data. Finally, we use our objects. The simplicity of this while loop is amazing. Since the code linking them together is all internal, using the objects together becomes very easy. Compare the example above with a version of the code that doesn't use the Observer pattern:

```
//Alternate code without Observer pattern
  while (!stageLogic.IsQuitting())
  {
    display.SetHeath(player.getHealth());
```

```
            display.Display();

            bar.setHealth(player.getHealth(), player.getMaxHealth());
            bar.Display();

            player.AdjustHealth(DECREMENT);

            stageLogic.SetQuit(player.GetHealth() <= 0);
    }
```

Using the Observer pattern allows us to write code that is more elegant and simple to use. Unfortunately, many programmers write code that is closer to the second version. They don't realize that with just a little thought as to how the objects will interact, the code is easier to use, easier to read, and is more efficient because it only gets data from the Player when the data changes.

In this simple example, it may not seem like the code is much different, but remember that this is just demonstrating the pattern as simply as possible. The second version looks reasonable because all the objects are in the same scope. Except for the constructor, in a real project, the Observer code stays the same. However, the second version can become a mess of Singleton method calls and object look ups.

Push versus Pull

One big problem with the Observer pattern that we have looked at so far is that the `Update` method in the base class is limited. In our case, it can only be used with Observers that expect two floats. If we want a different style of Observer, we need to create a new `Observer` class and a new Subject to work with it.

This Push version of the pattern is great because the classes are completely decoupled. The derived classes don't need to know about each other at all. The price to pay for this decoupling is that we need to write lots of `Subject` and `Observer` base classes for each method signature we want to use. An alternative version of this pattern lets the Observers pull the data they want from the Subject. In the Pull version, the Subject sends itself as a parameter in the `Update` method, and the Observer uses `Getter` methods from the Subject to only pull the data it wants.

That is exactly what is happening in our next example. The `PlayerHealthBar` class now takes a pointer to a Subject. In this case, we are expecting the Subject to be of type Player. The `Update` method can then use any Player data it needs to complete its task:

```cpp
//Now the update method takes a pointer to the subject
class Observer
{
public:
  virtual ~Observer(void) {}
  //Pull version of the Observer Pattern
  virtual void Update(Subject* pSubject) = 0;
};

//Example of an Observer Update method that pulls data
void PlayerHealthBar::Update(Subject* pSubject)
{
  //Make sure we have a Player
  Player* pPlayer = dynamic_cast<Player*>(pSubject);
  if(pPlayer == 0)
    return;

  m_percent = (pPlayer->GetHealth() / pPlayer->GetMaxHealth());
   m_percent *= 100.f;

  if (m_percent >= 75.0f)
    m_color = "Green";
  else if (m_percent < 75.0f && m_percent > 35.0f)
    m_color = "Yellow";
  else
    m_color = "Red";
}
```

In the Pull version of the pattern, the `Observer` is dependent on the derived `Subject` class (in this case the Player), but the `Update` method is more flexible. Additionally, this Observer could be observing many different Subjects. The `Update` method could have a series of `if` statements to determine which of the many possible Subjects performed the call. The classes are more tightly coupled to specific objects. However, since an Observer can now observe multiple Subjects, the same `Observer` class can be used for a wider range of objects. For example, a single `Observer` class could be used to keep track of how many objects of each type in the game have died by registering itself with every game object that gets created and monitoring the health of all Subjects.

Benefits of using the Observer pattern

At the start of this chapter we saw three problems with interacting gameplay code. As we said before, these problems aren't that big, but they creep up all over the place and can lead to inflexible code as the project moves forward. The Observer pattern solves these problems in a very simple way.

The biggest benefit of using the Observer pattern is that we can reduce dependency and coupling. By using the Push version of the Observer pattern, our classes can interact completely through interfaces, so they don't depend on each other at all. In the preceding example, the Player and Player Display are completely decoupled. This means that changes to one won't affect the other. For starters, this makes each class easier to test and debug because they can be worked on separately. However, this also means that as the game changes, these classes can change independently. This means the individual class can easily be reused within the current project or in separate projects. The only problem with the Push version is that we are stuck with a single `Update` method signature.

Using the Pull version of the Observer pattern increases the dependencies; however, the Subject/Observer system is much more flexible. An Observer can now listen to multiple Subjects, and a Subject can share different data with each of its Observers. Even though the dependencies are increased, this is only on the Observer side, since Subjects still don't need to know about their Observers. These increased dependencies are still better than the alternative, because they are limited to only the two classes that need to interact. Without using the Observer pattern, a third class would need to be used to link these two classes together.

The second benefit of this pattern is that we no longer need to hardcode methods or requirements. Since the event is broadcast to any object that registers, there is no need to recompile if a new object needs the event. This reduces compile times as well as limits the chance of breaking code.

This isn't just limited to connecting systems to other systems. Since Observers can register and unregister at runtime, game objects can register themselves with other game objects. Imagine an Enemy Space Station that continuously spawns Raiders. By registering Raiders with the station that spawned them, each station can act as a mini commander, easily coordinating units for attack and defense.

The last benefit is that there is no need to poll objects. In the preceding example, we saw two `while` loops--one using the Observer pattern, and one polling for data every frame. We saw how much cleaner the code looked when using the Observer pattern. Besides just looking cleaner, the first example is less likely to have bugs because once registered, the Observer will always receive the updated data. In a larger project, the alternative requires that every object constantly asks for the data all over the code base. Ensuring that every object that needs the data asks every frame in many locations can be a Herculean task.

In addition to being very difficult to find and maintain each poll occurrence, this method leads to less efficient code. We shouldn't try to prematurely optimize our code, and most likely this won't be the bottleneck of our game, so that is why we mentioned it last. However, the fastest code is the code that never runs. When using the Observer pattern, if the data never changes and the event never occurs, the `Update` methods never get called. So, using the Observer method has the chance to boost our performance compared to polling dozens or hundreds of times per frame.

Problems using the Observer pattern

Of course, the Observer pattern isn't a perfect solution. There is no perfect solution, if there was, this would be a very short book. As with every pattern, it is important to learn how to use it but also how not to use it. It is equally as important to learn when to use a pattern as it is to learn when not to use a pattern.

The Observer pattern has some things that you need to look out for when using it. The goal of all patterns is to simplify the development cycle. However, if a pattern isn't fully understood, lots of time can be wasted debugging layers and layers of code that were meant to save time.

Dangling references

The first major problem that everyone should be aware of is the problem of dangling references. We must ensure that the pointers held by our objects never become invalidated. The best way to understand this problem is to look at the Command pattern and compare it with the Observer.

The biggest difference between the Command pattern and the Observer pattern is a difference in ownership. In the Command pattern, the client or user of the command owns a pointer. This means that the client is responsible for deleting the command. The reason this is important is because no other class owns the command pointer, so it should never become invalidated. In the Mach5 Engine, the `UIButtonComponent` owns a command. It deletes that command in the destructor or when it is given a new command pointer.

Contrast this with the Observer pattern. The Subject contains a pointer to an Observer, and the Observer can hold a pointer to the Subject. Neither object owns the other, and either object can be deleted at any time. They are separate objects that just happen to communicate with each other via pointers.

Before an Observer is deleted, it must be unregistered from every Subject it is observing. Otherwise, the Subjects will keep trying to Update it via the invalid pointer, causing undefined behavior. In the example, we do this by having the Observer hold a pointer to the Subject and unregistering itself in the destructor. This causes a problem if the Subject gets deleted first. In the example, there is no way for the Subject to tell the Observer that it will be deleted. If the Subject does get deleted first, the Observers will still try to unregister in their own destructor, causing undefined behavior.

There are two solutions to this problem. First, we could ensure the Subject never gets deleted before the Observers. Second, we could remove the Subject pointer from the Observer and ensure that the Observer still gets unregistered from the correct Subject before it is deleted. Both solutions can be difficult to guarantee. If you implement the Observer pattern in your game, you must consider this problem.

Overuse

The second problem with the Observer pattern is the danger of overuse. We stated before that the Observer pattern is a great choice when the requirements of a method aren't completely known or are likely to change. While it is true that anything in a game can change, taking this to the extreme would create a project that is impossible to program in and that will never be completed. In the most extreme case, every object could be both a Subject and an Observer. Every method would be ultimately flexible because we could change everything about it at runtime. Every call would notify Observers, which in turn would notify more Observers.

Of course, no one would implement their engine to that extreme, but overuse of the Observer pattern is still a problem. It can be difficult to debug a method that notifies a long list of Observers. This becomes even worse if there are multiple layers to traverse before finding any real code. It can be difficult to find the right balance. If you feel like your code is becoming a spider web of interconnected pointers, it might be time to look for a better solution.

Implementing interfaces

The next thing to consider is the implementation of the Observer pattern. In the above example, the Subject and the Observer were designed to be interface classes. C++ doesn't have a language feature that supports interfaces but that doesn't mean we can't write code that uses them.

An interface is a class that contains no data members and has no method implementations. C++ does allow for the concept of abstract base classes. This is any class that marks at least one method a pure virtual, but using the = 0 notation. This means that the class can't be instantiated and instead must be derived from. This is different from an interface because abstract base classes can contain member data as well as implementations for methods (including pure virtual methods).

This distinction is important to us because C++ allows for multiple inheritance, although it is strongly recommended that you do not use this feature. Inheriting from multiple base classes means that you could be inheriting data members and methods with the same name. Since each of the parents could also be inheriting from multiple classes, it can be difficult to fully understand the entire tree that any derived class gets the implementations from. This will almost certainly lead to unexpected behavior. That is why you should avoid multiple inheritances and instead stick with a single parent class that your implementation derives from.

Interfaces are a little different. Many languages do not let you inherit from multiple classes that contain implementations, but they do let you implement multiple interfaces. Since interfaces do not contain method implementations or data members, there is no chance of having name clashes or inheriting unexpected behavior. By implementing an interface, you are simply promising that your class will respond to a method call. It is the responsibility of the derived class to write the behavior.

The Subject and Observer were written as interface classes in case they need to be used with Stages, Components, or any other class that already needs to derive from a base class. Of course, instead of using multiple inheritance, you could always find another solution. For example, you could create a new class that derives from the Observer and have your component contain, as opposed to inherit, that new class.

When to notify

The final thing to consider when using the Observer pattern is when to notify the Observers. The first option is to notify the Observers after any data has changed. In the above example, the Player called `Notify` within the `AdjustHealth` method. This means that the Observers will have the most up to date information immediately. However, if the `AdjustHealth` method is called many times in one frame, time is wasted updating the Observers many times. This problem becomes worse if the Observers were observing more than just the Player's health.

The other option would be to notify the Observers after all data has changed. This solution is obviously more efficient but a lot depends on how your system works. In the preceding example, it could be possible to update all the Player information (in this case, just the health) first, then call `Notify` before displaying anything.

In a game engine with many different Subjects and Observers that interact in different ways every frame, it can be difficult to know when all data has been updated. There might not be a way to sort the game objects such that all Subjects are updated before the Observers. It is possible that a HUD object that is an Observer has already been updated before the Subject gets updated. This becomes even more difficult since other systems such as physics can affect the data inside game objects.

In the end, there isn't a correct time to notify the Observers. It can be more efficient to only notify them once. However, if the system is complex, it probably isn't worth the programming trouble trying to batch all `Notify` calls together.

Summary

In this chapter, we focused on the communication between reusable engine code and game specific gameplay code. We learned that it can be difficult to make a clear distinction between these two parts because the gameplay code has the potential to creep into every system. This makes sense because to make a game, you must write code that interacts with every other system. However, this means reusing code is a little difficult.

We saw that the solution to this was to decouple our engine and gameplay code by having all communication go through interface classes. These interface classes were the basis for what is known as the Observer pattern. By using this pattern, we can make our code much cleaner and easier to use, and reuse.

The Observer pattern is as easy as it gets when it comes to design patterns. Few patterns are as simple to implement or understand. Once you start using it you will wonder how you ever programmed without it. However, we also learned there are some things to watch out for when using the pattern, the worst of which is dangling references.

Now that we have a great tool for separating gameplay from our engine, let's move onto another problem related to code reuse. In the next chapter, we will talk about a pattern that allows us to reuse objects and save memory. Along the way, we will learn about making great particle systems.

10
Sharing Objects with the Flyweight Pattern

We previously learned about object pools in `Chapter 7`, *Improving Performance with Object Pools*, and that they are great for avoiding slowdowns in our game due to dynamic memory allocation. But, there are still other steps that we can take to reduce the amount of memory that we use to begin with.

When creating projects, you'll often run into times where you want to have many objects on the screen at once. While computers have become much more powerful over the past few years, they still can't handle thousands of complex game objects on the screen by themselves.

In order to accomplish this feat, programmers need to think of ways to lighten the memory load on their program. Using the Flyweight pattern, we abstract the common parts of our object and share them with only the data that's unique to each instance (such as position and current health) being created.

Chapter overview

In this chapter, we will construct a particle system consisting of two parts: the particle itself, which will be a simple struct, as well as a particle system class that contains the system's data.

We will construct two different types of particle system: an explosion that moves on its own, and a static one that spawns at the position of our player's ship. We will also explore two ways to deal with the system data. The first will be for each particle system to contain its own copy of the system data. Then, after learning about the Flyweight pattern, we will use it to construct separate system data classes that we can assign using files or code. Then, each particle system will simply reference an instance of the system data that it needs.

Your objectives

This chapter will be split into a number of topics. It will contain a simple step-by-step process from beginning to end. Here is the outline of our tasks:

- Introduction to particles
- Implementing particles in Mach5
- Why memory is still an issue
- Introduction to the Flyweight pattern
- Transitioning to ParticleSystems

Introductions to particles

In game development, you may have heard of particles. They are typically small 2D sprites or simple 3D models that are created in order to simulate *fuzzy* things such as fires, explosions, and smoke trails to add visual flair to your projects. This visual flair is sometimes referred to as *juiciness*. Made popular by indie developers *Martin Jonasson* and *Petri Purho*, making a game *juicy* makes it more enjoyable to play and increases the feedback the player receives by playing the game.

This is usually something worked on more toward the end of development of titles in order to polish the project and add more feedback, but it's a good example of how we can want to have many things on the screen at one time.

 For more information on juiciness and to watch their Martin and Petri's GDC talk on the subject, check out
http://www.gamasutra.com/view/news/178938/Video_Is_your_game_jui
cy_enough.php.

The reason that these objects are so simple is because they are spawned hundreds and sometimes thousands of times, and this is done over and over again.

Implementing particles in Mach5

Now that we know what particles are, let's put them into Mach5 so we can get an example of how they work. We will be creating particles to follow our ship while it moves in a similar fashion to a smoke trail. This will be a great way to show an example of particles on the screen but, to have something to show, we will first need to bring a new archetype into the game.

To do that, open up the `Example Code` folder for this chapter and bring the `particle.tga` file into the `EngineTest/Textures` folder of your Visual Studio project.

After that, open up the `EngineTest/ArcheTypes` folder, create a new text file called `Particle.ini`, and fill it with the following info:

```
posX   = 0
posY   = 0
velX   = 0
velY   = 0
scaleX = 2.5
scaleY = 2.5
rot    = 0
rotVel = 0
components =  GfxComponent ParticleComponent

[GfxComponent]
texture = particle.tga
drawSpace = world
```

After that, we need the Mach5 engine to support our new object, so go to the `EngineTest` folder and then double-click on the `PreBuild.bat` file. The `M5ArcheTypes.h` file will be updated to include our particle:

```
//! AutoGenerated enum based on archetype ini file names
enum M5ArcheTypes {
AT_Bullet,
AT_Particle,
AT_Player,
AT_Raider,
AT_Splash,
AT_INVALID
};
```

Nice! Now that we have the object in the game, there's still the issue of putting in the Particle component. Since this component is not exclusive to our game, let's move over to the Core/Components filter and create a new filter called `ParticleComp`. From there, create two new files, `ParticleComponent.h` and `ParticleComponent.cpp`, making sure their locations are set to the `Mach5-master\EngineTest\EngineTest\Source\` folder.

In the `.h` file, use the following code:

```
/*****************************************************************************
****/
/*!
\file    ParticleComponent.h
\author John Doran
\par     email: john@johnpdoran.com
\par     Mach5 Game Engine
\date    2016/12/06

Used to display a single particle on the screen.
*/
/*****************************************************************************
****/
#ifndef PARTICLE_COMPONENT_H
#define PARTICLE_COMPONENT_H

#include "Core\M5Component.h"
#include "Core\M5Vec2.h"


class ParticleComponent : public M5Component
{
public:
  ParticleComponent();
  virtual void Update(float dt);
  virtual M5Component* Clone(void);
  virtual void FromFile(M5IniFile& iniFile);
  bool activated;
  float lifeTime;
  float endScale;
private:
  M5Vec2 startScale;
  float lifeLeft;
  float Lerp(float start, float end, float fraction);
};


#endif // !PARTICLE_COMPONENT_H
```

This class looks similar to other components that we've added in the past, but this time we've added a `startScale` property to keep track of what scale our object had at the start of its life, and an `endScale` property to be a modifier on how to change the scale. We also have `lifeTime`, which will be how long this object should live before we remove it, and `lifeLeft`, which will be how much longer this object has to live. Finally, since we are going to change our scale, we added another function, `Lerp`, to linearly interpolate between a starting and ending value.

In the `.cpp` file, use the following code:

```
/***************************************************************************
****/
/*!
\file    ParticleComponent.cpp
\author  John Doran
\par     email: john@johnpdoran.com
\par     Mach5 Game Engine
\date    2016/12/06

Particle system component. Allows you to draw many particles on the screen.
*/
/***************************************************************************
****/
#include "ParticleComponent.h"
#include "Core\M5Gfx.h"
#include "Core\M5Math.h"
#include "Core\M5Object.h"
#include "EngineTest\M5ObjectPool.h"
#include "Core\GfxComponent.h"
#include "Core\M5IniFile.h"


/***************************************************************************
****/
/*!
Construtor for ParticleSystem component.  Sets default values
*/
/***************************************************************************
****/
ParticleComponent::ParticleComponent() :
  M5Component(CT_ParticleComponent)
{
}


/***************************************************************************
****/
/*!
Takes care of the particle system, decrease lifetime and adjust scaling.
```

```
Will mark for destruction if needed.

\param [in] dt
The time in seconds since the last frame.
*/
/*********************************************************************
****/
void ParticleComponent::Update(float dt)
{
  // Decrease our life by the change in time this frame
    // (dt stands for delta time)
  lifeLeft -= dt;

  // Change our size based on where we want it to be
  float currentPercentage = 1 - (lifeLeft / lifeTime);
  m_pObj->scale.x = Lerp(startScale.x,
     startScale.x * endScale, currentPercentage);

  m_pObj->scale.y = Lerp(startScale.y,
     startScale.y * endScale, currentPercentage);

  // If there is no life left, destroy our object
  if (lifeLeft <= 0)
  {
    m_pObj->isDead = true;
  }

}
```

This code will modify the object's scale by using the `Lerp` function to interpolate between the starting and ending scale. We also will modify how much life the particle has left, and if it has none, mark the particle for deletion:

```
/*********************************************************************
****/
/*!
Will give you the percentage of the fraction from start to end

\param [in] start
What value to start from

\param [in] end
What value to end from

\param [in] fraction
What percentage of the way are we are from start to finish

*/
```

```
/*************************************************************************
****/
float ParticleComponent::Lerp(float start, float end, float fraction)
{
   return start + fraction * (end - start);
}
```

Linear interpolation (Lerp) allows us to obtain a value between `start` and `end` using the `fraction` property for how far along the transition it should be. If `fraction` is 0, we would get the value of `start`. If we give 1, we will get the value of `end`. If it's `.5`, then we would get the half-way point between `start` and `end`.

 For more information on interpolation including linear interpolation, check out *Keith Maggio*'s notes on the topic at `https://keithmaggio.wordpress.com/2011/02/15/math-magician-lerp-slerp-and-nlerp/`.

```
/*************************************************************************
****/
/*!
Clones the current component and updates it with the correct information.

\return
A new component that is a clone of this one
*/
/*************************************************************************
****/
M5Component * ParticleComponent::Clone(void)
{
   ParticleComponent * pNew = new ParticleComponent;
   pNew->m_pObj = m_pObj;
   pNew->startScale = m_pObj->scale;
   pNew->lifeTime = lifeTime;
   pNew->lifeLeft = lifeTime;
   pNew->endScale = endScale;
   return pNew;
}
```

The `Clone` function allows us to create a copy of this object. It will create a new version of this component, and we will initialize the values of the new component with the values we currently have. This is used by the Mach5 engine in the creation of new game objects:

```
/*************************************************************************
****/
/*!
Reads in data from a preloaded ini file.
```

```
\param [in] iniFile
The preloaded inifile to read from.
*/
/********************************************************************
****/
void ParticleComponent::FromFile(M5IniFile& iniFile)
{
  // Get our life time value
  std::string lifeTimeText;
  iniFile.SetToSection("ParticleComponent");
  iniFile.GetValue("lifeTime", lifeTimeText);

  // Convert the string into a float
  lifeTime = std::stof(lifeTimeText);
  lifeLeft = lifeTime;

  // Then do the same for endScale
  std::string endScaleText;
  iniFile.GetValue("endScale", endScaleText);
  endScale = std::stof(endScaleText);

}
```

Just like before, the `FromFile` function will read in our `ini` file we created previously and will use the values from it to set the properties of this component. In our case, here we set `lifeTime`, `lifeLeft`, and `endScale`.

Finally, let's start putting these objects into our game. Open up the `PlayerInputComponent.cpp` file and add the following to the top of the `Update` function:

```
M5Object* particle = M5ObjectManager::CreateObject(AT_Particle);

particle->pos = m_pObj->pos;
```

This will cause a particle to get spawned in every single frame and have the same position as our ship. Now, if we run the game, we should see some cool stuff! We can see this in the following screenshot:

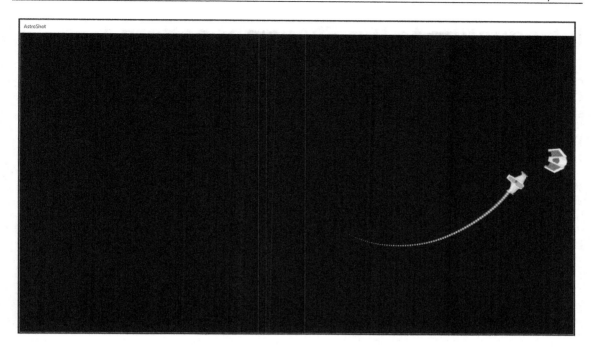

As you can see, our ship now has a trail following behind it. Each part is a particle!

Why memory is still an issue

The particle system that we are currently showing is probably running well enough on some computers, but note that a large number of the variables that we have created hold data that will never change once we've initialized them. Now, generally in programming we would mark a variable that wouldn't change as `const`, but we don't set the variable until we read from a file. We could potentially make the variables static, but there's also the chance that we may want to have more particle systems in the future and I don't want to create an archetype for each one.

If we continue to spawn many particles, the memory that it takes up will increase and we will be wasting valuable space in memory that we could be using for other purposes. To solve this issue, we will employ the Flyweight pattern.

Introduction to the Flyweight pattern

The Gang of Four states that a Flyweight is a shared object that can be used in multiple contexts simultaneously. Similarly to flyweight in boxing, which is the lightweight boxing category, we can have a lighter object that can be used in different places in our system simultaneously.

While not used terribly often nowadays, the Flyweight pattern can be very helpful in scenarios when memory is constrained.

A Flyweight will consist of two parts: the intrinsic state and the extrinsic state. The intrinsic state is the part that can be shared. The extrinsic state is modified based on the context it's being used in and, as such, cannot be shared.

Let's take a look at a UML diagram to see a closer look:

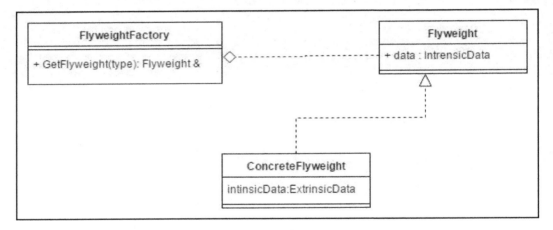

We have the **FlyweightFactory** class, which is used to manage the Flyweights. Whenever we request one, we will either give one that's been created or create a new one ourselves.

The **Flyweight** object itself has data that is of whatever type is needed, as long as it won't change depending on the object that we're working with.

Finally, we have the **ConcreteFlyweight**, which acts as our extrinsic information that can access and use our **Flyweight** via the **FlyweightFactory**.

Transitioning to ParticleSystems

So with that in mind, what we will do is separate the information that will be shared by each particle, which we will call a `ParticleSystem`:

```
// Abstract class for us to derive from
class ParticleSystem
{
public:
  float lifeTime;
  M5Vec2 startScale;
  float endScale;

  // Pure virtual functions
  virtual void Init(M5Object * object) = 0;
  virtual void Update(M5Object * object, float dt, float lifeLeft) = 0;

  float Lerp(float start, float end, float fraction);

};
```

The class acts as our intrinsic state, which is shared. Since the starting scale, end scale, and lifetime of our object never change, it makes sense for these variables to be shared instead of each object having one. In our previous example, we only had one particle system, but we may want the ability to have more as well, and it's when we start using it that some of the benefits of the Flyweight pattern become even more apparent. That's why we gave this class two virtual functions: `Init` and `Update`. We can have our extrinsic state call these functions, giving the function information about the particular object we're dealing with, and then we can modify it using these properties.

Creating different system types

Let's add a new type of particle system in addition to our current one that doesn't move. Let's call it `Moving` and our previous one, `Static`. To differentiate between the two, let's add an `enum`:

```
enum ParticleType
{
  PS_Static,
  PS_Moving
};
```

We can now modify the original `ParticleComponent` class, by removing the previously created variables and instead including a reference to the kind of `ParticleSystem` we wish to use:

```
class ParticleComponent : public M5Component
{
public:
  ParticleComponent();
  virtual void Update(float dt);
  virtual M5Component* Clone(void);
  virtual void FromFile(M5IniFile& iniFile);
  bool activated;
  float lifeLeft;

private:
  ParticleType particleType;
};
```

The `ParticleComponent` class acts as our extrinsic state, holding information about how much time it has left and the properties from the `M5Component` class, such as a reference to the object we want to create.

At this point, we need to create two classes to refer to each of these:

```
class StaticParticleSystem : public ParticleSystem
{
  void Init(M5Object * obj);

  void Update(M5Object *, float, float);

};

class MovingParticleSystem : public ParticleSystem
{
  void Init(M5Object * obj);

  void Update(M5Object *, float, float);

};
```

Developing the ParticleFactory

We need some way for our `ParticleComponent` to access this information. With that in mind, we will make use of the Factory design pattern that we learned about in Chapter 5, *Decoupling Code via the Factory Method Pattern*, and create a `ParticleFactory` class:

```
class ParticleFactory
{
public:
   static int objectCount;
   static std::map<ParticleType, ParticleSystem *> particleSystems;

   // Getting our Flyweight
   static ParticleSystem & GetParticleSystem(ParticleType type);
   ~ParticleFactory();
};
```

This `ParticleFactory` class is what we use to manage the creation of these Flyweights and to ensure that, if the object is already located in our map, we will return it. Otherwise, we will create a new object to be able to access it. I also added an `objectCount` variable to help us know how many objects currently exist and to verify that no memory leaks are occurring.

The `ParticleSystems` variable is of type map, which is actually one of my favorite containers in the `stl` and can be considered an *associative array*. By that, I mean instead of memorizing numbers in order to access certain indexes of an array, you can use a different type, such as a `string`, or in this case, an `enum`.

For more information on the map container, check out
`http://www.cprogramming.com/tutorial/stl/stlmap.html`.

After this, we will need to define the two static variables:

```
#include <map>

// Define our static variables
int ParticleFactory::objectCount = 0;
std::map<ParticleType, ParticleSystem *> ParticleFactory::particleSystems;
```

Using the ParticleFactory

Next, we will need to adjust our previously created Particle archetype and component to reflect these changes.

First, we want to change our `.ini` file. Since the `Particle` object is meant for all particle types, instead of having the properties being set there, we will instead set a base type for us to use:

```
posX   = 0
posY   = 0
velX   = 0
velY   = 0
scaleX = 2.5
scaleY = 2.5
rot    = 0
rotVel = 0
components =  GfxComponent ParticleComponent

[GfxComponent]
texture = particle.tga
drawSpace = world

[ParticleComponent]
type = Moving
```

This simplifies the particle object itself, but it's for a good cause. We will now update the code of the `ParticleComponent` class as follows:

```
/******************************************************************
****/
/*!
Construtor for ParticleSystem component.  Sets default values
*/
/******************************************************************
****/
ParticleComponent::ParticleComponent() :
  M5Component(CT_ParticleComponent)
{
}


/******************************************************************
****/
/*!
Takes care of the particle system, decrease lifetime and adjust scaling.
Will mark for destruction if needed.
```

```
\param [in] dt
The time in seconds since the last frame.
*/
/***************************************************************
****/
void ParticleComponent::Update(float dt)
{
  // Decrease our life by the change in time this frame (delta time, dt)
  lifeLeft -= dt;

  ParticleFactory::GetParticleSystem(particleType).Update(m_pObj, dt,
lifeLeft);

  // If there is no life left, destroy our object
  if (lifeLeft <= 0)
  {
    m_pObj->isDead = true;
  }

}
```

In this instance, you'll notice that instead of modifying the scale and/or movement being done here, we use the `ParticleFactory` to update our code based on the `particleType` property:

```
/***************************************************************
****/
/*!
Clones the current component and updates it with the correct information.

\return
A new component that is a clone of this one
*/
/***************************************************************
****/
M5Component * ParticleComponent::Clone(void)
{
  ParticleComponent * pNew = new ParticleComponent;
  pNew->m_pObj = m_pObj;
  pNew->particleType = particleType;

  ParticleSystem & system =
      ParticleFactory::GetParticleSystem(particleType);
  system.Init(pNew->m_pObj);
  pNew->lifeLeft = system.lifeTime;
  return pNew;
}
```

Here, we call the `Init` function for our particle system based on its type from the factory:

```
/******************************************************************
****/
/*!
Reads in data from a preloaded ini file.

\param [in] iniFile
The preloaded inifile to read from.
*/
/******************************************************************
****/
void ParticleComponent::FromFile(M5IniFile& iniFile)
{
  // Get our initial particle type
  std::string particleTypeText;
  iniFile.SetToSection("ParticleComponent");
  iniFile.GetValue("type", particleTypeText);

  if (particleTypeText == "Static")
  {
    particleType = PS_Static;
  }
  else if(particleTypeText == "Moving")
  {
    particleType = PS_Moving;
  }

}
```

We are now going to set our particle type based on what is marked on the `ini` file.

But, of course, now that we are using the `GetParticleSystem` function, we need to implement it for our code to compile:

```
/******************************************************************
****/
/*!
Used to get our Flyweight object and access the shared properties of the
particles.

\param type
What kind of particle we want to get access to

*/
/******************************************************************
****/
ParticleSystem & ParticleFactory::GetParticleSystem(ParticleType type)
```

```
{
  // If our object exists, return it
  if (particleSystems.find(type) != particleSystems.end())
  {
    return  *particleSystems[type];
  }

  ParticleSystem * newSystem = nullptr;

  // Otherwise, let's create one
  switch (type)
  {
  case PS_Static:
    newSystem = new StaticParticleSystem();
    newSystem->endScale = 0;
    newSystem->lifeTime = 1.5;
    newSystem->startScale = M5Vec2(2.5, 2.5);

    particleSystems[PS_Static] = newSystem;

    objectCount++;
    break;

  case PS_Moving:
    newSystem = new MovingParticleSystem();
    newSystem->endScale = 0;
    newSystem->lifeTime = 1.5;
    newSystem->startScale = M5Vec2(2.5, 2.5);
    particleSystems[PS_Moving] = newSystem;
    objectCount++;
    break;
  }

  return *newSystem;

}
```

In this script, we make use of the `particleSystems` map that we talked about earlier. The first thing that we do is check if there is an object in the map that has our `ParticleType` in it. If not, then we need to create one. In this case, I added a `switch` statement that will assign different values depending on the value mentioned in the `case` statement, but you could easily read these values from a text file in a similar manner to how files are read for archetypes. You'll notice that we are calling new in order to create these, so we will need to call `delete` on them as well in order to avoid any memory leaks. To accomplish this, I've added in a destructor for the `ParticleFactory` class:

```
/*********************************************************************
****/
/*!
Deconstructor for the ParticleFactory. Removes all of the elements in
ourparticleSystems map

*/
/*********************************************************************
****/
ParticleFactory::~ParticleFactory()
{
   for (auto iterator = particleSystems.begin();
      iterator != particleSystems.end();
      iterator++)
   {
     // iterator->first = key
     // iterator->second = value
     delete iterator->second;
   }

}
```

Finally, we need to write the implementations for our different `ParticleSystems`:

```
/*********************************************************************
****/
/*!
Will give you the percentage of the fraction from start to end

\param start
What value to start from

\param end
What value to end from

\param fraction
What percentage of the way we are from start to finish
```

```
*/
/*******************************************************************
****/
float ParticleSystem::Lerp(float start, float end, float fraction)
{
  return start + fraction * (end - start);
}
```

The `Lerp` function does the same for either particle type, so it's fine the way it was:

```
/*******************************************************************
****/
/*!
Used to initialize the particle system and set any parameters needed

\param obj
A reference to the object

*/
/*******************************************************************
****/
void StaticParticleSystem::Init(M5Object * obj)
{
  obj->vel = M5Vec2(0, 0);
}


/*******************************************************************
****/
/*!
Used to update the particle system. Called once per frame

\param m_pObj
A reference to the object

\param dt
Amount of time that has passed since the previous frame

\param lifeLeft
The amount of lifetime the object has left

*/
/*******************************************************************
****/
void StaticParticleSystem::Update(M5Object * m_pObj,
    float /*dt*/, float lifeLeft)
{
  // Change our size based on where we want it to be
  float currentPercentage = 1 - (lifeLeft / lifeTime);
```

```
    m_pObj->scale.x = Lerp(startScale.x,
        startScale.x * endScale, currentPercentage);
    m_pObj->scale.y = Lerp(startScale.y,
        startScale.y * endScale, currentPercentage);
}
```

The static version of the `Init` and `Update` functions will just set our velocity to 0 so we don't move:

```
/****************************************************************
****/
/*!
Used to initialize the particle system and set any parameters needed

\param obj
A reference to the object

*/
/****************************************************************
****/
void MovingParticleSystem::Init(M5Object * obj)
{
  obj->vel = M5Vec2(M5Random::GetFloat(-1, 1),
    M5Random::GetFloat(-1, 1)) * 10;
}

/****************************************************************
****/
/*!
Used to update the particle system. Called once per frame

\param m_pObj
A reference to the object

\param dt
Amount of time that has passed since the previous frame

\param lifeLeft
The amount of lifetime the object has left

*/
/****************************************************************
****/
void MovingParticleSystem::Update(M5Object * m_pObj, float /*dt*/, float
lifeLeft)
{
  // Change our size based on where we want it to be
  float currentPercentage = 1 - (lifeLeft / lifeTime);
```

```
    m_pObj->scale.x = Lerp(startScale.x,
        startScale.x * endScale, currentPercentage);
    m_pObj->scale.y = Lerp(startScale.y,
        startScale.y * endScale, currentPercentage);
}
```

For our moving particle system, we will set our velocity to a random number in the x and y axis, causing a nice explosion effect!

Now, instead of creating a copy of this data each time, we will have one copy that we will access, as shown in the following screenshot:

As we play, you'll notice that we now have a new particle system working and it's doing its job quite well.

Summary

Over the course of this chapter, we learned about particles and how they can be used in order to improve the polish of our game project. We learned how we can implement a particle system inside of the Mach5 engine, and then learned about the Flyweight pattern and how it can be used effectively in order to reduce the memory usage on your projects. We saw how to do this by making use of the Factory pattern too, while making it a lot easier for us to create new particle system types as well. Keeping this in mind, it will be a lot easier in the future to break apart pieces of your programs that stay consistent and only create additional variables when you need to!

Moving forward, in the next chapter we will dive into graphics and the concepts needed to understand how our code will affect moving and animating game objects.

11

Understanding Graphics and Animation

Over the last 10 chapters, we have dived deeply into some of the most popular design patterns. The goal of each chapter was to understand and solve some common problems that everyone encounters when creating games. Along the way, we have created component-based game objects with flexible State-based, decision-making capabilities. We have created core engines such as the `StageManager` and `ObjectManager` using the Singleton pattern, so that communication between game objects, components, and engines is incredibly simple. We also looked at Object Pools and the Flyweight pattern, which allow our game to use memory more efficiently.

In this chapter, we will focus on graphics. However, we will not be focusing on how to implement a graphics engine. That would require more than a single chapter. Instead we will focus on concepts that need to be understood, regardless of which graphics **Application Programming Interface (API)** you use.

Graphics is a large part of any game engine and is very likely the performance bottleneck of the game. However, whether we are using DirectX, OpenGL, or some other graphics API, we must understand what is happening behind the scenes. We shouldn't fall into the trap of thinking that just because we didn't write the graphics API, there are no design decisions to be made.

Chapter overview

This chapter is a little different than the ones before because it isn't focused on a design pattern. Instead we will focus on the low-level details of graphics so we can better understand how our code affects moving and animating our game objects.

First, we will look at how a computer monitor works. We will dive into the details of pixels and screen resolutions. We will look at how pixels are drawn on screen as well as understand the concept of tearing, learn why we hear so much about **frames per second (fps)**, and why games try to achieve 30 or 60 frames per second.

Next, we will look at timing in games. We will learn why we want a consistent frame rate. We will also look at what happens when our frame rate isn't consistent and how we can ensure that our frame time stays consistent throughout the game.

Your objectives

- Learn how computer monitors work and what a refresh rate is
- Learn about double buffering and why it is used for graphics
- Learn about time-based movement and animation, and why we want a consistent frame rate

Introduction to monitor refresh rates

These days, flat screen **Liquid Crystal Display (LCD)** monitors are very common. However, to understand refresh rates and double buffering, we need to understand how older monitors display an image. Along the way, we will learn about common graphics terms, such as pixels and screen resolution:

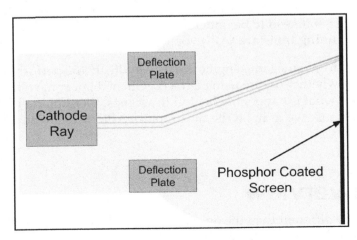

Figure 11.1 - Simplified cathode ray tube diagram

Cathode Ray Tube (CRT) monitors contain screens with millions of tiny red, green, and blue phosphor dots. These dots glow for a short time when struck by an electron beam that travels across the screen to create an image. The *cathode* is a heated filament inside a vacuum sealed glass tube. The *ray* is a stream of electrons generated by an electron gun, which is directed by magnetic deflection plates. By adjusting the magnetic field of the plates, the electron beam can be moved around and adjusted to strike every part of the screen.

The screen is coated with phosphor, an organic material that glows for a short time when struck by the electrons. It contains many groups of red, green, and blue dots. By varying the intensity of the electron ray on each dot, different colors can be generated. For example, with red, green, and blue fired at maximum strength, the color white is produced.

Since one color is produced by a group of red, green, and blue dots, the maximum number of these dot groups limits how many colors can be displayed horizontally or vertically. The diagonal distance between two dots of the same color is known as the dot pitch.

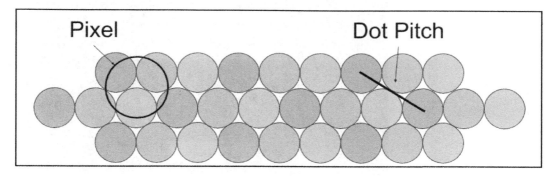

Figure 11.2 Close of view of the Pixel on the screen

What is a pixel?

A pixel, or *picture element*, is the basic unit of programmable color on a computer image or display. It is better to think about a pixel as a logical unit, rather than a physical unit. This is because the size of a pixel depends on the current resolution of the display screen. At the maximum resolution of the screen, one pixel maps exactly to one dot group. This means the size of a pixel at maximum resolution is equal to the dot pitch. Smaller resolutions will use more than one dot group to create a single color.

The resolution of the screen is the number of horizontal pixels multiplied by the number of vertical pixels, and is usually written as **width x height**. For example, a 640 x 480 resolution means that the screen is 640 pixels wide and 480 pixels high for a total of 307,200 pixels. Of course, the color data for each pixel must be stored in computer memory, so a higher resolution uses more pixels and more memory. For example, if each pixel used one byte of memory, our 640 x 480 display would need 300 kilobytes of memory. A 1280 x 1024 display would need 1.25 megabytes. Let's have a look at the following screenshot:

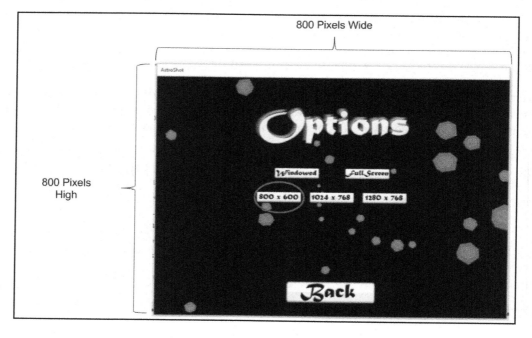

Figure 11.3 - An example of 800 x 600 screen resolution

The location in RAM that stores pixel color information is called the **framebuffer**. The framebuffer is written by a program and then transmitted to the monitor. The cathode ray interprets the pixel color and fires the electron ray at the proper intensity. The deflection plates direct the electron beam to the proper dot groups on the phosphor screen.

In the examples above, the size of each pixel was only 1 byte. However, a pixel can be, and usually is, more than 1 byte. As computers get faster and memory gets cheaper, we can use more bits per pixel. With 8-bit color, red and green each use 3 bits or a total of 8 levels of color each, while blue only uses 2 bits or 4 levels. This totals 256 possible colors for each pixel.

16-bit color, or high color, offers a few different options. One possibility is 4 bits for each red, green, and blue. These 4 bits provide 16 levels for each color for a total of 4,096 (16 x 16 x 16) colors, with an optional 4 bits for transparency. Another possibility is 5 bits per color and 1 bit for transparency for a total of 32,768 colors. Finally, a total of 65,536 can be achieved with 5 bits for both red and blue, and 6 bits for green.

True color is defined at 8 bits per color. This means that red, green, and blue all have 8 bits, or 256 possible color levels. If 24 bits are used, we get a total of 16,777,216 possible colors. These days, 32 bits per pixel are often used. The last 8 bits are for transparency. The transparency allows for different levels of blending with the background colors. This allows for a total of 4,294,967,295 colors per pixel.

The size of the framebuffer is calculated by multiplying the resolution and the numbers of bytes per pixels (color depth). For a game using a 1280 x 1024 display, we need 1280 x 1024 x 4 bytes, or 5 megabytes for the framebuffer. This might not seem like much considering that modern computers often have 8 to 12 gigabytes of RAM. However, it is worth remembering that if we are updating every pixel on screen, we are updating 1,310,720 pixels, or 5,242,880 bytes of data. This is assuming we only fill in each color one time and don't need to blend with overlapping colors.

The horizontal and vertical blank

The display is updated by reading data from the framebuffer and updating in sequence, starting from the left to right and top to bottom. We can think about this exactly as if we were iterating through a 2D array in C or C++. At the end of each scan line, the electron gun is adjusted to point at the start of the next scan line. Another adjustment must be made after the last pixel is lit so the beam can start again at the top.

The time it takes for the electron gun to move from the rightmost pixel of scan line X to the leftmost pixel of scan line $X + 1$ is called the **Horizontal Blank Interval**. This is because the electron gun is blanked, meaning that it is outputting zero electrons during this interval. This is to prevent pixels from being lit up while traveling from scan line to scan line. Similarly, the time it takes for the electron gun to move from the end of the last scan line back up to the first scan line is called the **Vertical Blank Interval**. Again, the electron gun is blanked to prevent pixels from being lit up while traveling back to the top scan line. The Vertical Blank Interval is a short period where the entire display has been updated and the framebuffer is not currently being read by the display:

```
//Example code drawing 640x480 display
//Including H Blank Interval and V-Blank Interval
for(int h = 0; h < 480; ++h)
{
```

```
    for(int w = 0; w < 640; ++w)
    {
        //Sets pixel color and moves to next pixel
        SetPixel(framebuffer[h][w]);
    }
//Resets to start of scan line and moves down one row
    ResetHorizontal();
}
//Resets to first pixel of first scan line
ResetVerticle();
```

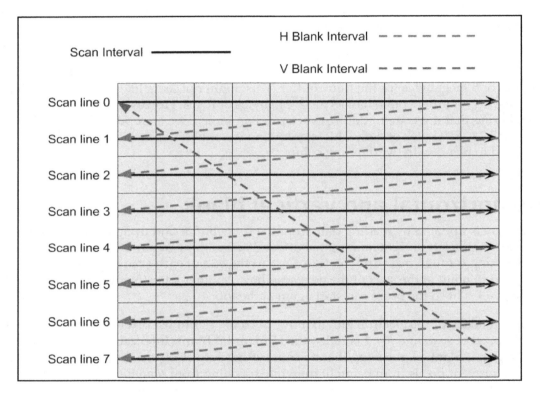

Figure 11.4-Showing the movement pattern of the electron gun including the Horizontal and Vertical Blank Intervals

The phosphor dots on the screen are only lit up for a short period, so the electron gun must constantly relight them. The gun moves from left to right and top to bottom many times per second to refresh each pixel and display the correct image. If this process is too slow, the display will appear to flicker.

Refresh rate

The number of times per second a monitor refreshes the display is known as it's vertical refresh rate, or just refresh rate. The refresh rate of a monitor is measured in hertz (Hz). So, a monitor that can refresh the display 30 times per second has a refresh rate of 30 Hz. Many monitors refresh at 60 Hz, however, it is becoming common to see monitors with refresh rates of 120 Hz or even 240 Hz.

It is important to realize that the refresh rate of a monitor has nothing to do with the performance of a game or program. Having a monitor with a higher refresh rate will not improve the frame rate of a game, unless the game itself can support higher frame rates. The number of times a program updates the framebuffer is measured in frames per second or fps, and is completely independent from the number of times the monitor refreshes. When these two numbers are out-of-sync, the display will not look correct. Let's look at the problem of when the frames per second is less than the refresh rate:

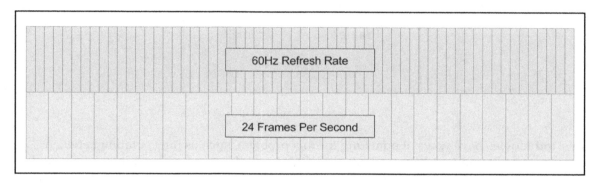

Figure 11.5 Comparing FPS versus Refresh Rate

These days, TV shows and movies are often displayed at 24 frames per second while the TV sets and monitors have a typical refresh rate of 60 Hz. In *Figure 11.5*, we have taken one second and split it into 60 red bars on the top to represent our refresh rate and 24 blue bars on the bottom to represent the frames of a movie. Each red bar represents the 1/60th of a second that the frame will be on screen. Each vertical dark red line represents when the monitor is refreshed.

As you can see, the refresh periods do not line up properly with the frames of the movie. In *Figure 11.5* we can clearly see that **Frame 1** is on screen for 3/60th (or 1/20th) of a second, while **Frame 2** is only on screen for 2/60th (or 1/30th) of a second. **Frame 1** is on screen longer than the original 1/24th of a second and **Frame 2** is on screen less. Since the frames are not on screen for an equal amount of time, the video seems jittery. While this may not seem like much of a difference, some people are sensitive enough to notice a slight speeding up and slowing down effect:

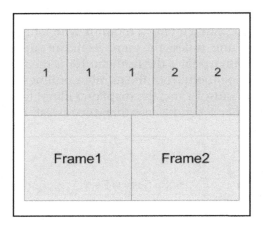

Figure 11.6 - Example of refresh rate and frames per second Out-Of-Sync

TVs and movies have ways of adjusting for this problem, such as interpolating between frames. Since **Frame 1** and **Frame 2** are already known, it is easy to blend, interpolate, and generate intermediate frames before displaying them. However, that doesn't help us when our games are out-of-sync with the monitor.

Since games are interactive, the player's actions determine what will be displayed next on screen. The details of **Frame 2** are determined by player input in response to **Frame 1**. This means that the contents of the framebuffer must be generated each frame, it can't be known ahead of time.

In the above example, we were simplifying a little by pretending that writing to the framebuffer was instantaneous. Of course, this isn't true. Even though the next frame of a movie is already known, it still takes time to write to the framebuffer. Unless we can copy to the framebuffer completely during the Vertical Blank Interval, we will need to write to the framebuffer while the display is being drawn on screen.

If we can time everything correctly, we can always write a pixel just after the electron gun has read it. However, if we are out-of-sync with the electron gun, eventually there will be a point when we haven't written the pixel for the current frame and the electron gun reads the old value. Let's look at this problem up close:

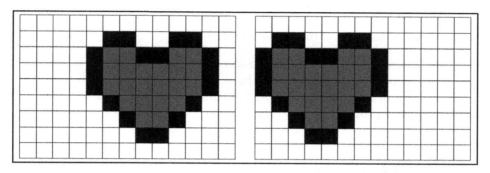

Figure 11.7 - Start position (Left) and End position (Right) in the framebuffer

Figure 11.7 shows what we would like to see on screen. The left image is the position of a game object in frame 1. The right image is the ending position after the object has moved. These are two discrete points in time that we want to show. However, if the display is reading the pixels as we are writing them to the framebuffer, we can see a tearing effect if we haven't finished writing the current frame:

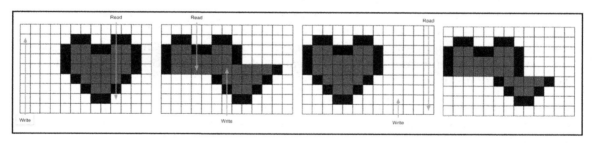

Figure 11.8 - Example of tearing in the framebuffer

As we can see in *Figure 11.8*, the first image is correct. We are writing to a pixel after the display has read it. In the second image, the pixel being read has almost caught up to the pixel that is being written. At this point, the framebuffer contains half of each image. The third image shows that the display has overtaken the write pixel. The correct pixels have been written but they were written too late. The fourth image shows what the user would see on screen. Since the display read faster than the pixels could be written, the image looks as if it has been torn in half. This effect is known as tearing.

Tearing occurs when our frames per second and our refresh rate are out-of-sync. Unfortunately, it can be very difficult to get these two values perfectly aligned, and being a little off will cause some tearing. To solve this problem, we need to write out an entire frame of pixels before the display reads them.

Double buffering

The solution to our read/write problem is double buffering. Double buffering is exactly what it sounds like. Instead of using only one framebuffer, we will use two: one for reading and one for writing. Of course, since we now have two framebuffers, we need twice the memory. For a 1280 x 1024 display using 4 bytes per pixel, we need 5 megabytes per framebuffer for a total of 10 megabytes.

Everything up to this point could have been implemented in software by using operating system commands. However, as displays started requiring more memory and more complex images, special hardware was created. Modern graphics cards can contain gigabytes of memory used for framebuffers, textures, 3D triangle meshes, and much more. They can also contain hundreds or even thousands of cores to transform 3D points into pixel data simultaneously.

It is important to understand this because, as a programmer, you don't need to implement double buffering yourself. It is implemented at a hardware level and our games will be double buffered automatically by using a 3D graphics API such as DirectX or OpenGL. However, we still need to understand how this process works so we can understand the implications to our frame rate.

The back buffer

As we said, double buffering works by using two framebuffers so that we are never setting pixels on the same buffer that is being used for the display. The framebuffer that is currently being displayed is called the front buffer or primary buffer, and the framebuffer that we are drawing to is called the back buffer or secondary buffer.

When drawing is completed on the back buffer, the buffers are swapped so that the back buffer is now the front buffer and the front buffer is now the back buffer. Of course, the buffers themselves are not swapped. Instead, pointers to the buffers are swapped. The monitor has a pointer to one buffer and is currently reading it. The graphics card has a pointer to another buffer that it uses for all draw operations. This pointer swap, or page flipping as it is sometimes called, is much faster than copying data from the back buffer to the front buffer:

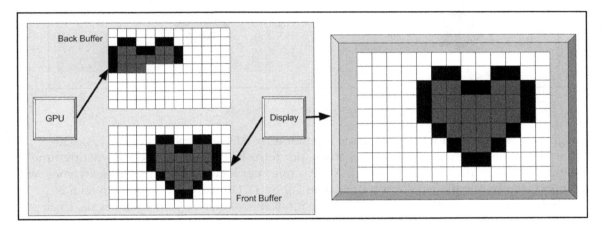

Figure 11.9 - Example of double buffering

As you can see in the next two images, the display can read the front buffer while the graphics processing unit or GPU draws to the back buffer. However, there is nothing about double buffering that has prevented tearing. We have prevented drawing to the same buffer that is being displayed but, if we swap buffers in the middle of a screen refresh, we will still have tearing. This is an important first step in solving the tearing problem. However, before we solve it, let's talk about what happens when we are out-of-sync with the monitor refresh rate because we are generating too many frames per second:

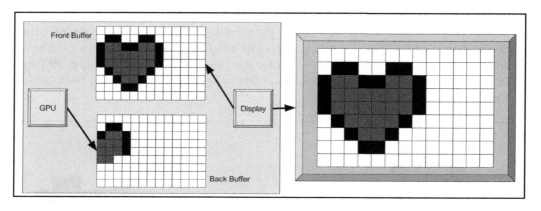

Figure 11.10 - Double buffering after the page flip

Imagine the situation in which our game is generating 90 frames per second. This is 30 frames more than we need to achieve 1 frame per refresh. This means we are wasting time creating frames that will never be seen. At 90 frames per second, one third of the frames will never be seen by the player. As you can see in *Figure 11.11*, every third frame, which is highlighted in green, will be skipped because it falls between two refresh intervals. Even more frames will be skipped if we are updating at 120 fps or more:

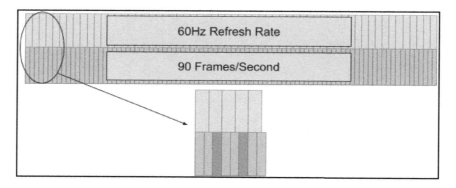

Figure 11.11 - Comparing 60 Hz refresh with 90 fps

At 90 frames per second, every frame takes 1/90th of a second to complete. From the player's perspective, the third frame that gets shown (which is really our fourth frame) has been updated for a total of 1/45th of a second, or double the amount of time. Just like with the movie at 24 fps, this can cause a jittery effect that some players may notice because all objects will appear to have moved twice as far.

When updating this many times per second, these time slices are very small. It is possible that they are so small that they may go unnoticed by the player. The real problem with skipping frames is that our game is doing work that it just doesn't need to. Since the frame will never be seen by the player, there is no point in wasting game time generating it.

It is worth pointing out that only the graphics part of the update is wasted. It is perfectly fine to update input, AI, or physics faster than the monitor can refresh. In fact, physics will be more accurate if the time step is smaller. We just want to really emphasize that there is absolutely no reason to draw frames faster than the monitor's refresh rate.

For most games this is never a problem. The usual solution to having a high frame rate is to do more work and make your game more interesting. If your game is too fast, draw more particles, have more enemies, calculate more accurate physics, or just do more physics effects. If you find that your game runs faster than 60 fps, your game probably isn't the best it could be. Again, there is no reason to draw more frames per second than can appear on screen.

VSync

So now we have seen both situations where our frame count is out-of-sync with our refresh rate. In both cases we can have tearing, and in the case of a very high frame rate, we are wasting CPU/GPU cycles that could be used to improve our game. We want to avoid tearing. We want to be in-sync with the monitor refresh. How can we solve this problem?

The solution is the Vertical Blank Interval. Remember that the Vertical Blank Interval is when the electron gun is repositioning itself from the last pixel on the display back to the first pixel. During this short period, the entire display has been drawn and the front buffer isn't being used. This period is too short to copy all the contents of the back buffer to the front buffer. However, it is long enough to swap the pointers, which is how the page flipping mechanism works.

Modern computer monitors and TVs can send a signal back to the computer when the Vertical Blank, Interval, or V-Blank occurs. The graphics card waits until a V-Blank before swapping the buffers after the back buffer is completely drawn. This guarantees that there will never be tearing because parts of different frames can never be read in a single refresh.

As we said, double buffering is implemented at the hardware level. This is also true of synchronizing with the Vertical Blank Interval. By using a 3D graphics API such as DirectX or OpenGL, you get this for free. This V-Blank syncing or VSync is an option that must be enabled when initializing graphics. Once VSync is turned on, we don't need to worry about tearing. Additionally, the game will never generate more than one frame per monitor refresh because the graphics card will always wait for the V-Blank signal before swapping the buffers.

Syncing with the refresh rate of the monitor is a great way to prevent tearing. If a game can update 60 or more times a second, the back buffer and the front buffer will always be able to swap and we will have a smooth, tear-free game. However, we haven't talked about what happens if the back buffer isn't ready to be swapped because the frame is taking longer than $1/60^{th}$ of a second to complete.

It is important to understand that the front and back buffers do not swap automatically every time the V-Blank signal arrives. Instead, the swap is performed at the request of the programmer. A function call is made to tell the graphics card that a new frame is prepared and the buffers should be swapped. This swap will happen immediately if VSync is turned off. However, if the VSync is turned on, the graphics card will wait for the V-Blank signal to arrive, no matter how long that is. If our update is just 1/100th slower, meaning a frame takes $1/59^{th}$ of a second to complete, we will miss the V-Blank and need to wait for the next one.

Since the current frame wasn't ready, the monitor displays the previous frame again. The same frame will be on screen for 1/30th of a second. Since the back buffer must wait to be swapped until the next V-Blank, our game can't start working on the next frame. Our game is idle while waiting for the V-Blank. This means that if our game is using VSync and it can't achieve 60 frames per second, our frame rate will drop down to 30 frames per second. If our game can't achieve 30 frames per second, our frame rate will take 3/60th of a second, or 20 fps.

For some programmers and some games, achieving 30 frames per second is perfectly fine. To implement more beautiful effects or more accurate physics, dropping to 30 frames per second might be an important trade off. Everyone must decide for their own game what is right. However, many players simply do not like 30 frames per second. Players often say they can notice more jittery movement and more importantly, they notice input lag.

Remember, if we can't achieve our goal of 60 fps, the graphics card must wait for the next V-Blank before returning from the swap call. This means that our game can't process physics, AI, or even input. The player is seeing half as many frames on screen, which means objects are moving more each frame. Additionally, input is now being gathered from the player once every 1/30th of a second instead of once every 1/60th of a second. While this may not seem like much, for fast, twitch response games such as *First Person Shooters*, this can be too long.

Figure 11.12 shows an example of the contents of both the front and back buffers in a VSync scenario where a game can't update at the same rate as the monitor. The display refreshes every 1/60th of a second or every 0.0167 seconds. The game can update every 1/50th of a second or every 0.02 seconds. In the image below, the monitor refreshes are colored red or green. The red refreshes are when the game frame isn't ready and so the previous frame is displayed. The green refreshes are when the game frame is ready and so the buffers are swapped.

The blue represents when the game frame is completed. This doesn't mean that the new frame is instantly displayed. This is because the graphics card waits until the next refresh to swap buffers. It is important to understand that the game doesn't update every 1/50th of a second for the same reason. Instead, each game update is 1/50th of a second after the last buffer swap:

Time (in Seconds)	Back Buffer	Front Buffer/Display
0.0	Frame 1 (Working)	Blank
1/60 = 0.0167(Monitor Refresh MISS)	Frame 1 (Working)	Blank
1/50 = 0.02(Game Update)	Frame 1 (Done)	Blank
2/60 = 0.0334(Monitor Refresh OK)	Frame 2 (Working)	Frame 1
3/60 = 0.0501(Monitor Refresh MISS)	Frame 2 (Working)	Frame 1
2/60 + 1/50 = 0.0534(Game Update)	Frame 2 (Done)	Frame 1
4/60 = 0.0668(Monitor Refresh OK)	Frame 3 (Working)	Frame 2
5/60 = 0.0835(Monitor Refresh MISS)	Frame 3 (Working)	Frame 2
4/60 + 1/50 = 0.0868(Game Update)	Frame 3 (Done)	Frame 2
6/60 = 0.1002(Monitor Refresh OK)	Frame 4 (Working)	Frame 3

Figure 11.12 - Showing contents of back buffer and front buffer when using VSync

Triple buffering

Turning on VSync in our games can improve the look of our graphics because we are guaranteed that tearing will never occur. Unfortunately, if our game frame isn't completed in time for the next refresh, the graphics card waits until the next V-Blank to swap buffers. This is true even if our game misses the refresh by only 1/100th of a second. If our frame is off by this short amount, our fps drops to 30. This is because the content of the back buffer hasn't been swapped yet, so we can't start drawing the next frame.

It would be nice if we could start drawing the next frame while still waiting for the V-Blank signal. To do this, we would need an extra framebuffer to draw to while we are waiting. This is exactly how triple buffering works.

For triple buffering we have a total of three framebuffers. For a 1280 x 1024 display with 4 bytes per pixel we would need a total of 15 megabytes. However, by using this extra memory, we will always have a framebuffer to draw to, so we should always be able to hit our fps goal.

In triple buffering, we have our primary and secondary buffers just like before but now we have a tertiary buffer as well. We start out drawing to the back buffer. If we finish the current frame before the refresh, we can immediately move on to drawing on the tertiary buffer. If we don't finish in time for the refresh we will need to wait for the next refresh, just as we did in the double buffer scenario. However, we only need to miss a refresh this one time. Once the back buffer is filled, we can immediately start working on the tertiary buffer. Either way, once the back buffer has been filled, we will be forever one frame ahead. The primary buffer will be used for display, the secondary buffer will be ready and waiting for the swap, and the graphics card will use the tertiary buffer for drawing:

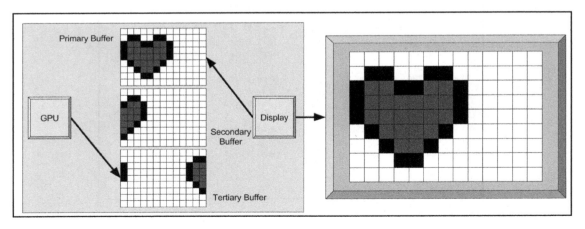

Figure 11.13 - Drawing to the tertiary buffer before the V-Blank

When the V-Blank occurs, all the buffers can swap if they are ready. The secondary buffer becomes the primary buffer for display. The tertiary buffer becomes the secondary buffer and waits to be displayed. Finally, the primary buffer becomes the new tertiary buffer used for drawing:

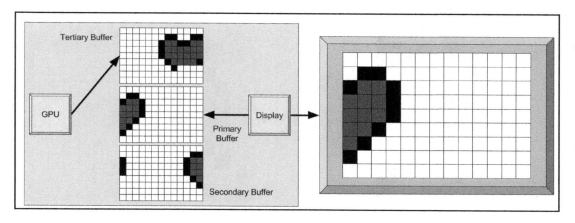

Figure 11.14 - Scenario 1 - Swapping all buffers after V-Blank

If the tertiary buffer isn't ready at the time of the V-Blank, it continues drawing until the frame is completed and can swap with the original primary buffer without waiting for the V-Blank:

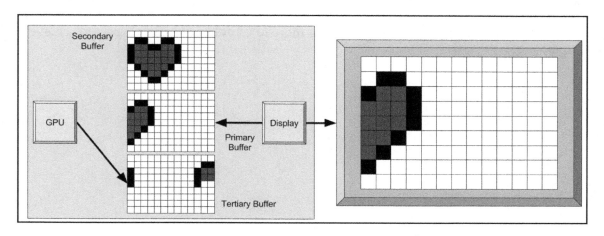

Figure 11 15 - Scenario 2A - Swap primary and secondary buffers after V-Blank

By using triple buffering, we solve the problem of suddenly dropping from 60 fps to 30 fps when there are a few slow frames in our game. This also allows us to avoid the drop to 30 fps and (almost) consistently achieve 60 fps in cases which are just below 60, since we don't need wait until a V-Blank before we can start the next frame:

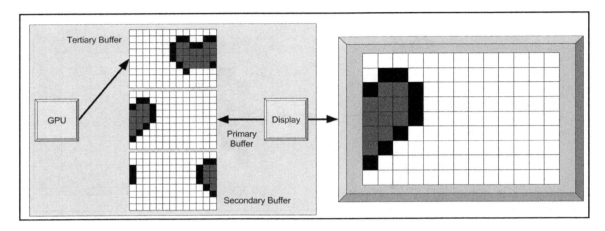

Figure 11.16 - Scenario 2B - Swap secondary and tertiary buffers when drawing is complete

However, as you can see in *Figure 11.17*, triple buffering still has the chance to miss a refresh. Using the same case as before where our game updates at 1/50th of a second and the monitor refreshes at 1/60th of a second, we still miss one out of every six refreshes. It should come as no surprise that the lower our frame rate, the more refreshes we will miss. If each of our frames takes 1/30th of a second or more to complete, we can't expect to achieve 60 fps:

Time (in Seconds)	Tertiary Buffer	Back Buffer	Front Buffer/Display
0.0	Idle	Frame 1 (Working)	Blank
1/60 = 0.0167(Monitor Refresh MISS)	Idle	Frame 1 (Working)	Blank
1/50 = 0.02(Game Update)	Frame 2 (Working)	Frame 1 (Done)	Blank
2/60 = 0.0333(Monitor Refresh OK)	Frame 2 (Working)	Idle	Frame 1
2/50 = 0.04 (Game Update)	Frame 3 (Working)	Frame 2 (Done)	Frame 1
3/60 = 0.05(Monitor Refresh OK)	Frame 3 (Working)	Idle	Frame 2
3/50 = 0.06(Game Update)	Frame 4 (Working)	Frame 3 (Done)	Frame 2
4/60 = 0.0667(Monitor Refresh OK)	Frame 4 (Working)	Idle	Frame 3
4/50 = 0.08(Game Update)	Frame 5 (Working)	Frame 4 (Done)	Frame 3
5/60 = 0.0833(Monitor Refresh OK)	Frame 5 (Working)	Idle	Frame 4
5/50 = 0.10(Game Update)	Frame 6 (Working)	Frame 5 (Done)	Frame 4
6/60 = 0.10(Monitor Refresh OK)	Frame 6 (Working)	Idle	Frame 5
7/60 = 0.117(Monitor Refresh MISS)	Frame 6 (Working)	Idle	Frame 5
6/50 = 0.12(Game Update)	Frame 7 (Working)	Frame 6 (Done)	Frame 5
8/60 = 0.133(Monitor Refresh OK)	Frame 7 (Working)	Idle	Frame 6
7/50 = 0.14(Game Update)	Frame 8 (Working)	Frame 7 (Done)	Frame 6

Figure 11.17 - Example of missing the refresh when using triple buffering

Even though triple buffering allows us to avoid tearing while maintaining 60 fps, there is an important factor that you must consider before deciding to use it. There is a two-frame delay between what has just appeared on screen and the current frame being processed. Triple buffering allows us to process another frame in the tertiary buffer while the next frame in the secondary buffer is waiting to be displayed, all while the primary buffer is currently being displayed. This puts us one frame ahead so we can avoid frame rate drop, but lowers response time for the player.

If the jump button is pressed, the player avatar won't appear to jump until the current frame and the next frame have been displayed. This is because the frame being processed, including game object responses to input, is being put into the tertiary buffer. If the primary and secondary buffers are on screen for 1/60th of a second each, there will be an effective lag of 1/30th of a second for player input. The game will look like it is running at 60 fps (because it is), physics will behave like the game is running at 60 fps (because it is), but because of the input delay, the game will feel like it is running at 30 fps.

It is up to you to decide what is best for your game. Many players may not even notice the input lag because the time slice is so small. However, for fast twitch games such as first person shooters, or games that require precision control for jumping or steering, this may be unacceptable.

LCD monitors

We spent a lot of time talking about how Cathode Ray Tube monitors work. This was important so that we could understand the Vertical Blank interval and how it relates to double buffering. However, it seems a little outdated since LCD and LED monitors are much more common. We aren't going to discuss how these two types of monitors work, because it has no effect on our frame rate. What is important is that these monitors fake the V-Blank signal. Even though they don't need to refresh and have no electron gun, they still send a fake signal to the graphics card. This way, your program can still be locked with the *refresh* rate of the monitor.

Time-based movement and animation

We have covered a lot so far in this chapter. We have been looking at the frame rate and refresh rate so we can understand how it relates to what is displayed on screen. However, the frame rate of a game has the chance to impact upon every engine of the game. It can even affect testing and debugging during development.

At the start of a game's development, the game logic isn't very complicated and the unit count is very low. For this reason, it is common to see thousands of frames per second. As development continues, this frame rate will slowly drop to hundreds and then (hopefully) settle around 60 frames per second. Imagine if there was some game logic to spawn an enemy once every 10 frames. Depending on where we are in the development cycle, we might be spawning six or sixty enemies every second. This makes the game very hard to test and debug because it is not consistent.

What makes this problem even more interesting is that, even within a single play session, nothing is guaranteed to be consistent. At the start of the game, there are no enemies, so the frame rate might be as high as 600 frames per second. This means we are spawning 60 enemies every second. After five seconds, there are 300 enemies on screen which makes both physics and graphics very slow. Suddenly our frame rate might drop to 30 frames per second, slowing down enemy creation. As the player kills more enemies, the frame rate will rise, causing enemies to spawn faster and dropping the frame rate again.

This problem isn't just limited to affecting game logic. It is a problem that affects anything that changes between frames. In particular, it is going to affect animation of game objects. Here, animation refers to anything that changes within a game object. This includes changing a game object's texture over time, which is how we typically think of animation. However, it also includes moving, scaling, rotating, or changing the color and transparency of an object over time. To understand this problem more, let's look at how moving a unit every frame can adversely affect game development.

Frame-based movement

When we want to move a game object, the simplest way to do it is to update the position at a constant rate. This can work fine for some games. However, for simulating cars, spaceships, or even gravity, it won't look correct. For now, we will use this method as an example then look at physics-based movement a little later. Since we are just updating the object's position, the code to move the player to the right will look like this:

```
//Move the player to the right
//This is just an example
//A game should not be hard-coded like this
pos.x += 5;
```

It is worth noting that the value 5 is not measured in inches or meters; it is in game units. Game units are completely arbitrary and are dependent on the size of objects in the game. 3D modeling programs will allow you to set up units of scale for your models. If the same units are used for every model, and the models are not scaled in the game world, it would be possible to think about the game world in terms of those units. However, it is more common to consider everything as arbitrary game units. The amount an object moves on the screen depends on the size of the object and how far it is from the camera. If everything looks and feels correct in relation to everything else, it is OK.

In the preceding example, assuming the size and camera distance are fixed, the distance on screen that the player moves will be completely dependent on our frame rate. For example, if we are getting 1,000 frames per second, as we might early in the development, our player will move 5,000 game units in the x direction. Later in development, when we are getting 100 frames per second, our player will only be moving 500 units in the x direction. To get the same amount of movement, we would need to change the speed of the player:

```
//Move the player to the right
//This is just an example
//A game should not be hard-coded like this
pos.x += 50;
```

As we get closer to finishing the game, we might only be getting 60 frames per second. This would mean the speed of the player would need to be changed again. To get the same amount of movement, the player speed would need to be 83.333 fps. Unfortunately, even after the game is released, we still have the same problem. As graphics cards and CPUs become faster, our game's frame rate will increase, meaning the player will be moving too fast. The gameplay experience is completely dependent on the computer hardware.

This problem could be solved by enabling VSync. As we saw earlier, using VSync will effectively lock our frame rate to the refresh rate of the monitor. This would guarantee that our frame rate has a maximum value. However, the player will be very confused when they upgrade to a 120 Hz monitor and the player moves twice as fast. Additionally, if the game runs slow for a few frames, VSync causes our frame rate to drop down to 30 fps. Suddenly, the player is moving at half speed. Even when using VSync, our gameplay experience is completely dependent on the hardware.

Obviously using frame-based movement is not the way to go. As our frame rate rises and falls, we must change the movement speed of the player. As we said, this same problem occurs in all animation. Rotational speed of spinning objects, scale, fade speed of particles, and the number of frames to display a texture before changing it all must be constantly modified during development, and still won't be consistent across different hardware.

Time-based movement

Instead of using frame-based movement, it is much better to base our movement on time. Time is guaranteed to be consistent throughout development and on all hardware, now and in the future. Whether our game is updating at three frames per second or 3,000 frames per second, one second will always be equal to one second.

Using time-based movement is great because it allows us to use equations that have existed for hundreds of years. We don't need to reinvent the wheel to simulate velocity and acceleration. As we said before, using a constant speed to move the player is OK for some games, but that isn't how real physics works. Cars and spaceships do not accelerate instantly. Gravity pulls you down faster and faster the longer you fall.

When you toss a ball to a ten year old child, they don't need to do complex calculations to catch the ball; they can just do it. Similarly, in a semi-realistic simulation, players will expect the physics to behave *normally*. To simulate realistic or semi-realistic physics in our game, we should understand how to incorporate velocity and physics into our movement.

We can calculate an object's velocity by subtracting the initial position of an object from the final position of an object, and dividing that by how long the displacement took. Another way to say this is that velocity is equal to the change in the position divided by the change in time. We can use this to create an equation that we can put in our code:

$$\frac{dx}{dt} = v$$

$$\frac{x1 - x0}{dt} = v$$

$$x1 - x0 = v * dt$$

$$x1 = x0 + v * dt$$

We can also calculate an object's acceleration by subtracting the initial velocity from the final velocity and dividing by the change in time. Acceleration is change in velocity over change in time:

$$\frac{dv}{dt} = a$$

$$\frac{v1 - v0}{dt} = a$$

$$v1 - v0 = a * dt$$

$$v1 = v0 + a * dt$$

We also know from Newton's second law of motion that force equals mass times acceleration. This also means that acceleration is equal to force divided by mass:

$$F = ma$$

$$a = F/m$$

What this means is that, if we know the current position, velocity, and the forces acting on an object, we can find the position and velocity at some point in the future. In our games, we can use these three equations to simulate motion:

$$x1 = x0 + v * dt$$

$$v1 = v0 + a * dt$$

$$a = Force/mass$$

The first two of these three equations are called Euler (pronounced Oiler) Integration. Specifically, it is called explicit Euler. In code, it will look something like this:

```
float EulerIntegration(float pos, float vel, float accel,
    float totalTime, float dt)
{
  float time = 0.0f;
  while (time < totalTime)
  {
    pos += vel * dt;
    vel += accel * dt;
    time += dt;
    }
  return pos;
}
```

The inner loop of this code is a close example of how we will use this in a game. Every frame, we will update our position and velocity based on dt and the acceleration. The velocity calculated in this frame will be used to update the position of an object in the next frame. Outside of a loop, these equations make perfect sense. If we are traveling at 55 mph down the freeway, after one hour we expect to be 55 miles further down the road. Similarly, if we are accelerating at 8 miles per hour per second then after ten seconds we expect to have a velocity of 80 mph.

However, inside of the loop we will have some errors. Euler Integration is only accurate if acceleration and velocity are held constant. In the preceding code example, velocity is changing every time through the loop, so it is inaccurate proportional to the square of the step size. That means that the larger the step, the more error it has.

Let's compare Euler Integration with one of the Kinematics Equations of motion to see how this error effects our results. The Kinematics Equation that we will test with is:

$$p = \frac{1}{2}at^2 + v_o t + p_0$$

Where p is our new position, p^0 is our initial position, v^0 is our initial velocity, a is our acceleration and t is our time.

Let's assume that our starting position is 0 and our starting velocity is 0. Typically, in physics equations, acceleration is in units of seconds per second instead of hours per second. So, let's say we are accelerating at 20 feet per second for 10 seconds. After 10 seconds, our car will have traveled 500 feet:

$$distance = \frac{1}{2}at^2 + 0 + 0$$

$$distance = \frac{1}{2}(10)*(10*10)$$

$$distance = 10*(100)$$

$$distance = 1000$$

So, the Kinematics equations say we will be 1000 feet from where we started after 10 seconds. Using this same data, let plug it into our Euler Integration function. We will be integrating every second for 10 seconds:

```
Time = 0   pos =     0.00 vel =     0.00
Time = 1   pos =     0.00 vel =    20.00
Time = 2   pos =    20.00 vel =    40.00
Time = 3   pos =    60.00 vel =    60.00
Time = 4   pos =   120.00 vel =    80.00
Time = 5   pos =   200.00 vel =   100.00
Time = 6   pos =   300.00 vel =   120.00
Time = 7   pos =   420.00 vel =   140.00
```

```
Time = 8  pos =  560.00 vel = 160.00
Time = 9  pos =  720.00 vel = 180.00
Time = 10 pos =  900.00 vel = 200.00
```

Euler Integration says we will be 900 feet from where we started. The Kinematics Equation and Euler Integration are 100 feet off. This is after only 10 seconds. The longer we integrate for, the more the error. Of course, we already explained why we have this problem. The error is proportional to the time step. If we use a smaller time step, we will have a smaller error. Luckily our game will be updating more than one frame per second. Let's integrate again, but let's use some more realistic time steps. Let's choose values for 30 fps, 60 fps, and 120 fps. These give us time steps of .0333, .0167, and .008 respectively:

```
 dt = 1.000000   pos = 900.00
 dt = 0.033333   pos = 996.67
 dt = 0.016667   pos = 998.33
 dt = 0.008333   pos = 1000.83
```

As you can see, by using a smaller time step, we come closer to the matching result. At 120 fps, we are pretty accurate but, even at 60 fps, we have calculated a few feet off. Unfortunately, even the Kinematics equations are not accurate unless acceleration is held constant.

For many games, Euler Integration will be all you need. The errors are small enough that players may not notice. This of course depends on gameplay and the frame rate. Creating an extremely accurate physics integrator is beyond the scope of this book.

 If your game requires very accurate physics, check out Verlet Integration or RK4 Integration at:
https://en.wikipedia.org/wiki/Verlet_integration,
https://en.wikipedia.org/wiki/Runge-Kutta_methods

Whichever integration method you choose, it will be better and more reliable than using frame-based movement. The important thing to remember is that anything that changes in the game must use time. This includes rotations, which can use similar rotational velocity and rotational acceleration if you want. It also includes scaling over time, animating a texture over time, and even changing color and transparency. This will give our game a very consistent look and feel, as well as making it easier to test and debug throughout development.

Summary

We have really covered a lot in this chapter. Now, you know more about how computer monitors work than you probably ever wanted. In this chapter, we dived into the nitty gritty details of framebuffers and how pixels are colored on screen. We saw that having a frame rate that was out-of-sync with the monitor can cause tearing. We also looked at how double buffering and using VSync can fix this problem. Unfortunately, we also saw that VSync can cause problems of its own. We also looked at triple buffering and saw the pros and cons there. In the end, there is no perfect answer. There will always be some trade-off. You must either accept tearing or the possibility of a drastic drop in frame rate due to VSync.

Finally, we finished this chapter by looking at how our frame rate affects the rest of our gameplay code. Specifically, we looked at physics and animation, and learned that we must use time-based physics and animation for a more consistent look and feel in our game.

In the next chapter, we are going to get away from the low-level details and look at the big picture of programming. This includes our coding philosophy and why we care about high quality code. We will look at a few tips and tricks that can help make developing a game less of a headache, as well as covering a few specific things in the Mach5 engine that aren't patterns but can still make your coding life much easier.

12
Best Practices

Learning to program is difficult for many reasons, but learning to program games is even more difficult, specifically because there are so many different systems and object types that need to interact with each other. Throughout this book, we have covered some of the most important design patterns to make those interactions as simple as possible. Each chapter focused explicitly on a design pattern to help make coding easier. However, buried within each paragraph and code sample are core ideas and techniques to help make our design easier to read and maintain.

These *Best Practices* can sometimes be found in other books; however, programming books often strive to teach you the grammar of a language, as opposed to style, design, and organization. Even books about design patterns may gloss over these fundamental techniques. Since they are so fundamental, it is easy to forget they are not necessarily explicitly discussed everywhere. That leaves you, the reader, forced to read dozens of books and scour the Internet for blog posts that talk about these fundamentals. Worse, you are required to spend hours and hours writing code with the feeling that it could be better, but you just don't understand why it isn't.

Of course, all those things will happen anyway. Part of being a programmer is constantly reading books like this. You should be looking for ways to improve by reading blogs and you will write code that you consider garbage after six months. This is all part of becoming better. It is our hope in writing this book that you can understand and incorporate these fundamentals into your programs sooner rather than later.

Chapter overview

In this chapter, we will be focusing on fundamental ideas and techniques that will improve your code and improve your game. These ideas come from years of programming as well as years of teaching. If these seem simple and obvious, that is great. However, we chose these topics because they are things that we, the authors, struggled with early on, or that our students struggled with.

Your objectives

Over the course of this chapter we will be discussing a number of topics:

- Learn fundamental code quality techniques
- Learn and understand the uses of the const keyword
- Learn how iteration can improve your game and code design
- Learn when to use scripting in a game

Learning fundamental code quality techniques

The process of moving from beginner to expert programmer can be challenging. In the beginning, you must learn not only the rules of the language, but also how to use a compiler and understand the error messages. Moreover, you are trying to solve increasingly difficult programming problems while following what might seem like arbitrary rules for writing *good* code. Most novice programmers are focused on solving a given problem, as opposed to making the code look nice. To many, it seems worthless to spend time making the code look clean, because it will almost certainly be deleted after writing it. Even more experienced programmers may ignore code style in the rush to complete an assignment or finish a project.

This is bad for a few reasons. First, well-written code is easier to read and understand. It almost certainly has fewer errors, and is more efficient than code that is carelessly mixed together and never polished. Just as we discussed in earlier chapters, the time you spend upfront making sure the code is bug free, is time you won't need to use debugging it later. The time you spend making sure the code is readable and easy to maintain is time you won't need to spend later making changes or deciphering old code.

Second, good programming style is a matter of habit. Taking time to read and debug your code is slow at first. However, the more you improve your code, the easier and quicker it becomes. Eventually, you will develop habits and writing quality code will happen naturally. Without this habit, it can be easy to push style aside and worry about it later. However, the code that is being written is almost always sloppy, and it can be hard to find the time later to go back and improve it, since there is always another deadline approaching. With good habits, you will be able to write clean, readable code in even the most time-constrained situations, such as an interview or a fast-approaching deadline.

Finally, at some point in the future you will almost certainly be working with other programmers. This could be a small team of two or three, or perhaps in a company with dozens of programmers all over the world. Even if you understand what your code is doing, it is not guaranteed that your teammates will. Writing code that is hard to understand will lead to people using your code incorrectly. Instead, strive to make your code easy to use and hard to break. Take pride in how much other people love to use your code, your teammates and boss will thank you. You will appreciate it if your teammates do the same thing. At some point, you will be required to maintain other programmers code after they have left the job. You will find it much easier to do if they wrote high quality code, so write code that will be easy to work with after you have left.

Over the next few pages, we will cover some very basic but extremely important code quality tips. As we said, these come from years of reading programming, as well as teaching. Use these techniques for every single line of code that you write. Think about these techniques for every piece of code that you read. Doing so will help you form great habits.

Avoid magic numbers

Hard coding number literals into code is generally considered a bad idea. The problem with using a number literal instead of a named constant is that the purpose of that number is unknown to the reader. The number appears in code as if by magic. Consider the following code:

```
M5Object* pUfo = M5ObjectManager::CreateObject(AT_Ufo);
pUfo->pos.x    = M5Random::GetFloat(-100, 100);
pUfo->pos.y    = M5Random::GetFloat(-60, 60);
```

It is hard to know why those four numbers were chosen. It is also hard to know how the program will be changed if the values are modified. Code like this would be much more readable and maintainable if the named constants or variables were used:

```
M5Object* pUfo = M5ObjectManager::CreateObject(AT_Ufo);
pUfo->pos.x    = M5Random::GetFloat(minWorldX, maxWorldX);
pUfo->pos.y    = M5Random::GetFloat(minWorldY, MaxWorldY);
```

After the change, it is much easier to understand that the position of the new UFO is being randomly placed within the world. We can understand that if we change the values, the possible starting location of the UFO would either be outside of the world, or constrained to a tighter rectangle around the center of the world.

Besides being hard to read and understand, using magic numbers makes the code hard to maintain and update. Let's say we have an array of size 256. Every loop that needs to manipulate the array must hardcode the value 256. If the array size needs to be larger or smaller, we would need to change every occurrence of 256. We can't simply do a *find and replace* because it is very possible that 256 is used elsewhere in the code for a completely different reason. Instead we must look through every occurrence of the number and make sure that we are changing the code correctly. If we miss even one, we could create a bug. For example, if we are changing the size of the array to something smaller, such as 128. Any loops that still treat the array as if it had size 256 will cause undefined behavior:

```
int buffer[256];

//Some function to give start values
InitializeBuffer(buffer, 256);

for(int i = 0; i < 256; ++i)
std::cout << i " " << std::endl;
```

As before, it is better to use a named constant instead of a magic number. The constant is more readable and easy to change because it only needs to be changed in one place. It is also less likely to cause bugs because we are only changing the values associated with the array. We won't accidentally change a value we shouldn't or miss a value that we should change:

```
const int BUFFER_SIZE = 256;
int buffer[BUFFER_SIZE];

//Some function to give start values
InitializeBuffer(buffer, BUFFER_SIZE);

for(int i = 0; i < BUFFER_SIZE; ++i)
std::cout << i " " << std::endl;
```

Another important reason we don't want to use magic numbers is that they are inflexible. Throughout this book, we try to emphasize the benefits of reading data from a file. Obviously, if you hardcode a value, it can't be read from a file. In the preceding example, if BUFFER_SIZE ever needs to be changed, the code needs to be recompiled. However, if the size of the buffer is read from a file at runtime, the code only needs to be compiled one time and the program will work for buffers of all sizes:

```
int bufferSize = GetSizeFromFile(fileName);

//we can Dynamically allocate our buffer
int* buffer = new int[bufferSize];

//Some function to give start values
InitializeBuffer(buffer, bufferSize);

for(int i = 0; i < bufferSize; ++i)
std::cout << i " " << std::endl;

delete [] buffer;//We must remember to deallocate
```

In the preceding example, we must remember to deallocate the buffer. Remember, that probably won't be the usual case because for arrays, we could always use an STL vector. The more general case is that we are reading ints or floats from a file. These could be used for anything from screen resolution, to player speed, or even the time interval between spawning enemies.

As with all rules, there are a few exceptions or special cases where it might be fine to hardcode numbers. The numbers 0 and 1 are generally consider OK. These might be used as the initialization values for ints or floats, or just the starting index for an array.

Your goal is to make your code as readable and flexible as possible, so a named constant is almost always going to be better than a hardcoded number. Do your best to make sure that your code can be understood by others. Your code isn't more readable if you simply have a variable named ZERO or TWO, so you should use your best judgment and perhaps ask another programmer if you think the meaning is unclear.

White space

When thinking about high quality code, white space is often forgotten. Maybe this is because white space isn't code you write, but is instead the empty space between your code. However, if you don't use white space correctly, your code will be unreadable. When we say white space, we are talking about the spaces, tabs, newlines, and blank lines within your program. How you use these can make the difference between code that is easy to read and maintain, and code that will give you nightmares. Here is a piece of code with very little thought about white space:

```
RECT rect={0};
int xStart= 0,yStart = 0;
rect.right=s_width;rect.bottom=s_height;
s_isFullScreen = fullScreen;
if (fullScreen) {DEVMODE settings;
settings.dmSize = sizeof(settings);
EnumDisplaySettings(0, ENUM_CURRENT_SETTINGS, &settings);
settings.dmPelsWidth=(DWORD)s_width;
settings.dmPelsHeight = (DWORD)s_height;
settings.dmFields = DM_BITSPERPEL|DM_PELSWIDTH|DM_PELSHEIGHT;
s_style = FULLSCREEN_STYLE;
if (ChangeDisplaySettings(&settings
,CDS_FULLSCREEN) !=DISP_CHANGE_SUCCESSFUL) {
s_isFullScreen = false;s_style = WINDOWED_STYLE;
ChangeDisplaySettings(0, 0);M5Debug::MessagePopup(
"FullScreen is not supported. "
"You are being switched to Windowed Mode"); }
}
  else {ChangeDisplaySettings(0, 0); s_style = WINDOWED_STYLE;}
```

The preceding code is perfectly acceptable to the compiler. For humans, however, the code above is hard to read because there is no line spacing, no indentation, and no consistency. Of course, this is an extreme example, but throughout our years of teaching, we have seen examples of code with just as little thought to style and formatting. When code looks like the example above, the quality of comments and identifier names doesn't matter because the entire block is difficult to read. Compare the preceding code with the following version, which has tried to code for human readability:

```
/*Set window rect size and start position*/
RECT rect    = { 0 };
rect.right   = s_width;
rect.bottom  = s_height;
int xStart   = 0;
int yStart   = 0;

/*save input parameter to static var*/
```

```
    s_isFullScreen = fullScreen;

    /*Check if we are going into full screen or not*/
    if (fullScreen)
    {
      /*Get the current display settings*/
      DEVMODE settings;
      settings.dmSize = sizeof(settings);
      EnumDisplaySettings(0, ENUM_CURRENT_SETTINGS, &settings);

      /*Change the resolution to the resolution of my window*/
      settings.dmPelsWidth  = static_cast<DWORD>(s_width);
      settings.dmPelsHeight = static_cast<DWORD>(s_height);
      settings.dmFields     = DM_BITSPERPEL | DM_PELSWIDTH  |
                              DM_PELSHEIGHT;

      /*Make sure my window style is full screen*/
      s_style = FULLSCREEN_STYLE;

      /*If we can't change, switch back to desktop mode*/
      if ( ChangeDisplaySettings(&settings, CDS_FULLSCREEN) !=
                              DISP_CHANGE_SUCCESSFUL )
      {
        s_isFullScreen = false;
        s_style        = WINDOWED_STYLE;
        ChangeDisplaySettings(0, 0);
        M5Debug::MessagePopup("FullScreen is not supported. "
        "You are being switched to Windowed Mode");
      }
    }
    else /*If we are already fullscreen, switch to desktop*/
    {
      /*Make sure I am in windows style*/
      s_style = WINDOWED_STYLE;
      ChangeDisplaySettings(0, 0);
    }
```

While the preceding example is by no means the perfect example of high quality code, it is certainly more readable and maintainable than the first example. When it comes to real-world programs and programmers, there is no such thing as perfect. Every programmer has their own style, which really means that every programmer believes their style is the easiest to read. However, as you read more code, you will notice that there are certain common elements to code that is readable. Let's look at some of those elements now.

Indentation

Block statements such as loops and conditionals should have the sub statements indented. This easily shows the program intent to the reader. The number of spaces to indent is less important than the indentation itself. Most programmers agree that 2 to 4 spaces are sufficient for readability. The most important thing is to be consistent with your spacing. Likewise, the placement of the starting curly brace isn't important, (although you can find some interesting arguments online), but it is important to consistently place it in the same location:

```
//This shows the purpose of the statement
if (s_isFullScreen)
{
   s_style = FULLSCREEN_STYLE;
   SetFullScreen(true);
}

//So does this
if (s_isFullScreen) {
   s_style = FULLSCREEN_STYLE;
   SetFullScreen(true);
}


//This does not shows the intent of the statement
if (s_isFullScreen)
{
s_style = FULLSCREEN_STYLE;
SetFullScreen(true);
}
```

It is important to remember that in C++, indentation has no meaning to the compiler. Without the curly braces, loops and conditionals will execute only one statement. For this reason, some programmers will always use the curly braces, regardless of how many sub statements are needed:

```
/*Single statement in the loop*/
while (i++ < 10)
   printf("The value of i is %d\n", i);


/*After adding another statement*/
while (i++ < 10)
   printf("The value of i is %d\n", i);
   printf("i squared is %d\n", i*i);
```

The preceding example is misleading, because only the first statement will be part of the loop. It can be a common mistake when writing a loop or conditional to forget to add curly braces after adding a second statement. For this reason, some programmers will use curly braces even for single statement loops and conditionals. The idea is that the code is more readable and easier to maintain, and so it is less prone to error.

Blank lines and spaces

As we said before, how you use white space will determine how readable your code is. Using indentation for code blocks is one way to show the logical structure of a program. Another good way to show this is by using blank lines. Just as a good piece of writing is separated into paragraphs, a good piece of code should be separated into some form of logical grouping. Group statements together that logically go together. Put blank lines between the groups to improve the readability:

```
//Save position and scale to variables for readability.
const float HALF = .5f;
M5Vec2 halfScale = m_pObj->scale * HALF;
M5Vec2 pos = m_pObj->pos;
//Get world extents
M5Vec2 botLeft;
M5Vec2 topRight;
M5Gfx::GetWorldBotLeft(botLeft);
M5Gfx::GetWorldTopRight(topRight);
//If object is outside of world, mark as dead
if (pos.x - halfScale.x > topRight.x || pos.x +
    halfScale.x < botLeft.x || pos.y - halfScale.y
    > topRight.y || pos.y + halfScale.y < botLeft.y)
{
  m_pObj->isDead = true;
}
```

The preceding code has no blank lines so the code seems to run together. It is hard to look at it and understand what the code is doing because your brain tries to understand all of it at once. Even though there are comments, they don't really help because they blend in to the rest of the code. The if statement is also hard to read because the conditions are separated by how they fit on the line instead of a logical alignment. In the following code, we have added some blank lines to separate the logic grouping of the statements:

```
//Save position and scale to variables for readability.
const float HALF = .5f;
M5Vec2 halfScale = m_pObj->scale * HALF;
M5Vec2 pos       = m_pObj->pos;

//Get world extents
```

```
M5Vec2 botLeft;
M5Vec2 topRight;
M5Gfx::GetWorldBotLeft(botLeft);
M5Gfx::GetWorldTopRight(topRight);

//If object is outside of world, mark as dead
if ( pos.x - halfScale.x > topRight.x ||
     pos.x + halfScale.x < botLeft.x  ||
     pos.y - halfScale.y > topRight.y ||
     pos.y + halfScale.y < botLeft.y  )
{
   m_pObj->isDead = true;
}
```

By using line breaks to group related statements together, the code is separated into easy to understand chunks. These chunks help the reader understand which statements should logically go together. In addition, the comment at the beginning of each chunk sticks out much more and explains in English exactly what will happen will contained in the chunk.

Complicated conditional statements should be separated and aligned based on the conditions so they are easier to understand. In the preceding code, each of the four conditions are aligned in the same way. This gives a clue to the reader as to how the condition will be executed. Using parentheses along with aligning the code further adds to the readability:

```
//If object is outside of world, mark as dead
if (( (pos.x - halfScale.x) > topRight.x ) ||
    ( (pos.x + halfScale.x) < botLeft.x  ) ||
    ( (pos.y - halfScale.y) > topRight.y ) ||
    ( (pos.y + halfScale.y) < botLeft.y  ))
{
   m_pObj->isDead = true;
}
```

Using parentheses isn't just helpful in conditionals. All complicated expressions should be grouped together with parentheses. Of course, everyone's definition of complicated differs, so a good general rule is *, /, and % are executed before + and -; use parentheses for everything else. In addition to being clearer to the reader, this will ensure that the code is executing exactly as you expect. Even if you understand all the C++ rules of precedence and associativity, your teammates may not. Parentheses don't cost anything but can improve the readability, so feel free to use them as much as possible to show the intent of the code.

Comments and self-documenting code

Comments and documentation seem to be more controversial than they should be. On the one hand, many people think comments and documentation are a waste of time. Writing documentation literally takes time away from writing code, and reading comments takes time away from reading the code. In addition, some people think that comments just don't help because they can become out of date, and don't explain anything that isn't already in the source code. The worst situation with comments is when they are flat out wrong. In that case, the code would be better off without the comments at all.

However, there are few things more frustrating than debugging code written by someone that didn't add comments. Even debugging your own code just a few months after you have written it can be difficult. In the end, the time spent writing and updating comments is time that you and your teammates won't need to spend deciphering code.

While the use of comments may be controversial, writing clean, high-quality code is important to everyone. As we have already seen earlier, using white space well can improve readability. However, white space alone doesn't make code readable. We really want our code to be self-documenting. Here is an example of that, which is difficult to read, even though it has proper white space:

```
void DoStuff(bool x[], int y)
{
  for(int i = 0; i < y; ++i)
    x[i] = true;

  x[0] = x[1] = false;

  int b = static_cast<int>(std::sqrt(y));

  for(int a = 2; a <= b; ++a)
  {
    if(x[a] == false)
      continue;

    for(int c = a * 2; c < y; c += a)
      x[c] = false;
  }
}
```

Can you tell what the algorithm is doing? Unless you happen to know this algorithm already, chances are that you may not understand the intent of the function. Comments would help here, but the bigger problem is the low quality of the identifiers. Good variable names provide a hint as to what they will be used for. The idea is that, with good variable names, you should be able to understand the code without the need for comments. This is how you make your code self-documenting:

```cpp
void CalculateSievePrimes(bool primes[], int arraySize)
{
  for(int i = 0; i < arraySize; ++i)
    primes[i] = true;

  primes[0] = primes[1] = false;

  int upperBound = static_cast<int>(std::sqrt(arraySize));

  for(int candidate = 2; candidate <= upperBound; ++candidate)
  {
    if(primes[candidate] == false)
      continue;

    int multiple = candidate * 2;
    for(; multiple < arraySize; multiple += candidate)
      primes[multiple] = false;
  }
}
```

Even if you don't understand every single line of the preceding code example, you can at least use the function name as a guide. The name CalculateSievePrimes is a big clue as to what the function is doing. From there you should be able to piece together what each line is doing. Names such as candidate, arraySize, and multiple are much more meaningful than a, b, and c. The best part about self-documenting code is that it can never be wrong, and never become out of date. Of course, the code can still contain bugs. It just can't be out of sync with the documentation, because the code is the documentation.

There are a few things that you can do to attempt to make the code self-documenting, as we said before. Good variable names are a start. The variable name should explain the exact purpose of the variable and they should only be used for that purpose. For Boolean variables, give a name that makes it obvious what true means. A name such as isActive is much better than simply active or activeFlag because the names gives a hint as to what true means for that variable.

Often there will be naming conventions that distinguish between types, local variables, constants, and static or global variables. Some of these naming conventions, such as using all capital letters for `const` variables, are very common and used by most programmers. Other naming conventions, such as beginning all static variable names with an `s_`, or adding a `p` at the beginning of pointers, are less common. Whether you think these styles look ugly or not, understand that they are there to help readability and make wrong code look wrong. The compiler will already catch some of the problems that these naming conventions aim to solve, but since they can still help readability they are worth considering.

When giving names to methods and functions, similar rules apply. Give a clear name that explains the purpose of the function. Make sure the function or method only has one purpose. Typically, the name should be an action. `CalculateSievePrimes` is a much clearer name than `SeivePrimes` or even just `Calculate`. As with Boolean variables, methods or functions that return Boolean values are often named with a hint. The name `IsEmpty` or `IsPowerOfTwo` are much more clear than `Empty` or `PowerOfTwo`.

Commenting

If the code is self-documenting, then why do we need to add comments at all? This is certainly the feeling of some programmers. When the comments aren't doing more than simply repeating the code, or when comments are out of date and difficult to update, then it is easy to understand why they feel that way. However, this is the opposite of what good comments should be.

Good comments should explain things that the code cannot. For example, copyright information, or author and contact information are things that can't be represented in code, but may be of use to the reader. Additionally, good comments do not simply repeat the code. The comment below is completely worthless. It adds nothing to the code:

```
//Assign START_VALUE to x
int x = START_VALUE;
```

Instead, good comments should explain the intent and purpose of the code. Even if you understand what a block of code is supposed to do, you can't know what the author was thinking when they wrote it. Knowing what the author was trying to accomplish can save you a lot of time when debugging someone else's code:

```
/***********************************************************/
/*!
Given an array of "arraySize" mark all indices that are prime as true.

\param [out] primes
```

```
The array to modify and Output.

\param [in] arraySize
  The number of elements in the array

\return
  None. Indices that are prime will be marked as true

*/
/******************************************************************/
void CalculateSievePrimes(bool primes[], int arraySize)
{
  /*Ensure array is properly initialized */
  for(int i = 0; i <size; ++i)
    primes[i] = true;

  /*Zero and One are never prime*/
  primes[0] = primes[1] = false;

/*Check values up to the square root of the max value*/
  int upperBound = static_cast<int>(std::sqrt(arraySize));

  /*Check each value, if valid, mark all multiples as false*/
  for(int candidate = 2; candidate <= upperBound; ++candidate)
  {
    if(primes[candidate] == false)
      continue;

    int multiple = candidate * 2;
    for(; multiple < arraySize; multiple += candidate)
      primes[multiple] = false;
  }
}
```

The comments above explain what the author was thinking while writing the code. They do not just repeat what the code is doing. Notice that some comments explain a single line, while other comments summarize entire code blocks. There aren't any hard rules about how many comments should be in your code. A rough suggestion is that every code block should have a comment explaining its purpose, with additional comments for more complex lines.

The comment blocks such as the one at the top of the method are the least likely to be used but they can serve an important purpose as well. Just as the section headers of this book help when you are scanning for something specific, function headers can help you when scanning a source code file looking for a specific function.

Functions headers can be very helpful because they summarize everything about the function without the need to look at the code. Anyone can easily understand the purpose of the parameters, return values, and even any exceptions that may be thrown. The best part is, by using a tool such as Doxygen, the header blocks can be extracted to make external documentation.

 Check out the Doxygen tool and documentation at
`http://www.stack.nl/~dimitri/doxygen/`.

Of course, these are the most difficult to write and maintain. It is comment blocks like these that often become out of date or are flat out wrong. It is up to you and your team if you want to use them. It takes discipline to keep up with them, but they can be worth it if you happen to be working on another programmer's code after they have left the team.

Learning and understand the uses of the const keyword

Using `const` is another area of programming that seems to be a little controversial. Some programmers argue that they have never had a bug where using `const` would have helped. Others feel that, since you can't guarantee that a `const` object won't be modified, it is completely worthless. The fact is that `const` objects can be modified. `const` is not magic. So, is `const` correctness still a good thing? Before we get into that, let's have a look at what `const` is.

When you create a `const` variable, you must initialize it. All `const` variables will be checked at compile time to make sure that the variable is never assigned a new value. Since it happens at compile time, it doesn't have an influence on the performance. These are a few benefits that we should consider. First, it improves readability. By marking a variable as `const`, you are letting the reader know that this variable is not supposed to change. You are sharing your intent about the variable and making your code self-documenting. `const` variables are also usually named in all capital letters, which further helps with readability. Second, since the variable is checked at compile time, there is no way for the user to accidently change the value. If someone tries to modify the variable, it will cause a compiler error. This is great for you if you were expecting the value to stay the same. This is great for the user if the modification was truly an accident.

Compiler errors should always be preferred over runtime. Anytime we can use the compiler to help us find problems, we should. This is the same reason that many programmers choose to set their compiler warnings to maximum and treat those warnings as errors. Time spent fixing a known compiler issue is time you won't have to spend finding the runtime error that it might cause.

Additionally, `const` variables should be preferred over C style `#define` macros. Macros are a blunt tool. Sometimes they may be the only tool for the job, but they are overkill for simple symbolic constants. Macros do a blind *find and replace*. Anywhere the symbolic constant is in the source code, the value will replace it. While these situations may be rare, they can also be frustrating. Since the values are replaced in the pre-processing phase, the source code is unchanged when you go to fix the problem.

The `const` variables, on the other hand, are part of the language. They follow all the normal language rules for types and operators. There is nothing mysterious happening. They are just variables that can't be reassigned:

```
int i1;            //No initialization, OK
int i2     = 0;    //Initialization, OK

const int ci1;     //ERROR: No initialization
const int ci2 = 0; //Initialization, OK

i1 = 10;           //Assignment, OK
i2 += 2;           //Assignment, OK

ci1 = 10;          //ERROR: Can't Assign
ci2 += 2;          //ERROR: Can't Assign
```

Const function parameters

Creating `const` variables as symbolic constants makes code more readable because we are avoiding magic numbers. However, `const` correctness is more than just creating symbolic constants. It is important to understand `const` in relation to function parameters.

It is important to understand the difference between these different function signatures:

```
void Foo(int* a);       //Pass by pointer
void Foo(int& a);       //Pass by reference
void Foo(int a);        //Pass by value
void Foo(const int a);  //Pass by const value
void Foo(const int* a); //Pass by pointer to const
void Foo(const int& a); //Pass by reference to const
```

The default behavior of C and C++ is to pass by value. This means that, when you pass a variable to a function, a copy is made. Changes made to function parameters do not modify the original variable. The function author has freedom to use the variable however they want, while the original variable owner can be sure that the values will remain unchanged.

That means, as far as the original variable owner is concerned, these two function signatures behave the same. In fact, the compiler doesn't make a distinction between these two when considering function overloading:

```
void Foo(int a);        //Pass by value
void Foo(const int a);  //Pass by const value
```

Since it is impossible for a pass by value variable to be modified when it gets passed to a function, many programmers do not mark these parameters as `const`. It can still be a good idea to mark them as `const`, because it signifies to the reader that the variable value shouldn't be changed. However, this type of parameter is less important to mark as `const` since it can't be changed.

What about when you want to pass an array to a function? Remember that one of the little quirks of C and C++ is the fact that arrays and pointers are sometimes treated similarly. When you pass an array to a function, a copy of the array is not made. Instead, a pointer to the first element is passed. One side effect of this default behavior is that the function can now modify the original data:

```
//A Poorly named function that unexpectedly modifies data
void PrintArray(int buffer[], int size)
{
   for(int i = 0; i < size; ++i)
   {
     buffer[i] = 0; //Whoops!!!
     std::cout << buffer[i] << " ";
   }
   std::cout << std::endl;
}
//Example of creating an array and passing it to the function
int main(void)
{
   const int SIZE  = 5;
   int array[SIZE] = {1, 2, 3, 4, 5};

   PrintArray(array, SIZE);
   return 0;
}
```

The output for the preceding code is as follows:

```
0 0 0 0 0
```

As you can see, there is nothing preventing the function from modifying the original data. The `size` variable in the function is a copy of `SIZE` in main. However, the `buffer` variable is a pointer to array. The `PrintArray` function is short, so finding this bug might be easy, but in a longer function that may pass the pointer to additional functions, this problem can be difficult to track down.

If the user wanted to prevent the function from modifying the data, they could mark array as const. However, they won't be able to use the `PrintArray` function, and they won't be able to modify the data either:

```
int main(void)
{
  const int SIZE  = 5;
  const int array[SIZE] = {1, 2, 3, 4, 5};//Marked as const

  array[0] = 0;//ERROR: Can't modify a const array

  PrintArray(array, SIZE);//Error: Function doesn't accept const
return 0;
}
```

Of course, sometimes the purpose of the function is to modify data. In that case, the user would just have to accept that if they wanted to use the function. With a name like `PrintArray`, the user probably expects that the data will be unchanged after the function call. Is the data modification on purpose or an accident? The user has no way of knowing.

Since the problem is with the poor function name, it is up to the function author to make the change. They can choose to make the name clearer, perhaps something such as `ClearAndPrintArray`, or fix the error. Of course, fixing the error doesn't prevent something like this from happening again, and it doesn't clarify the intent of the function.

A better idea would be for the author to mark buffer as a const parameter. This will allow the compiler to catch any accidents like the one above, and it will signal to the user that the function promises not to modify the data:

```
//Const prevents the function from modifying the data
void PrintArray(const int buffer[], int size)
{
for(int i = 0; i < size; ++i)
{
  //buffer[i] = 0; //This would be a compiler error
  std::cout << buffer[i] << " ";
```

```
    }
std::cout << std::endl;
}

int main(void)
{
  const int SIZE  = 5;
  int array[SIZE] = {1, 2, 3, 4, 5};

  array[0] = 0;//Modifying the array is fine

  PrintArray(array, SIZE);//OK. Can accept non-const
return 0;
}
```

As we said before, the `size` variable could also be marked as const. This would more clearly demonstrate that the variable shouldn't change, but it isn't necessary because it is a copy. Any modification of size will not change the value of `SIZE` in main. For this reason, many programmers, even the ones that strive for const correctness, do not mark *pass by value* parameters as const.

Const classes as parameters

We have now discussed the default behavior when passing arrays to functions. The compiler will automatically pass in a pointer to the first element of the array. This is good for both speed and flexibility. Since only a pointer is passed in, the compiler doesn't need to spend time copying a (possibly) large array. This is also more flexible, because the function can work with arrays of all sizes instead of just a specific size.

Unfortunately, when passing structs or classes to a function, the default behavior is *pass by value*. We say unfortunately, because this will automatically evoke the copy constructor, which may be expensive and unnecessary if the function is only reading data from the data type. A good general rule to follow is when passing structs or classes to functions, do not pass by value, pass by pointer, or reference. This avoids the possibly expensive copy of the data. There are certainly exceptions to this rule, but 99% of the time, passing by value is the wrong thing to do:

```
//Simplified GameObject struct
struct GameObject
{
M5Vec2 pos;
M5Vec2 vel;
int     textureID;
std::list<M5Component*> components;
```

```
std::string name;
};

void DebugPrintGameObject(GameObject& gameObject)
{
//Do printing
gameObject.textureID = 0;//WHOOPS!!!
}
```

We would like to avoid the expensive copy constructor call when passing GameObjects to functions. Unfortunately, when we pass by pointer or reference, the function has access to our public data and can modify it. As before, the solution is to pass by pointer to const or reference to const:

```
void DebugPrintGameObject(const GameObject& gameObject)
{
//Do printing
gameObject.textureID = 0;//ERROR: gameObject is const
}
```

When writing functions, if the purpose is to modify the data, then you should pass by reference. However, if the purpose is not to modify the data, then pass by reference to const. You will avoid the expensive copy constructor call, and the data will be protected from accidental modification. Additionally, by making a habit of passing by reference or reference to const, you code will be self-documenting.

Const member functions

In the previous example, we kept the struct very simple. Since the struct didn't have any member functions, we only needed to worry about when non-member functions want to modify the data. However, object-oriented programming suggests that we shouldn't have data be public. Instead, all data should be private and accessed through public member functions. Let's look at a very simple example to understand this concept:

```
class Simple
{
public:
Simple(void)
{
  m_data = 0;
  }
void SetData(int data)
{
  m_data = data;
}
```

```
int GetData(void)
{
  return m_data;
  }
private:
int m_data;
};

int main(void)
{
Simple s;
const Simple cs;

s.SetData(10);            //Works as Expected
int value = s.GetData();//Works as Expected

cs.SetData(10);           //Error as expected
value = cs.GetData();     //Error: Not Expected
return 0;
}
```

As expected, when our class is not marked as const, we can use both the SetData and GetData member functions. However, when we mark our class as const, we expect that we won't be able to use the SetData member function, because it modifies the data. However, unexpectedly, we can't use the GetData member function, even though it doesn't modify the data at all. To understand what is going on, we need to understand how member functions are called and how a member function modifies the correct data.

Whenever a non-static member function is called. The first parameter is always the hidden this pointer. It is a pointer to the instance that is calling the function. This parameter is how the SetData and GetData can act upon the correct data. The this pointer is optional within the member function, as programmers, we can choose to use it or not:

```
//Example showing the hidden this pointer. This code won't //compile
Simple::Simple(Simple* this)
{
  this->m_data = 0;
}
void Simple::SetData(Simple* this, int data)
{
  this->m_data = data;
}
int Simple::GetData(Simple* this)
{
  return this->m_data;
}
```

This is completely true. The `this` pointer is actually a `const` pointer to a `Simple` class. We didn't talk about const pointers, but it just means the pointer can't be modified, but the data it points to (the `Simple` class) can be. This distinction is important. The pointer is `const`, but the `Simple` class is not. The actual hidden parameter would look something like this:

```
//Not Real Code. Will Not Compile
Simple::Simple(Simple* const this)
{
   this->m_data = 0;
}
```

When we have code like this that calls a member function:

```
Simple s;
s.SetData(10);
```

The compiler is really turning it into code that looks like this:

```
Simple s;
Simple::SetData(&s, 10);
```

This is the reason we get errors when we try to pass a `const` `Simple` object to the member function. The function signature is not correct. The function does not accept a `const` `Simple` object. Unfortunately, since the `this` pointer is hidden, we cannot simply make the `GetData` function accept a `const` `Simple` pointer. Instead we must mark the function as `const`:

```
//What we would like to do but can't
int Simple::GetData(const Simple* const this);

//We must mark the function as const
   int Simple::GetData(void) const;
```

We must mark the function as const within the class as well. Notice that `SetData` is not marked const, because the purpose of that function is to modify the class, but `GetData` is marked `const` because it only reads data from the class. So, our code would look something like the following. To save space, we didn't include the function definitions again:

```
class Simple
{
  public:
  Simple(void);
  void SetData(int data);
  int GetData(void) const;
  private:
```

```
    int m_data;
};

int main(void)
{
    Simple s;
    const Simple cs;

    s.SetData(10);            //Works as Expected
    int value = s.GetData();//Works as Expected

    cs.SetData(10);           //Error as expected
    value = cs.GetData();     //Works as Expected
    return 0;
}
```

As you can see, by marking the GetData member function as const, it can be used when the variable instance is marked const. Marking member functions as const allows the class to work correctly with non-member functions that may be attempting const correctness. For example, a non-member function (possibly written by another programmer) trying to display a Simple object by using the GetData member function:

```
//Const correct global function using member functions to access
//the data
void DisplaySimple(const Simple& s)
{
    std::cout << s.GetData() << std::end;
}
```

Since DisplaySimple isn't intending to change the data in the class, the parameter should be marked as const. However, this code will only work if GetData is a const member function.

Being const-correct takes a little work and may seem difficult at first. However, if you make it a habit, it will eventually become the natural way that you program. When you are const-correct, your code is cleaner, more protected, self-documenting, and more flexible, because you are prepared for const and non-const instances. As a rule, if your function isn't going to modify the data, mark the parameter as const. If the member function isn't going to modify the class data, mark the member function as const.

Problems with const

As we said before, const isn't magic. It doesn't make your code 100% secure and protected. Knowing and understanding the rules related with const parameters and const member function will help prevent mistakes. However, failing to understand the rules and behaviors of const can lead to bugs.

The biggest problem with const in C++ is a misunderstanding of bitwise const versus logical const. This means that the compiler will try to ensure that the bits and bytes will not change through that specific variable. This doesn't mean that those bits won't change through another variable, and it doesn't mean that the data you may care about won't change. Consider the following code:

```
//Example of modifying const bits through different variables.
int i = 0;
const int& ci = i;

ci = 10; //ERROR: can't modify the bits through const variable
i  = 10; //OK. i is not const

std::cout << ci << std::endl;//Prints 10
```

In the preceding example, i is not const, but ci is a reference to a const int. Both i and ci are addressing the same bits. Since ci is marked const, we cannot change the value through that variable. However, i is not const, so we are free to modify the value. The fact that we can have a multiple const and non-const variables pointing to the same address has consequences for const member functions:

```
class Simple
{
public:
     Simple(void);
   int GetData(void) const;
private:
   int m_data;
   Simple* m_this;
};
Simple::Simple(void):m_data(0), m_this(this)
{
}
int Simple::GetData(void) const
{
   m_this->m_data = 10;
   return m_data;
}
```

```
int main(void)
{
  const Simple s;
  std::cout << s.GetData() << std::endl;
  return 0;
}
```

In the preceding code, we have given the `Simple` class a pointer to itself. This pointer can be used to modify its own data in a const member function. Remember, in a `const` member function, the `this` pointer is marked `const`, so data can't be changed through that variable. However, as in this case, the data can still be changed through another variable. Even if we didn't use another variable, the use of `const_cast` could also allow us to change the data:

```
int Simple::GetData(void) const
{
  const_cast<Simple*>(this)->m_data = 10;
    m_data;
}
```

It is very important to understand that you should never write code like this. It is undefined behavior to try to modify a const variable with `const_cast` or using a non-const pointer to a `const` object. The original data could be placed in read-only memory, and code like this could cause the program to crash. It is also possible that the compiler could optimize away multiple reads to memory that shouldn't change. Therefore, the old value may be used for any future calculations. Casting away const with `const_cast` is meant for backwards compatibility with old C++ libraries. It should *NEVER* be used to modify const values. If there is a piece of data that needs to be modified even when the class is `const`, use the `mutable` keyword.

Even when avoiding undefined behavior, bitwise constness can get us into trouble with const member variables. Consider a simple class that will contain some dynamic memory. Since it contains dynamic memory and pointers, we should add a copy constructor, destructor, and other things to prevent memory leaks and memory corruption, but we will omit those for now since they aren't important for our discussion on const:

```
class LeakyArray
{
public:
LeakyArray(int size)
{
  m_array = new int[size];
  }
void SetValue(int index, int value)
{
  m_array[index] = value;
```

```
  }
  int GetValue(int index) const
  {
    //function is const so we can't do this
    //m_array = 0;

    //but we can do this!!!!!!!
    m_array[index] = 0;

    return m_array[index];

  }
  private:
    int* m_array;
  };
```

As you can see, bitwise const only prevents us from modifying the actual bits inside the class. This means we can't point m_array to a new location. However, it doesn't prevent us from modifying data in the array. There is nothing preventing GetValue from modifying the array in the const function, because the array data isn't part of the class, only the pointer is. Most users aren't concerned about where the data is located, but they would expect a const array to remain unchanged.

As you can see, being const, correct is certainly not a guarantee that the data will never be modified. If you are diligent about using const, as well as understand and avoid the problems that can arise, the benefits are worth it.

Learning how iteration can improve your game and code design

While it's nice to imagine it to be this way, games never come fully-formed from the mind of a designer/developer. A game is made up of many different ideas from many different people. While in the past people could develop games with only a single person, now it's much more common for teams to be made up of many different disciplines and every game developer on your team has ideas, many of them good that can contribute to the final product that gets made. But with that in mind you may be wondering how does a game get to the final point with all those different changes made? The answer to that is iteration.

The game development cycle

Game development is a process, and different people have different names and/or phrases for each of these steps, but most people can agree that, for commercial game development, there are three main phases:

- Pre-Production
- Production
- Post-Production

Each of these states has their own steps within them as well. Due to page constraints, I'm unable to write about the entire process, but we will be focusing on the Production aspect of development, since that's where the most relevant content will be for our readers.

 If you are interested in learning more about the different aspects of the game development process, check out
`https://en.wikipedia.org/wiki/Video_game_development#Development_process`.

During game development, you'll see a lot of companies use an agile development process, which is based on iterative prototyping, using feedback and refinement of the game's iterations while gradually increasing the game's feature set. A lot of companies enjoy this method as there is always a version of the game playable every couple of weeks, and you can make adjustments as the project is being worked on. If you have heard of Scrum, it is a popular method of agile software development, and one that I use with my students as well as what I used in the game industry.

Production phase

Upon entering the production phase, we have come up with our base idea for our project and have created our proposal and game design document. Now that we have this information, we can start doing the following three steps:

- Prototyping
- Playtesting
- Iterating

Each of these steps serves a valuable process and will be completed in this order. We will be repeating these steps repeatedly until release, so it's a good idea to have an understanding of them.

Prototyping

Prototyping is when you make the simplest version of your ideas in a quick manner to prove if your concept works well or not. For some people, they will do this via index cards, paper, chits, and boards, which is called a paper prototype. This can be quite useful, as you don't have to think about the code side of things to begin with, and instead it allows you to experience the core of the game without having all the nice art and polish. A game that is fun to play with bad graphics will only be improved when you add to it.

Of course, assuming you have purchased this book, you are probably already a developer, but it's still a good idea to think of it as an option. *Jesse Schell* wrote about paper prototypes in his book *The Art of Game Design: A Book of Lenses*, where he explained how you could create a paper prototype of the game Tetris. To do so, you could cut out cardboard pieces and then put them into a pile and pick them out randomly, and then slide them down the board, which would be a piece of paper. Once you completed a line, you would grab an X-acto knife and then cut the pieces. While it doesn't give you the same experience entirely, it captures enough of the experience to see if you are using the right kinds of shapes and how fast the pieces should drop. The big advantage would be that you could create this prototype in 10 to 15 minutes, while programming it may take a lot longer.

It's a lot easier to justify 30 minutes of work rather than a day for something that doesn't work out. This can be done with 3D games as well, such as First Person Shooters, by creating maps in a similar way to how you create combat encounters in a pen and paper role playing game such as Wizards of the Coast's *Dungeons and Dragons* (which is a great thing to learn how to play as a designer, as you learn about telling a story and developing interesting encounters).

A prototype's job is to prove if your game works and, specifically, how it works. Don't invest in only one idea specifically, but rather create a number of small prototypes that are quick to make, without worrying if it is polished or you've made it the best possible.

For some more information on building a prototype and an example of a prototype that was created in seven days about *Tower of Goo*, which was the prototype for their indie hit *World of Goo*, check out `http://www.gamas utra.com/view/feature/130848/how_to_prototype_a_game_in_under_ 7_.php?print=1`.

One of the most vital skills as a game developer is being able to create rapid prototypes, to see how it works, and then test it. We call this process of testing out a game idea playtesting.

Playtesting

Once we have a prototype, we can then begin the playtesting process. Playtest as soon as possible in your development, and do it often. As soon as you have something playable, get people in front of it. First play the game yourself and see how you feel about it. Then invite some friends over to your house and have them play it as well.

Oftentimes, I find my students have difficulty at first actually doing playtests and may be hesitant to show people their projects as it's not *ready* yet or because they won't get it. Or they know that their project isn't finished so they think they know what they should be working on already, so there's no need to do playtesting. I find this usually comes from them being shy, and one of the first major obstacles you'll need to overcome as a developer is being able to show your ideas to the world.

If the play testers of your game aren't your close friends and/or family, it is likely that people will say negative things about the game. This is a good thing. They will also mention many things that you already know your game doesn't have yet or that you don't have the budget for. This isn't a time for you to defend any points, or explain why things are the way they are, but instead a time for you to accept the points and note them, as you can take them into consideration in the future.

As a game developer, one thing that's important to note is that you are one of the worst judges of your games, especially when just starting out. A lot of times I see starting developers trying to justify the problems in their games, stating that it is their vision and people don't get it because it's not in a final game. It's a very important skill of a game developer to be able to get feedback, take criticism, and evaluate if things are worth changing or not.

Conducting a playtest

Now that we know how valuable it is to do a playtest, you may wonder how to go about doing one. First, I do want to note that it is vitally important that you are in the room while your project is being playtested. While they are playing the game, you can see not only what someone thinks, but also how they react to things as well as what they do with your game. This is the time where you find out what works well and what doesn't. If for some reason, you are unable to be there in person, have them record themselves playing, both on the PC and from the webcam if possible.

When someone comes to a computer to playtest your game, you may be tempted to tell them things about your project, such as the controls and the story, and the mechanics, and anything else, but you should resist these urges. See what the player does without any prompting to begin with. This will give you an idea of what players will want to do naturally given the environment that you created and what needs to be explained more. Once they play for a while and you've gotten the information you need on that end, then you can tell them some things.

When playtesting, it's a good idea to get as much information from the player as you can. When they finish, ask them what they liked, what they disliked, if they found anything confusing, where they got stuck, and what was the most interesting thing to them. Do note that what a player says and what they actually do are two different things, so it's important that you are there and watching them. Getting your game played and seeing what those players do is where you will start to see the cracks in your design's form, and seeing what people do will show how they experience the things you have created. While doing this testing, I've seen a lot of people do the exact opposite of what I expected and not understand something that I thought was quite simple. The player isn't wrong in this regard though, I was. The player can only do what they know from prior playing or from what is taught in the game.

All of the information that you get during a playtest is important. Not just what they say, but also what they don't say. Once they finish playing, give them a survey to fill out. I find using Google Sheets does a good job at storing this information and isn't too difficult to set up, and you have hard data from which you can make decisions without having to remember what people say. Plus, it's a lot easier for people to select a number from 1-10 for how they enjoyed different aspects of the game than to ask their thoughts for everything and doesn't require them to write paragraphs of info (unless they want to in a comments section at the end).

In case you'd like to see an example playtesting form, while this form is for board games, I feel it does a good job of making it easy for play testers to give information that can be useful:
https://www.reddit.com/r/boardgames/comments/1ej13y/i_created_a_streamlined_playtesting_feedback_form/.

If you're looking for some ideas of questions to ask, *Wesley Rockholz* wrote some examples of questions that may be useful for you to use:
http://www.gamasutra.com/blogs/WesleyRockholz/20140418/215819/10_Insightful_Playtest_Questions.php.

In addition, the order in which players give their feedback is also important as it communicates how important different things are to them. You may find that what was intended to be the main mechanic isn't as engaging and/or fun as something else. That is valuable feedback, and you may decide to focus on that secondary mechanic instead for the title, as I've seen happen repeatedly on projects. It's better to do this as early as possible so you will waste as little of your time as possible.

Iteration

At this point, we've playtested our project and have gotten our player's feedback, and, if we have set it up, gotten data and analytics from which we can build upon. Now we need to take this information into consideration, make some changes to our current prototype, and then bring it back to be play tested again. This is what's known as the iteration stage of development.

In this stage, you'll need to take this feedback and then decide how to incorporate it into your design. You'll need to decide what should be changed as well as what shouldn't. While doing so, keep in mind the scope of the project, realistically evaluating how long it will take to make the changes, and be willing to cut features, even those that you love, to have the best project.

After making these decisions again, we will once again create a new prototype, which you will then playtest again. Then iterate again. Then build another prototype, where you will continue to test, removing prototypes that don't work and features that don't work well for the project. You'll also try adding new features using feedback and remove previous features that would no longer fit the game in its current state. You will keep doing this cycle repeatedly until you reach your final release!

If you're waiting for your game to be *perfect* before releasing it, you'll never release it. Games are never finished, they're only abandoned. If the project is at a point where it is good enough, you should ship, because it's only when you ship a project that you can finally say you've developed a title.

 If you'd like to see an example of this process and how it can benefit a title, check out:
`http://www.gamasutra.com/blogs/PatrickMorgan/20160217/265915/Gur gamoth_Lessons_in_Iterative_Game_Development.php`.

Meeting milestones

When working on a commercial game project, especially when you have a publisher, you often times will have a schedule to keep and milestones to meet. Milestones are ways for everyone to know if the game is on track or not, because certain things need to be accomplished by them. Not making a milestone can often be a horrible thing, because your publisher usually will only pay your team if the milestone has everything in it that was agreed upon. There's no standard milestone schedule, as every company is different, but some of the most common ones are as follows:

- **First-playable**: This is the first version of the game that can be played. Has the main mechanic of the game in and can demonstrate how it works.
- **Alpha**: When all the features of your game are in, known as being feature complete. Features can change slightly, and make revisions based on feedback and testing, but at this point, unimplemented things may be dropped to finish the title on time.
- **Beta**: The game is complete, with all assets and features completed and finished. At this point you are only doing bug testing and fixes for potential problems that would prevent your game from being shipped.
- **Gold**: This is the final version of the game, which you'll either be releasing, or sending to your publisher to create copies on disks, cartridges, or whatever your device uses.

Do note that every company is different and these milestones may mean different things to different people, so be sure to clarify before diving into development.

Learning when to use scripting in a game

Scripting languages are something that can be quite beneficial to developers when working on a team with multiple disciplines in it. But before we dive into what they are and how they work, and the pros and cons of using a scripting language, it's best to get a bit of a history lesson in terms of how code executes.

Introduction to assembly

Underneath the hood, all the code that we have written over the course of this book is ones and zeroes indicating what switches should be marked as on and off by our computer's processor. Low-level programming languages such as machine language use these switches to execute commands. This was the only way to program to begin with, but we have developed more readable languages for us to work with instead.

Starting with assembly languages, low-level languages have a very strong connection between the language's instructions and the machine code's instructions. While more readable than a sequence of 0s and 1s, it was still quite difficult to write code. For example, here is some assembly code used to add two numbers in Assembly Language:

```
push    rbp
mov     rbp, rsp
mov     DWORD PTR [rbp-20], edi
mov     DWORD PTR [rbp-24], esi
mov     edx, DWORD PTR [rbp-20]
mov     eax, DWORD PTR [rbp-24]
add     eax, edx
mov     DWORD PTR [rbp-4], eax
nop
pop     rbp
ret
```

Each computer architecture has its own assembly language, so writing code in low-level languages has the disadvantage of not being portable as they are machine dependent. Back in the day, people would have to learn many different languages in order to port your program to another processor. Program structures became more complicated, as the demands of functionality increased over time, making it quite difficult for programmers to implement efficient programs that were robust enough.

Moving to higher-level programming languages

As programmers, we are inherently lazy, so we seek ways to make our job easier or rather to find the best use of our time. With that in mind, we have developed other higher level languages, which are even easier to read. By higher level, we mean closer to the way that humans think or closer to the problem we are trying to solve. By abstracting the machine details from our code, we simplify programming tasks.

Introducing the compiler

Once we have finished our code, we use a compiler to translate that high-level code into assembly, which in turn will get turned into machine language that our computer can execute. Afterwards, it will translate that program into an executable file that the user can run. Functionally, it looks something like this:

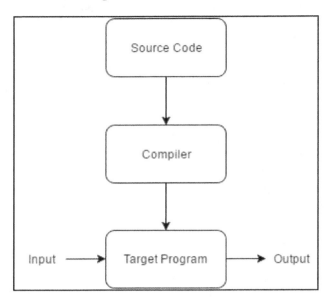

This has several advantages, as it provides abstraction from the hardware details. For example, we don't need to work directly with registers, memory, addresses, and so on anymore. It also makes our code portable in that we can use the same program and have it translated by different assemblers for the different machines that use it. This was one of the reasons C took off and became so popular, because it allowed people to write code once and then have it work everywhere. You may notice that Unity has taken the same thought process to game development, and that's one of the reasons that I feel they've been so successful as of this writing.

This is a much more efficient use of time than writing assembly language code as it allows us to create more complex programs and machines, and modern compilers such as Microsoft's produce some highly efficient assembly code in most circumstances. This is what we have been using over the course of this book.

Writing code in assembly can still have its benefits though. For instance, after you've written your game in a higher-level language, you can start profiling it and seeing what aspects of the game are the bottlenecks, and then determine if rewriting it in assembly will give you a speed boost. The point of using a lower-level language is the fact that you can gain some substantial speed advantages.

 For a real-life example as to how assembly was used to optimize a game engine, check out the following article from Intel:
https://software.intel.com/en-us/articles/achieving-performance-an-approach-to-optimizing-a-game-engine/.

One of the issues with writing code that needs to be compiled before running is the fact that as projects increase in size, so do compile times. Recompiling a full game can take minutes to hours depending on the size of the project, and while that's going on, you are unable to work on your project, or else you'd need to recompile again. This is one of the reasons why scripting languages can be useful.

Introduction to scripting languages

A scripting language is a programming language that allows scripts to be written for it. A script is a program that can be executed without being compiled in one of a few different ways. Scripting languages are also sometimes referred to as very high-level programming languages, as they operate at a high level of abstraction, being very fast to learn how to write in.

Scripting languages also have the advantage of taking care of a lot of things that programmers would need to take care of, such as garbage collection, memory management, and pointers, which often confuse non-developers. Even a visual editor such as Unreal 4's blueprints is still a scripting language, as it accomplishes the same thing as a written one does.

Most games use scripting languages in some form, but other games may use it a lot more, such as how GameMaker uses **Game Maker Language** (**GML**) for their logic.

Using interpreters

To use a scripting language, we need to be able to execute new code on the fly. However, unlike a compiler, there's also another way to convert code into something that can be understood by a machine that is called an interpreter. Interpreters do not produce a program themselves, and rather stay around for the execution of a program. This program will either:

- Execute the source code directly
- Translate the source code into some other efficient intermediate representation (code) and then immediately execute it
- Explicitly execute stored precompiled code made by a compiler that is part of the interpreter system

The interpreter translates one line at a time, as opposed to the compiler doing it all at once.

Visually, it looks a bit like the following:

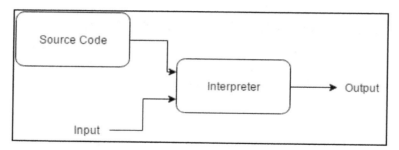

As you can see here, the **Interpreter** takes in the **Source Code** and any **Input** that has been received, and will then **Output** what is expected of it.

Just in time compilation

There is yet another way to run code, using what's called a **just in time compiler**, or **JIT** for short. A JIT caches the instructions, that have been previously interpreted to machine code, and reuses those native machine code instructions thus saving time and resources by not having to re-interpret statements that have already been interpreted.

Visually, it looks similar to this:

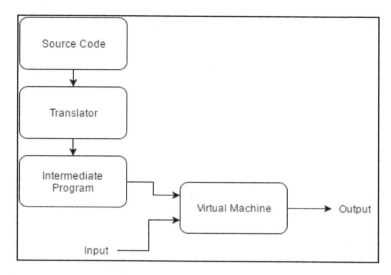

Now, Unity uses a JIT and AOT compiler to convert code into machine code, which can then be read by the machine. The first time that a function is called, the game will convert that code into machine language and then the next time it is called, it will go directly to the translated code, so you only need to do conversions to things that are happening. Due to this happening at runtime, this may cause your project to lag when using a lot of new things.

 A great talk about how scripting works inside of the Unity game engine can be found here: https://www.youtube.com/watch?v=WE3PWHLGsX4.

Why use a scripting language?

C++ is often overkill when it comes to building things for your game, such as tools, or for high-level game tasks that could be handled by your technical designers. It has some definite advantages for ease of development. Specifically, that you don't have to worry about a lot of the low-level things, as the language takes care of it for you; there's also fewer errors by the programmer due to the limited options available. There's less of a technical programming knowledge required, and it can be customized to fit your game's needs. This also makes the game more data driven instead of hardcoding things into the game engine, and allows you to patch the game without having to send over the entire project.

Often in game development, game logic and configurations can be found in script files. This way, it's very easy for scripts to be modified and adjusted by people on the team that aren't programmers (such as designers), allowing them to playtest the game and tweak the gameplay without having to recompile the game.

Many games also have a console window, which uses a scripting language to do things like this even at runtime. For instance, Unreal Engine has a console window open by default when you press Tab and in Source engine, pressing the ~ button at the pause menu will open one up.

Scripting languages are also often used in areas that have level design as well, such as having triggers for when you enter certain areas, or for controlling cinematics. It also allows you to let players of your game mod the game as well, which could potentially increase the lifespan of your game and help foster your game's community.

When to use C++

C++ is a great language to be using, as performance is a crucial first step. This used to be all aspects of game engines, but now is used primarily with graphics and AI code. Scripting languages also have the problem of being slower than C++, sometimes even 10x slower than what it would be otherwise. Due to scripting languages having memory management taken care of for them automatically, there could be times when commands are interrupted or take a while to complete garbage collection, causing lag and other problems.

C++ also has the advantage of much better IDEs and Debuggers, making it a lot easier for you to find mistakes and fix them when they do occur.

There's also the possibility that you are working with a legacy code base. Most game companies aren't starting with a fresh slate. It can also be useful to make use of the middleware libraries that C++ has, such as FMOD and AntTweakBar.

Compiled versus scripting

For some game engines, the game engine itself is programmed in C++, but the game logic is entirely done in a scripting language, like most development for Unity, for example. This allows you to iterate on gameplay much faster, and allows technical designers and artists to modify behaviors without having to bother a programmer. Also, depending on the language, it can allow people to use a more appropriate language for the problem's domain (for example, AI may not be the easiest thing to implement in C++).

Different companies handle working with languages differently. When I was working at a AAA (pronounced triple-A) studio, we would have designers prototype ideas for mechanics and get it working in the best possible way making use of scripting languages. Upon approval from the leads as something to add to the project, if the script had performance issues, programmers would use the scripting language code as a base and then create a super-efficient version using C++ that would work in all levels. However, when I was working on an indie title, all of the code for the project was written in a scripting language (C#), since we didn't have access to the engine's source code (Unity). Also, if you are wanting to target devices that are limited in memory and processing power (such as the Nintendo 3DS), you are likely wanting to care about performance a lot more so it's more important to use more optimized code. It's a good idea to be familiar with both options and be comfortable working either way.

If you are interested in using a scripting language for your project, Lua is very widely used in the game industry because it's very easy to learn and fairly easy to incorporate into your engine. Lua started off as a configuration language. This has some nice quirks, in that it's great for creating and configuring things - which is what you want to do in a game. It's important to note, though, that it's not object-oriented but uses a small amount of memory.

 A list of games that use Lua as a scripting language can be found here: `https://en.wikipedia.org/wiki/Category%3aLua-scripted_video_games`.

If you are interested in integrating Lua into your project or would like to see how it works, I highly suggest checking out `http://www.lua.org/start.html`.

Summary

In this chapter, we covered a lot of best-practice information, which we hope will give you a good foundation when building your own projects in the future. We touched on why hardcoding values is a bad idea, in addition to making a number of other code-quality suggestions, to ensure that your code is easy to understand and easy to extend from in the future, when it needs to be.

We also learned how iteration is useful in game development, talking about the traditional game development cycle, with tips and tricks about playtesting and how it can be immensely useful when developing your projects.

We also looked into low-level and high-level programming languages, learning about how scripting languages run inside another program that we have to build into our project. They are not compiled but rather interpreted, and are generally easier to use and write code for than a compiled language, but come at the cost of performance. Depending on how complex your game is, it may be a good idea to stick to just C++, but if you are working with designers, it can be quite useful to give them the tools to do things on their own.

With that, we've reached the end of the book. We hope that you found the information both interesting and useful. As you go out there and build your own projects, make use of the design patterns and best practices that we've talked about over the past 12 chapters, and make the best games that you can!

Index

Made in the USA
Columbia, SC
19 May 2018